SURVIVAL

SURVIVAL

**HOW A CULTURE OF PREPAREDNESS CAN SAVE
YOU AND YOUR FAMILY FROM DISASTERS**

Lt. Gen. Russel L. Honoré (U.S. Army, retired)

with Ron Martz

ATRIA BOOKS
NEW YORK • LONDON • TORONTO • SYDNEY

ATRIA BOOKS

A Division of Simon & Schuster, Inc.
1230 Avenue of the Americas
New York, NY 10020

First Atria Books hardcover edition May 2009

ATRIA BOOKS and colophon are trademarks of Simon & Schuster, Inc.

For information about special discounts for bulk purchases,
please contact Simon & Schuster Special Sales at
1-800-456-6798 or business@simonandschuster.com.

Designed by Paul Dippolito

Manufactured in the United States of America

10 9 8 7 6 5 4 3 2 1

Library of Congress Cataloging-in-Publication Data

Honoré, Russel L.
    Survival : how a culture of preparedness can save you and your family
from disasters / by Russel L. Honoré with Ron Martz.
        p.   cm.
    1. Emergency management—United States. 2. Disasters—United States.
3. Survival skills—United States. I. Martz, Ron, 1947– II. Title.
    HV551.2.H66 2009
    363.34'70973—dc22   2008043269

ISBN: 978-1-4165-9900-5

To the victims of Katrina, who suffered far more than they should have and endured one of the worst natural disasters this country has ever seen.

And to my wife, Beverly, for all she has done for me and our family since our marriage in January 1971. She has been the consummate Army wife through countless moves and sometimes less-than-ideal living conditions. She has been a warm and loving mother to our children. She has served dutifully as a coach and counselor to me. She has been a social aide-de-camp, and, in her own right, a general officer in charge of our household. She helped me understand that I need to let other people do their jobs and not try to do those jobs for them. She is strong, opinionated, caring, loving, and deserves much of the credit for the success that I now enjoy.

Contents

Glossary of Abbreviations

C2V—Command and Control Vehicle
DCO—Defense Coordinating Officer
DEA—Drug Enforcement Administration
DHHS—Department of Health and Human Services
DHS—Department of Homeland Security
DMORT—Disaster Mortuary Operational Response Team
DOD—Department of Defense
DSCA—Defense Support to Civil Authority
EMAC—Emergency Management Assistance Compact
EOC—Emergency Operations Center
EPLOS—Emergency Preparedness Liaison Officers
FEMA—Federal Emergency Management Agency
FORSCOM—U.S. Army Forces Command
JFCOM—Joint Forces Command
JFHQ-HLS—Joint Forces Headquarters–Homeland Security
JTF—Joint Task Force
MRE—Meal Ready to Eat
NGB—National Guard Bureau
NORTHCOM—U.S. Northern Command
NTC—National Training Center, Fort Irwin, California
OSD—Office of the Secretary of Defense
PAO—Public Affairs Officer
ROE—Rules of Engagement
TAG—The Adjutant General, commander of a state's National Guard forces
VTC—Video Teleconference

SURVIVAL

Prologue

Why America Needs a New Culture of Preparedness

EARLY ON THE MORNING OF SUNDAY, AUGUST 28, 2005, HURRICANE Katrina moved into position to attack the Gulf Coast with all the precision of a well-planned and well-coordinated military assault. What had been a relatively large but slow-moving Category 3 storm with winds just over 110 miles per hour exploded over the next few hours as it neared the mouth of the Mississippi River and the Louisiana coastline, becoming a Category 5 storm with winds approaching 175 miles per hour. By early that evening the storm was pushing tropical storm–force winds more than 230 miles out from its center and hurricane-force winds more than one hundred miles. The storm also began to pick up speed as it neared land, increasing its northward momentum from a leisurely five to six miles per hour to more than twelve miles per hour.

At 6:10 A.M. on August 29, Hurricane Katrina made its initial assault on the Gulf Coast at Buras, Louisiana, a small fishing village about sixty-five miles southeast of New Orleans in the Mississippi River delta. Buras sits at sea level in Plaquemines Parish on low-lying marshlands with the river to its west and the Gulf of Mexico to its east. It is extremely vulnerable to storm surges from both directions and the people who live there are seasoned hurricane veterans who respect these storms enough to evacuate their homes and businesses when one with the size and power of Katrina is bearing down on them. Just before Katrina came ashore at Buras it dropped to a Category 3 storm for reasons that puzzled scientists at the National Hurricane Center. They thought it might have been a result of slightly lower water temperatures in the northern Gulf of Mexico, a phenomenon they had seen before, or the initial brush with

1

land, which usually causes hurricanes to diminish quickly in strength and size.

Then Katrina did something that any military commander would have considered a tactical stroke of genius. It took a turn to the right, went back into the open waters of Breton Sound, and began moving northeasterly, bearing down on the Mississippi coast. It maintained its Category 3 intensity with winds of about 120 miles per hour and headed for Biloxi, which had suffered a devastating blow in 1969 from Hurricane Camille, a Category 5 hurricane and one of the deadliest ever to hit the mainland United States. As Katrina moved ashore near the Louisiana-Mississippi line about ten o'clock the morning of August 29, it pushed ahead of it a tidal surge that in some places was more than thirty feet high.

One of the fundamental concepts of war is to surprise the enemy. Katrina created that surprise in its movement, first by increasing speed when least expected and then making the right turn after hitting Buras. Military commanders also try to create shock and awe during an attack with overwhelming force. The storm created that overwhelming force with its high winds and massive tidal surges. It created shock and awe by knocking out communications. It toppled cell phone towers throughout southern Louisiana and from Biloxi more than 175 miles inland to Jackson. It cut electricity by tossing trees onto power lines in an area the size of England, denying people in those areas access to radio, television, or Internet reports of what was happening, leaving them in the dark and in fear for their lives.

The most vulnerable part of any formation when it makes a right turning movement in the attack is the left flank. Katrina protected its left flank by kicking up a seventeen-foot storm surge in Lake Pontchartrain east of New Orleans and set back technology eighty years by flooding the city and knocking out essential services such as water, electricity, and telephone. Residents of the city thought early Monday morning they had dodged yet another bullet when the eye of Katrina went ashore east of them, leaving them to deal only with wind and rain damage. But that tidal surge easily overwhelmed the levee system in New Orleans and created unprecedented flooding that chased tens of thousands of people from their homes and onto any high ground they could find. Katrina was not yet finished with its attack. As it came inland and slowly started to die, it moved north and east, trapping military helicopters and fixed-wing aircraft that had been moved out of southern Florida, Louisiana, and Mississippi for safekeeping. Now those vital assets that were needed for immediate search-and-rescue missions were trapped on the ground for crucial hours.

Some weeks later, after the accountants had punched all their numbers, the economic losses from the storm—most of it in Louisiana and Mississippi—was approaching $100 billion. It was the costliest hurricane ever to hit the United States. The toll in human life was even greater— more than 1,800 people died, about 1,600 of them in Louisiana—making Katrina one of the five deadliest storms on record.

For six weeks in the late summer and early fall of 2005, I was the commander of Joint Task Force–Katrina (JTF-Katrina), the officer on the ground in charge of all active-duty military forces sent to Louisiana and Mississippi to save lives, facilitate evacuations of at-risk civilians, and help provide an environment in which civil control was restored so recovery and rebuilding efforts could begin in the storm-ravaged areas. Initially, my primary role was overseeing federal military response to Katrina in Mississippi. My staff and I were working on that when the order came down from Admiral Timothy Keating, commander of U.S. Northern Command (NORTHCOM) in Colorado Springs, Colorado, to go to Louisiana and head up the task force. I had recommended several days earlier, while Katrina was still brewing in the southern Gulf of Mexico, that a joint task force commander be considered in the event the storm hit more than one state. That was not my way of volunteering for the job, however. I had enough on my plate at the time. As the three-star commander for United States First Army, headquartered just southeast of Atlanta at Fort Gillem, I was responsible for the mobilization and training of thousands of National Guard and Army Reserve soldiers east of the Mississippi River who were heading overseas to the wars in Iraq and Afghanistan. In addition, First Army provided support to civil authorities in that same region in times of disaster. We were right in the heart of hurricane season and the potential for more storms was significant in the states along the east and Gulf coasts.

Besides, Louisiana was outside the First Army area of responsibility and expertise. Louisiana disaster response was the province of Lieutenant General Robert Clark, commander of U.S. Fifth Army in San Antonio, Texas. Its staff had done the tabletop exercises and was familiar with the terrain and the local and state officials. Although I was born in Lakeland, Louisiana, in Pointe Coupee Parish little more than a hundred miles northwest of New Orleans, I had spent the last thirty-four years stationed everywhere but Louisiana and was not as familiar with the state or the city as I once had been. But as soon as the order came down, my staff and I set out to ensure that the federal military response met the needs and desires of the elected officials of Louisiana and New Orleans, for whom we were working.

Once we got to New Orleans it seemed as if my entire career leading up to that moment had prepared me for this role as task force commander. I had worked in a number of joint military assignments, including on the joint staff at the Pentagon, and as commander of Joint Forces Head-quarters–Homeland Security, so I was familiar with the inner workings of numerous federal agencies and how interagency groups function. I had undergone media training early in my career and although I had a tendency at times to say things that made my superiors cringe, I was well versed in dealing with the media and had learned valuable lessons from mistakes made along the way. I had spent a number of years as a trainer at the Army's National Training Center at Fort Irwin, California, where armor and mechanized infantry units honed their skills in incredibly difficult and complex exercises, and I knew how to deal with large and difficult problems. And, in my most recent command at First Army, I oversaw the training and mobilization of many of the National Guard units sent to Louisiana in Katrina's wake and had good working and personal relationships with many of their commanders.

I was not in charge of the post-Katrina effort, despite media perception to the contrary. My role was as commander of the active-duty forces sent there. That's all. I went where assigned to help save lives and became a coordinator and collaborator with federal, state, and local officials. Since Katrina, I have often been complimented by people who are still under the impression that I was in charge of operations in New Orleans. Whenever I hear that I get goose bumps because it's a hell of a compliment. There may have been that appearance, but I certainly did not take any control from Louisiana Governor Kathleen Blanco, New Orleans Mayor Ray Nagin, or any of the officials from the Federal Emergency Management Agency (FEMA). JTF-Katrina worked for them.

The impression that I was in charge most likely is a result of my willingness to stand in front of the media and answer their questions. Earlier in my career it was impressed on me that in times of crisis the media can be a valuable asset—what is often referred to as a combat multiplier—in getting information out to the public and to those most affected by a disaster. They get their stories out and we get our information out. There were times when I felt the message coming out of New Orleans and Baton Rouge was close to spinning out of control because Nagin and Blanco, like the poor souls of the 7th and 9th wards, were victims of Katrina. I took it upon myself to try to present a voice of calm and reason when the politicians could not. And, unlike many other general officers and politicians, I was not afraid to address reporters and their questions in my blunt and sometimes direct manner of speaking.

General Peter Schoomaker, then the chief of staff of the Army and my boss at the Pentagon, told me in a telephone conversation we had at one point early in those six weeks: "Russ, don't become a celebrity. Whatever you do, don't become a celebrity." I told him I would do my best to avoid it, but my name and my face became forever linked to Hurricane Katrina and disaster response.

One reason that it did was that soon after my arrival Nagin referred to me in one interview as "a John Wayne dude" who flew into town and with straight talk and some forceful guidance tried to focus on moving forward and getting things done rather than trying to figure out who was to blame. I was being likened to a movie star when my goal was to save lives. This was no movie. I was a general, not some movie actor playing a general. John Wayne got to reshoot scenes whenever he needed to. We did not have that opportunity in New Orleans. I think a lot of John Wayne and am a big fan of his movies but definitely did not want to be put into that box. For some people, though, my legacy will likely be as that "John Wayne dude."

This book is not intended to be the definitive history of Hurricane Katrina. Nor is it strictly about me and the federal military response to the disaster. It is simply my story of what happened before and after Hurricane Katrina; what I saw and heard in my role as JTF-Katrina commander. I also will not point the blame at anyone for things that went wrong. Blame will eventually find its rightful owners, and while this book may provide some sense of who those owners are, it is not my intent to focus on them. If there is anyone or anything to blame, it is Katrina. She broke the disaster response mold and forced us to think of new ways to deal with major catastrophes such as this. Besides, my field of vision was relatively narrow and crowded with new problems every day. I heard a lot but did not have the time or resources to chase down every accusation. I purposely have not read any of the numerous books written about Katrina because I did not want to alter my own judgment and assessment of what was done right and what was done wrong.

Although I will delve briefly into my background growing up in Louisiana and my years of military service, it will be done in such a way as to demonstrate that even as a child in the 1950s and 1960s, despite the poverty and segregation that my family endured, the Honoré clan knew full well of the need to be prepared for the next big storm, whether it was a hurricane, a crop failure, a death in the family, or some other unforeseen disaster. That culture of preparedness was ingrained in our family by our parents because of the indigent conditions in which we grew up. It was much the same in the Army—we trained and prepared for the unexpected so we knew what to do when we confronted it on the battlefield. I was surrounded and embraced by that culture of preparedness throughout my life.

It is still a major part of the military, but among citizens in this country that culture has all but disappeared. This book is being written with the hope that it will help initiate a national conversation about the need to re-create the culture of preparedness. We have a National Response Framework for natural and man-created disasters. Now we need a National Preparedness Plan to ensure that Americans are ready for hurricanes, tornadoes, earthquakes, pandemics, or attacks by terrorists.

Katrina was a watershed event for many Americans. It made us realize the frailty and insufficiency of our disaster preparedness plans. The storm simply overmatched and exposed many of the shortcomings of the federal, state, and local governments, as well as the business community, when it comes to responding to major disasters. It also exposed the lack of preparations by the poor, who often cannot afford to make those necessary preparations, and revealed the need for a comprehensive National Preparedness Plan for individuals, local, state, and federal government agencies, and the business community. As a nation, we need to do a better job of preparing for disasters. Had Katrina been a Category 5 storm and not a Category 3, and scored a direct hit on New Orleans, the outcome likely would have been much worse than it was for the poor, the disadvantaged, the ill, and the elderly. We need to ensure that disaster preparedness plans are specially tailored to provide for their safety.

It is understandable that the competing nature of what people deal with on a daily basis makes it difficult for them to focus on disaster preparedness until after the fact. Until someone is a victim, or knows a victim, or comes close to being a victim, preparedness often is an abstract thought. It's a human condition our society has come to accept. This is a discipline that people will think about occasionally but it is difficult to get them to focus on it for any length of time or with any sense of purpose. The day-to-day business of the people is to think about the here and now—the mortgage, the job, the kids at school, and the economy.

But even a minor amount of preparation can pay major dividends. In Cameron Parish in southwestern Louisiana, after Hurricane Rita had blown through there in late September 2005, houses built above the floodplain often survived. The others did not. In subdivisions between Abbeville and Erath in Vermilion Parish many homeowners who had spent a few thousand dollars to bring in fill dirt and elevate the foundations four or five feet above the surrounding area often survived without major flood damage. Their neighbors were tossing water-logged furniture and carpet into the street. Even in the 7th and 9th wards of New Orleans, homes that were elevated just a few feet off the ground fared much better than those built with the foundation slab on grade.

Those issues speak directly to the culture of preparedness. It's the individual, it's local government, and it's state and federal governments that need to get involved in re-creating that culture. It is also the business community, which has yet to find this type of preparation to be an attractive financial opportunity despite the obvious need for it.

Category 3 Katrina left in its wake Category 5 confusion, chaos, and conflicting and competing interests in the business and political communities from New Orleans to the state capital in Baton Rouge to Washington, D.C. The storm severely damaged portions of two states, left tens of thousands of people homeless and more destitute than they had been previously, and kept New Orleans uninhabitable for months. I was not sure what to expect when the message from NORTHCOM was passed to me to create and command JTF-Katrina. My staff and I arrived in Mississippi only that Tuesday morning, August 30, after a long and arduous overnight drive from Atlanta. We received a warning order from NORTHCOM earlier in the day about the impending move to create the task force, so it was not unexpected. But we had spent the day assessing the situation in Mississippi with the state's National Guard commander, Major General Harold A. "Hac" Cross, and knew little about the extent of the problem in Louisiana, especially in New Orleans. The message from NORTHCOM was sent out about 10 P.M. Central Daylight Time (CDT) and reached me shortly thereafter at Camp Shelby, Mississippi, a staging area for our efforts in that state and where my headquarters was setting up.

During the movement Monday night and Tuesday morning from Atlanta to Camp Shelby we monitored news reports from CNN and Fox Television News on XM radio while making telephone calls to the staff back in Atlanta, which had gone to Condition Red and was manning our headquarters around the clock. We were hearing frequent reports of the Mississippi River levees being violated and the bowl in which New Orleans sits slowly filling with water. But we had no access to video and did not realize how desperate the situation had become for tens of thousands of people in one of America's most popular and unique cities. That came the next morning, when the havoc that Katrina had wrought and the enormity of the need to do something about it, and to do it quickly, became all too evident. I flew into downtown New Orleans and was confronted with what had all the makings of a third-world disaster in a first-world nation.

1

The Patience of the Poor

THE SLATE-GRAY NAVY SH-60 SEAHAWK HELICOPTER CAME IN FAST and low over New Orleans. Rushing beneath me were rivers of dark, stagnant water that three days earlier had been the streets and alleys of this vibrant city. In some areas only the roofs of houses were visible above the waterline. Elevated portions of Interstate 10 rose out of the murky water like the bleached spine of some elongated humpbacked sea serpent. People who had been chased from their homes by the floodwaters were scrambling to reach the highest levels of the highway overpasses in search of islands of dry concrete. It was shortly after 9:30 A.M. on Wednesday, August 31, and what could be seen from the air was not good. But much worse was waiting just a few minutes away at the Louisiana Superdome.

As the helicopter approached the business district of downtown New Orleans and the hulking round mound of concrete and glass that is the Superdome, thousands of people packed together and looking up at the helicopter from the upper plaza level outside the building that bills itself as "Louisiana's Most Recognizable Landmark" came into view. Just a few feet below the crowd, at street level, were the rising waters flowing into the city from nearby Lake Pontchartrain.

My initial reaction to the scene was to mutter to myself, "Oh, my God!" This was my first view of the situation here. All my knowledge to this point had come from reports written by my staff. Their words failed to describe adequately the magnitude of the disaster that Katrina inflicted on New Orleans. But, in their defense, no one could have done justice in words to what was unfolding that morning.

Some of the thousands of people standing outside the Superdome had come there over the weekend when New Orleans Mayor Ray Nagin ordered the first-ever mandatory evacuation of the city after it appeared Katrina was going to score a direct hit. Many of them were poor and African-American, their only means of transportation the buses and streetcars of the New Orleans Regional Transit Authority. They had no way to escape the storm's fury, no way to get out of the city ahead of the hurricane. And those on welfare had little money to buy their way out of town because it was the end of the month and the subsistence checks would not arrive for another few days. The Superdome, which can seat more than 72,000 football fans for New Orleans Saints games and the Sugar Bowl, was converted into a temporary shelter and became their refuge of last resort.

By Monday morning that refuge was a double-edged nightmare. Sunday night and early Monday morning, as about 9,000 city residents and tourists and more than five hundred Louisiana National Guard soldiers huddled inside, Katrina's winds began peeling away the rubber membrane that covers the roof. Holes opened and torrents of hurricane-driven rainwater poured in. People moved quickly to find dry spots. Some of those who came early to the Superdome were encouraged by city officials to bring food, water, and sleeping bags so they could ride out the storm with some amenities since few would be available at the stadium. But when the storm violated the roof and knocked out power throughout the city, the lights went out and the toilets stopped working. This refuge of last resort quickly became a foul-smelling, water-soaked place of suffering instead of a safe haven.

Then, when the levees failed on Monday morning flooding much of the city, the homes of many inside the Superdome became uninhabitable and those people had nowhere else to go. Many came believing they would simply ride out Katrina in the safety of the Dome and go home the next morning. Katrina had other ideas. She not only took their refuge, she took their homes and all their possessions. As the waters rose throughout the city, thousands more were chased from their homes and came looking for shelter and help. But these latest arrivals were chased from their homes on short notice and had not prepared to evacuate. They came with only what they wore and what they could carry. They were unprepared for the disaster that had descended on New Orleans.

The numbers of evacuees grew throughout Monday and Tuesday from the original 9,000 to more than 15,000. Some estimates ran as high as 20,000. Despite gate checks at every entrance for those early arrivals, in which National Guard soldiers searched for weapons and alcohol among those allowed into the Dome, there was no accurate head count, although most estimates had the total at around 16,000–17,000. By Monday morning, when the crowd inside began moving outside to get away from the fouled toilets and dark, water-soaked interior, the new arrivals whose homes had been inundated by the levee breaks were crowding onto the already jammed plaza.

By Wednesday morning people were standing elbow to elbow and hip to hip. They were surrounded by water with no place to go and no way to get there. They were trapped, with the fouled inside of the Dome to their back and the National Guard and floodwaters all around them. They had no working toilets. Their food and water were dwindling. Their only hope was in the government that had encouraged them to come here. But what we were all about to discover was that Katrina was so massive and so destructive that even the federal, state, and local agencies that might have come quickly to the aid of these poor souls were terribly overmatched and had themselves become victims of the storm.

At about 1,500 feet the helicopter made two quick turns around the Superdome before dropping into a steep dive for a small, concrete landing pad on the northwest corner of the upper parking lot near Poydras Street. The clatter of the Seahawk's rotor blades echoed and reverberated off the nearby buildings and water. It seemed abnormally loud, like a helicopter on steroids. Despite the noise, I could hear in my headset calls from the pilots of other helicopters talking to one another about people they had seen standing on their roofs, trapped by the water, waiting to be rescued. The pilot threw the helicopter onto the landing pad with a solid thump and I quickly deplaned and headed for a small white security trailer to meet with Mayor Ray Nagin and officials from FEMA and the Louisiana National Guard to get their assessment of the situation.

A wall of humidity hit me as soon as I was clear of the helicopter's rotor wash and I broke out in a sweat. This was summer in Louisiana, just as I remembered it as a child growing up on the farm. The overpowering stench of brackish water and human waste was thick in the air. It was a collective smell of noxious odors that reminded me of the smell of a full garbage can when the lid is lifted on a hot summer morning.

Just a few yards to my left were the masses of people. They looked at the helicopter and at my uniform hopefully, expectantly, pleading with their eyes to be rescued. Many of the faces were faces of color, like mine. Except for the grace of God, I might have been among them. These were the people I had grown up with. Now they were looking for help. They had that look of people who were trapped and had lost their freedom of movement. They wanted in the worst way to get out but knew there was nothing they could do but wait. They looked at the helicopter as if to say, "Maybe that's our ride out. Maybe they'll take us with them." But they stood quietly behind the flimsy metal barricades, with only a few National Guard soldiers between them and the helicopter, and they waited with a patience that only the poor know.

Turning to walk up the few steps to the security trailer, I looked over a low concrete retaining wall to the street below. A young African-American woman was wading slowly but deliberately through waist-deep water along West Stadium Drive near Cypress Street pushing a grocery cart with a child standing in it. They were searching for an entrance ramp to the Superdome, searching for shelter and rescue.

Already in the trailer were Nagin; Major General Bennie Landreneau, The Adjutant General (TAG) of the Louisiana National Guard, whom I had known for many years; Scott Wells, FEMA's Federal Coordinating Officer (FCO) for Katrina (and later Hurricane Rita); and Wells's deputy, Philip Parr. In addition, members of Landreneau's staff and mine crowded into the trailer along with Coast Guardsmen handling the FM radios and coordinating helicopter search-and-rescue missions throughout the city. Those radios were the only communications systems working in New Orleans at that time except for satellite telephones, because the storm had knocked out virtually all cell phone towers and downed electrical and telephone lines in much of southern Louisiana.

It was stifling in the trailer. The single toilet was fouled and unusable. Only one small generator was working. But the Coasties had somehow managed to scrounge up a coffee pot and hooked it up to the generator and had fresh coffee brewing. It was one of the few obvious signs of initiative, but it was a good sign.

Nagin looked like a man under a great deal of stress, which was understandable. He was tired, edgy, and in need of a shave. It had not been a good few days for him or the city of New Orleans. But he was the senior elected official on the ground and nominally would be my boss, or one of them, for the duration of this mission. It was not my intent to give him the impression that JTF-Katrina was the cavalry riding in to rescue him or that we were coming here to take charge. JTF-Katrina was in a support role and would do what it could to assist him, other elected officials, and the FEMA representatives while working in coordination with Landreneau's Louisiana National Guard soldiers.

For the first thirty minutes I simply sat and listened as Nagin, Wells, Parr, and Landreneau talked about their concerns and their needs and how they thought the numerous problems confronting them should be addressed. The mayor's focus was on getting people out of the Superdome. "We need to start some flow," he said more than once. "We need to start moving people any way we can." He talked about the horrific conditions inside the Superdome and how people could not go back inside because of the filth, water, and lack of electricity. More and more people were coming to the Superdome every hour seeking help as the flooding got worse throughout the city. Though I didn't know it at that moment, an equal number of people were heading to the sprawling Ernest N. Morial Convention Center, which stretched for blocks along the Mississippi River just a short distance away. The mayor's focus in that first meeting was almost entirely on evacuating the Superdome. It was unclear whether there was any solid information about the crowd at the convention center.

Landreneau's concern was to maintain the flow of National Guard troops into the city to assist with security because reports were starting to come in about looting. He also stressed the importance of getting additional food and water to the people at the Superdome. The Coast Guard, which was taking the lead on the search-and-rescue mission, and Landreneau's Louisiana National Guard forces seemed to understand their roles in this disaster and were working with all the speed they could muster and what few resources were available to them at that time.

At one point the discussion turned to using helicopters to start evacuating people from the Superdome. But the helicopters, which eventually would number more than three hundred, were heavily involved in search and rescue, plucking people off rooftops and taking them to the nearest dry ground. In my mind diverting the helicopters from that mission in order to start moving people out of the Superdome was not a wise use of limited resources. The people at the Superdome had dry feet and were in no danger of drowning. Those who were injured or ill, or who needed medications left behind when they evacuated their homes, could be evacuated by helicopter to where they could get medical aid. Other than that, the people on the rooftops were the priority.

The helicopter idea was one of just many thrown out and batted around in that meeting. It was the kind of thing that happens whenever a group of people is trying to solve a complex problem; people bring up all sorts of ideas about how to do things and out of that they figure out what will really work and what won't. But some months later, Parr gave a statement to congressional investigators that he had worked out a plan with a National Guard official, who was never identified, to evacuate people from the Superdome using helicopters. Parr said that they could have cleared out the 16,000–17,000 people within thirty hours and that I came in and nixed the plan, resulting in a delay in the evacuation of at least twenty-four hours.

Parr's comments during the meeting about helicopter evacuation were not something that resonated with me. It seemed more like a bright-ass idea than a plan. But he later confused his bright-ass idea for a plan and told Congress about it. We all get those kinds of ideas. The city had already ordered the buses from FEMA and Parr had been a part of that. But to later say I delayed evacuation by twenty-four hours is unconscionable. Nobody wanted those people at the Superdome to stay in those conditions any longer than was necessary, least of all me, because I, more than anyone else in that room, except for Nagin, identified with those people.

Parr simply did not know what he was talking about when it came to helicopters. The numbers just did not work out. In that weather, with that kind of humidity, using medium-lift helicopters like UH-1 Hueys and Army Black Hawks and Navy Seahawks, we might have been able to move ten to twelve people at a time from the Superdome. Then, once we got them out of there, the question was where we would take them. The nearest likely spot was Baton Rouge, seventy-five miles and thirty minutes away. Then there was the thirty minutes back, refueling, crew changes, loading and unloading, and occasional maintenance. The math was not there. When my staff later heard about Parr's testimony before Congress we called bullshit on it all the way to the bank.

As the meeting went on, it began to descend into the blame game. Nagin, Wells, and Parr went back and forth about who was responsible for what and who should have done what and when. Nagin said FEMA was responsible for the buses but the buses were not there. Parr said the buses were en route but he did not know how many or when they would arrive. Finally, I stood up and said firmly, "Okay guys, let's get off our asses and do something." We left the trailer with the situation unresolved but I knew that we had to start building capacity in order to take care of all the issues that confronted us.

I flew immediately from the Superdome to the USS *Bataan*, an amphibious assault ship sitting about eighty miles offshore, to check it out as a possible site for my forward headquarters. The ship had been in the Gulf of Mexico before Katrina and rode out the storm at sea. It was ordered to stay in the area to assist if it was needed. I had a staff back in Atlanta and a smaller headquarters at Camp Shelby, Mississippi, but was looking for something that would give me more command and control for the operations in New Orleans. After about a ninety-minute visit it became clear that the *Bataan* did not suit my needs and I returned to the Superdome to meet with National Guard officials and police about additional security.

For the second time that day I was met by those same haunting stares and that same look of expectancy from the people massed outside the building. Their eyes seemed to follow me and the more I looked back at them the more I wanted to get them out of there quickly and safely.

There was a brief discussion with National Guard officials about the possibility of using high-water trucks to evacuate people. But the trucks had the same problems as the helicopters; too few people could be evacuated on each run and there was no place close to New Orleans to take them. The hotels and motels that had survived Katrina were full. Baton Rouge was overflowing. Putting people on charter buses and taking them to the Houston Astrodome, a solution worked out by FEMA, was the quickest, safest, and most logical way to go at that point. But I made it clear to the National Guard that the people should be able to walk directly from the Superdome onto the buses without getting their feet wet. A plan eventually was worked out so the evacuees would walk through the Hyatt Regency hotel next door and onto the buses waiting on Loyola Avenue to take them to Houston.

Late that afternoon I flew to Baton Rouge to meet with Governor Kathleen Blanco at the state Emergency Operations Center (EOC) to get her assessment of the situation and hear what priorities she thought needed addressing. She was the senior elected official in the state, so JTF-Katrina was working for her as well as Nagin. I could not unilaterally start making decisions about how we would be employed because of the restrictions on the use of active-duty military troops within the continental United States under the Posse Comitatus Act. Essentially, active-duty troops are able to assist and provide support to civil authorities in times of disaster to save lives. But they cannot do law enforcement and are not in charge of anything except themselves. Under the provisions of the Stafford Act, federal officials, civilian and military, have to be invited by a state's governor to come into his or her jurisdiction to perform specified missions unless it involves saving lives that are in imminent danger. Law enforcement is not one of those missions for active-duty military forces.

Blanco was a pleasant, amiable woman but it was clear that, like Nagin, she was under a great deal of stress and also was a victim of the storm. Victims tend to act and speak like victims and that becomes quite apparent to those who are not victims. Still, Blanco seemed well aware of the immediate needs and priorities. They were to save lives, evacuate people from the Superdome, provide assistance to those in need of it, and tend to the dead, in that order. Brigadier General Mark Graham from Fifth Army in San Antonio, Texas, was with me and it became his job to stay in Baton Rouge and ensure the evacuation plan worked smoothly from that end. He also was responsible for helping track the buses to the Houston Astrodome.

What I did not realize at the time, and what Blanco did not mention in that meeting, was that she was quite disappointed that I had not brought a large number of troops to handle what appeared to her, based on what she was seeing on television, to be a situation in New Orleans where civil authority was breaking down and the city was on the verge of chaos from looters, arsonists, and roving gunmen. It was an impression that many people were beginning to develop as a result of media coverage of Katrina's aftermath. But as will be recounted in detail later in the book, much of that was overhyped and unsubstantiated rumor breathlessly passed on to the world by news media more intent on feeding the insatiable 24/7 news cycle monster than on verifying potentially explosive information.

Had Blanco asked me in that meeting why I had not brought in more troops, a complaint she later repeatedly made to members of Congress and numerous others, I would have told her it was simply a matter of priority and capacity. The priorities were to save lives and evacuate people. We needed helicopters, boats, and buses to do that. Additional troops would merely have taken up space, food, water, and transportation assets. Even if we had been able to get them into the city, there was no place to house them. And there was little for them to do in those first few days since they were prohibited from doing law enforcement.

From the outside the situation may have appeared maddeningly dysfunctional, and at times it seemed that way from the inside. But FEMA was working the evacuation issue with the buses, and the Louisiana National Guard was working with the overextended New Orleans Police Department to provide more security in and around the city. Things were beginning to work, but we were in the process of building capacity and because of the magnitude of the problems dropped in our laps by Katrina, the responses were moving slowly.

There is a National Response Framework for situations such as hurricanes and floods. There is no National Preparedness Plan for disasters. A disaster breaks everything, including the response plan, just as Katrina did. But even a good response plan is just what it says it is: a response. It is not a preparedness plan. The response plan does not provide for the prepositioning of key assets, military or civilian, in areas that are prone to hurricanes, floods, tornadoes, wildfires, earthquakes, or any number of other natural disasters. FEMA did not have two hundred buses sitting around waiting for the next hurricane. It has to contract for those buses and those buses have to be driven in. Governors in hurricane-prone states chafe at the idea of federal troops being sent in prior to a storm. They see it as an insult to their first responders and National Guard forces. Until we as a nation develop a sense that preparedness means actual preparation, not just thinking about it, there will come a time when other communities find themselves in the same situation as New Orleans did after Hurricane Katrina.

Shortly after 7 P.M. my staff and I flew back to New Orleans to talk to the mayor, police, fire, and National Guard officials about the evacuation plan that had been developed. Nagin had to sign off on it, as did the police, before it could be implemented. Louisiana National Guard officials had expressed concerns in my meeting with them earlier that day about security. They felt we needed a significant number of police to help control the crowd at the critical point where evacuees would pass out of the Superdome plaza, through the Hyatt Regency, and onto the buses on Loyola Avenue in front of the hotel. They wanted police to be used, rather than uniformed National Guard soldiers, because if there was any trouble the police could quickly intervene.

I hopped into a Humvee for the short drive to the police department and before we had gone very far the water was up to my butt in the low-slung vehicle. We plowed through the water slowly, watching as people continued to wade through the flood in search of high ground or the refuge of last resort at the Superdome. Once we got to police headquarters we learned the mayor was not there. His house had been flooded and he had been given a room at the Hyatt Regency, even though the hotel had shut down and most of the staff had gone home. But the hotel was close to both the Superdome and City Hall and from there Nagin could easily monitor situations as they developed, even though there were no working communications systems except for military radios and satellite telephones.

We linked up with police superintendent P. Edwin "Eddie" Compass III; his top deputy, Steven Nicholas; Fire Department superintendent Charles Parent; and the New Orleans homeland security chief, Terry Ebbert. Ebbert is a retired Marine Corps colonel and Vietnam veteran who had been awarded the Navy Cross, the nation's second-highest military decoration for valor in combat. He was a good man to have around in a time of crisis. Ebbert was not given to wild statements and overexaggerations as were Compass and Nicholas. Both resigned only a few months after Katrina.

The discussion centered on the evacuation plan and the need for security as the crowd passed through the Hyatt Regency and onto the buses. The National Guard believed the presence of local police would help preserve order and prevent people from rushing the buses and trampling others ahead of them. There was also concern that people might try to inflict some damage on the hotel or surrounding businesses. We reached agreement relatively quickly on the details of the plan and we returned to the Superdome, butt-wet again, to meet with the mayor, tell him what had been decided, and see if he approved of it.

In order to get to the Hyatt Regency I had to walk through the crowd. By now it had grown into a sea of humanity pressed together uncomfortably close in the stifling heat and humidity. Some people were standing in their own filth, unable to move. Only a few small, flimsy metal barricades, each manned by two National Guard soldiers, held them back. Darkness was coming on quickly and some of the National Guard soldiers wanted to put together an armed escort to help me get through the crowd.

"All I want is somebody who can walk through here and show me the way. I don't want any weapons drawn," I told them.

I picked two soldiers, had them sling their weapons, and we moved into the crowd, walking slowly. "I don't want you pushing people out of the way," I told the two. It was so crowded people could not lie down or sit down. These guardsmen knew what they were doing and it was my sense as well that we needed to be as respectful as possible. We offered a polite "Excuse me" and "Pardon us" as we passed through the crowd. How else are you going to act when you're in the middle of 16,000 or 17,000 people, many of whom have just lost their homes and most of their belongings and are about to be shipped out to parts unknown? They hadn't done anything wrong. They had just survived a horrific event. They were waiting for the system to help them but the system was responding slowly.

That walk of just a few hundred yards from one side of the Superdome plaza to the other was amazing. Once again the look of helplessness and despair was obvious in the eyes of many. Their pain was not only physical, it was emotional. The storm had basically broken their morale. Their frustration filled the plaza. I know if I had been among them I would have been the first to be angry. I get upset when I have to wait at the grocery store for the cashier to change the tape in the register. Still others gave me a look that said, "Hey, I'm still alive."

These were mostly poor people, people who were used to having nothing but patience. Their tolerance for these horrible conditions and their calmness while waiting for help were amazing. There was never a harsh word for us, never a sense that we were going to be attacked.

"Hey, brah," one man called out in the vernacular of the street. "Are you going to get us out of here?"

"Yep," I replied, "we're going to get you out."

Walking through the crowd I realized these people were in an information vacuum. They had no real idea of what had happened, what was happening, or what was about to happen. They needed information as much as they needed help, but they had neither. People in Chicago and New York knew more about what was going on in New Orleans than they did. The media were beaming this story around the world, but not one bit of that information was being delivered here, to the people who needed it most.

In any national-level natural disaster such as Katrina or major man-created disaster such as a terrorist attack or mass shooting, there is usually an unspoken, implicit contract between the news media and the individuals and agencies that deal with the response and recovery. The media use these individuals and agencies to get access so they can report their stories and get them out to the general public. The media in turn are used by those who respond and assist in the recovery to get out information that is vital for the public at large and for those most affected.

But for the first few days after Katrina hit, the information flow was all one way. The media had the equipment and the technology to get the information from a storm- and flood-ravaged New Orleans to the world. But it did nothing to provide information to the people most in need of it, those at the Superdome and later at the convention center.

There are those within the media who would argue that that is not their role. But I would argue that it is their responsibility as good citizens. They had the technology and the necessary equipment to bring in loudspeakers or wide-screen televisions so the people trapped at the Superdome could have had some sense of what was going on. Even some radio broadcasts or quickly printed leaflets would have helped immensely. None of this would have gotten the buses there any faster. Nor would it have gotten people the toilets they needed. But it would have provided a sense that a great number of people were working furiously on behalf of those who were trapped. The media are fond of saying it is their role to afflict the comfortable and comfort the afflicted. They did a lot of the former but absolutely none of the latter for the survivors in the first few post-Katrina days.

That sense of wanting some news, any news, was evident during my walk through the crowd that night. Many asked what was going on and how quickly they would be getting out of there. One man, who apparently had some military experience, saw the three silver stars on my black beret and remarked to someone else, "That's a three-star general. Something's going to happen now."

When people saw my name tag with HONORÉ stitched in bold, black thread on the green background they recognized it as a Louisiana name with a long and distinguished heritage. Some would ask if I knew this Honoré or that Honoré that they knew. Usually I did not, but simply having that Louisiana name meant something to them. It seemed to provide a sense of hope that things would get better.

When we got to the hotel only two guards were at the door. The crowd was not pushing at them or trying to break through. These people had come through an incredible shock and were not rioting and were not on the verge of panic. They had been put in a helpless, almost hopeless situation. Still, they waited with that patience that is so much a part of the culture of the poor.

After meeting briefly with the mayor and explaining what would happen the next morning when the buses started arriving, he agreed to the plan and we returned to the Superdome. I talked again with National Guard officials to make sure we were all on the same page, then shortly before 10:30 got back into the helicopter for the return flight to Camp Shelby and a few hours of sleep.

As the helicopter sliced through the thick night air, the ground below us eerily dark because of the lack of electricity in much of southern Louisiana and Mississippi, I ran through the events of the day in my head. It was clear that no one, least of all the people most affected, had been prepared for the wrath of Katrina. The storm had overwhelmed the ability of both the system and the people to deal with it. Whatever any government agency or individual had put in place to cope with storms such as Katrina had simply been overmatched. Some families had prepared, but their preparations usually had not been sufficient to deal with this storm. The governments of Louisiana and New Orleans had talked about the worst-case scenario but prepared for the best-case scenario. The people had thought about the worst-case scenario, but few had actually prepared for it.

In order to change that, in order to mitigate the effects of storms like Katrina or other disasters, there would have to be a cultural shift in how governments, businesses, the education system, and individuals prepared for them. Preparation would have to become as important as response. It was something that had been bred into me growing up on a subsistence farm in central Louisiana. Disaster was always one storm, one bad crop, one untimely death away. But how well we survived that disaster was in direct relation to how we prepared for it. In my family, disaster preparedness, even if we didn't call it that, was the key to survival in rural Louisiana.

CHAPTER 1
Lessons Learned for Building a Culture of Preparedness

1. Remember lessons from the Superdome: shelters must be able to keep people alive in the worst-case scenario.

2. Be aware of a thirty-foot tidal surge coming ashore with the eye of a hurricane.

3. When a hurricane hits at the end of the month, the poor, elderly, and disabled people who depend on government checks will not have the money to evacuate.

4. Don't stage response equipment inside an area prone to tidal surges or floods.

5. The federal government, led by FEMA, needs to stage supplies, buses, and IBBs (itty-bitty boats) on the flanks of the projected storm landfall area.

6. When evacuating a city, government personnel should evacuate last. All bus drivers and public service personnel should remain behind to help with evacuation of disabled, poor, and the ill.

7. During an evacuation, no car should leave with an empty seat . . . take a neighbor, a friend, an employee.

8. First responders need satellite based communication in the event cell towers are down.

9. Police stations, hospitals, and fire stations should have generators large enough to provide power for the entire building.

10. Generators should be on upper floors of buildings and not at ground level or in basements.

11. The U.S. Navy should have standing orders to follow hurricanes ashore with Wasp-class amphibious assault ships that have helicopters and Marines onboard.

12. State and local governments need to work with in-state businesses for help with evacuation and response. Colleges in high-risk areas should offer a Red Cross First Aid and Disaster Response Course. The students would earn college credit and be trained to keep people alive during a disaster.

2

Hurricane Born and Hurricane Bred

THE STORM WAS KNOWN SIMPLY AS HURRICANE FOUR. IT BEGAN AS a tropical wave off the west coast of Africa on September 4, 1947, and slowly made its way across the Atlantic, taking aim at the Bahamas and coastal Florida. On September 15, two days before the storm slammed ashore at Fort Lauderdale, Florida, with winds of more than 160 miles per hour, Eudell St. Amant Honoré of Lakeland, Louisiana, with the aid of a local midwife, gave birth to me, the eighth of her twelve children and her eighth consecutive son. Like all my brothers and my sisters, I was born in a clapboard house about twenty-five miles northwest of Baton Rouge in the middle of fertile bottomland that for centuries was repeatedly flooded and enriched by the nearby Mississippi River until protective levees were built in the late 1930s.

My father, Lloyd Honoré, was a man everyone in Pointe Coupee Parish knew as "Chief." He was a hardworking, no-nonsense subsistence farmer who invested his life in the land in order to provide for his family. He grew cotton and sugarcane to sell and raised cows for milk, and pigs and chickens and a garden full of vegetables to eat. My father always had a truck of some type to haul cargo for other farmers. It might have been a load of furniture for residents who were moving to nearby Alma Plantation, cattle or hogs to the slaughterhouse, or cotton to the nearby gin for processing. Those trips meant extra cash for him and his family.

My father was an icon in our family and our small community. People of all races liked him because he always tried to find the middle ground and help others find it as well. He was a natural negotiator. He was also a tremendous storyteller. He and my relatives would sit on our porch or under a tree and start telling stories early in the afternoon and go on until well after dark. They told stories about growing up during the really hard times. They particularly liked the tales about their mules. They spoke with great pride about how hard their mules worked and how strong they were. They had great affection for those animals. But sometimes the stories they told were not about animals. They were stories about a time when people of color were found dead for no apparent reason. Their stories were sometimes frightening but always captivating. Those stories became part of the Honoré family legacy and heritage.

My birth in 1947 coincided with the time of year in Louisiana that is the worst for hurricanes. Come September each year, poor farmers like my father kept a worried eye on the sky and listened to weather reports on the radio in an effort to stay ahead of hurricanes and get the cotton and corn harvested before the winds and rain got to them. There was no reliable early warning system in those days except for the radio and our relatives. We had relatives who lived in the 7th and 9th wards of New Orleans and we knew that a bad storm was going to hit when they showed up at our house, which they called "the country," with their cars packed with clothes and enough food to outlast the flooding in the city.

Hurricane Four, later to become known as the 1947 Fort Lauderdale Hurricane, made landfall as a Category 3 storm near Louisiana's Chandeleur Islands four days after my birth. The storm pushed inland across New Orleans and on through Lakeland. That storm killed fifty-one people and did more than $110 million damage, and for the rest of my childhood the rhythm of my life was dictated by hurricanes and tropical storms that swept through the area on a regular basis.

That was a different era. It was an era of self-sufficiency, when people were expected to fend for themselves and prepare themselves and their families for disasters, natural or man-made. We were poor but we learned at an early age that we needed to be prepared for the worst nature could give us. It became part of our culture to be adequately prepared. During hurricane season my father tried to make sure that he had harvested what he could before the storms hit. If he was not able to get all the harvesting done and the crops were badly damaged by a storm, there were always a few hogs to sell for enough money to buy the supplies we needed to get through the lean months. Only on rare occasions did we have to dip into the surplus foodstuffs the Department of Agriculture handed out to families when things got tougher than they normally were. My father would get these big logs of cheese, sacks of flour, syrup, and peanut butter in gallon cans. He would have to document how many people were living at home so he could get enough for all of us.

That food was not handed out every year. It usually was available only after a big storm came through or the boll weevils ruined the cotton crop. When those disasters struck, they affected everybody, whether big farmers, middle-class farmers, or poor farmers like my father, who rented the land he farmed. The farther down that food chain you were, the bigger the impact that storm had on you and your family.

In most years, though, my father depended on the land to supply what we needed. The good thing about that part of Louisiana is that we could raise vegetables such as mustards and cabbage well into the winter. We would store potatoes to eat during the cold months and kill the pigs that we did not have to sell at market. Through the winter and holiday period we would be eating off those animals. We would butcher them right there in the yard and my mother would cook them up in the kitchen. At the time it seemed the most natural thing to do, but there probably are few people today who know how to kill and pluck a chicken, much less butcher a hog.

When you're poor you have to learn how to be innovative in order to survive. You learn how to adapt to the situation you are in and overcome it. In our home we had two black-and-white television sets. The sound worked in one and the picture worked in the other. We could not afford to get either fixed so we put both on the same channel and had our television, the sound coming from one and the picture from the other.

On Sunday afternoons entertainment was three kids, a ball, and two cotton sacks. We'd play ball all afternoon with one guy hitting, one pitching, and one in the outfield. If more kids showed up we might have two in the outfield. These days kids won't play, or their parents won't allow them to play, without uniforms, helmets, umpires, and adult supervision. The fun and spontaneity is gone. So too are those life's lessons of learning how adapt to the circumstances in which you find yourself and making them better by finding a way to overcome adversity.

People to a great degree have become too dependent on others. They don't have the self-sufficiency that we once had. To my own slap in the face I have not passed that on to my son, Steven. If we needed something to eat when I was growing up and didn't have money to buy groceries we would simply go outside, kill a chicken in the yard, bring it inside, cook it, and eat it. Or we would go to the chicken coop and get some eggs. My son can cook an egg, but he's never harvested one.

But, to be fair, I did not want my kids to have to deal with the same things I did. In the process I made them more dependent on others. I did not want them to have to learn how to fix an old broken car. I did not want them living in an old wooden house. I did not want them to have bad teeth, like I did. By the time I was thirty-two years old many of my teeth had been pulled because of the lack of dental care earlier in life. My kids now have beautiful teeth. Their life is better than mine was. What they call a *Survivor* television show today was a way of life back in southern Louisiana in the 1950s and 1960s. It's not that my kids have to suffer the same pain I did growing up as a second-class citizen. Things are a lot more complex now. We can't have chickens in the backyard where we live now. My children will just have to learn to overcome and adapt in a different way.

Although I often was referred to during the Hurricane Katrina operations as "The Ragin' Cajun," my heritage is Creole. There is a significant difference. Cajuns are Louisianans who trace their ancestry back to the French Acadians who came to the region starting in the mid-eighteenth century. Creoles are something of a racial and ethnic gumbo, with French, African, Spanish, and Native American thrown into the mix. Creoles for many years were considered neither all white nor all black and frequently were shunned by both races.

My family referred to itself as *les Creole,* which means we were people of mixed blood and therefore considered "colored" or black. The high Creoles were white, a mixture of Spanish and French. Our brand of Creole was made up of people who came through the port of New Orleans by way of the West Indies and ended up in Pointe Coupee Parish. There exists among the Creoles a common bond in religion, speech, and food. There is a shared culture and we tend marry within that culture and the Creole community. It is a culture difficult for outsiders to understand and tends to defy description and classification.

There were only two designations of people in Pointe Coupee Parish—"colored" and white. Inside the "colored" community were Creole families and black families, the latter now known as African-Americans.

They had no French lineage. In our church, the Immaculate Conception Catholic Church in Lakeland, we had two separate seating sections— one for whites, one for "coloreds." We self-segregated and all sat in our own sections. That did not change until after the *Brown v. Board of Education* Supreme Court decision in 1954 desegregated schools and society was forced to change with it.

My official military records list me as African-American even though I am Creole. But if my picture were placed side by side with that of John James Audubon, the famous painter, writer, and ornithologist, we would appear to have no common characteristics. He was a white Creole. The famous Civil War general P. G. T. Beauregard, who was instrumental in Confederate victories at Fort Sumter and in First Manassas, was a Creole, as was the pirate Jean Lafitte. The musicians Jelly Roll Morton and Fats Domino are of Creole heritage. So too was Ernest Morial, the former mayor of New Orleans for whom the convention center was named.

The Honorés' Creole roots in Louisiana, particularly in Pointe Coupee Parish, ran deep into the ground at least as far back as the early eighteenth century. The name is common and quite recognizable in that part of the state. Although our family tree can not document any direct relations to them, at least three Honorés fought as "free men of color" under the banner of Andrew Jackson in the Battle of New Orleans in 1815 to beat back British efforts to capture the city.

For several generations before my birth, my family knew of the ferocity of the occasional hurricanes that hit Louisiana. They came to respect those storms and passed on that respect and wisdom of how to deal with them to future generations. Whenever my relatives got together they inevitably told stories about memorable storms of the past and what the next year might bring. It was not unusual for conversations over Christmas dinner to turn to hurricanes. People just naturally thought about things like that throughout the year because those conversations provided everyone with insights about what they should have done that year or how they could better prepare for future storms. It was a part of our life cycle to be concerned about and aware of hurricane preparedness.

My parents often talked about the times the Mississippi River spilled over its banks, usually in the spring, and washed over Point Coupee Parish. They used to say some floods were so bad and the water covered so much of the lower Mississippi River valley that it was possible to take a boat in a straight line across the farm fields from Jackson, Louisiana, just north of Baton Rouge, to Lafayette, a distance west of more than ninety miles. In those years the poorer farmers would lose everything. Their crops and their livestock, and often their homes, would be washed away by the muddy water. But as soon as the water backed out they would return and start working the land again. It was a tough life but those who lived here, like my parents, were tough people.

The worst flood in their memory was in 1927, when heavy spring rains in the South and ice melt in the North sent the Mississippi River sprawling over its banks for miles. More than twenty-six thousand square miles were covered in water, over two hundred people died, and an estimated six hundred thousand people were chased out of their homes. The damage was more than $1.5 billion in today's dollars. After that the U.S. Army Corps of Engineers made flood mitigation one of its priorities through the use of levees to hold back water and the creation of floodways to control excess water flow. The Corps put in a spillway at Morganza not far from our home so it could divert water into the swamp in case the river got too high. When it built the flood control system it also left considerable land on both sides of the channel so that the river could spread out before it got to the levees.

As kids we used to go to the river in the spring, after the water had gone down, to seine for crawfish in the deep pits left by workers who dug up soil for the levees. We'd spend hours down there and come home with big tubs of crawfish and boil them immediately. What was not apparent to me then was that that land between the channel and the levees acted as part of the flood control plan. Farther south along the river in New Orleans there is no land between the river and the levees. The levees are built right up to the river channel so there is no place for the water to go when the river rises except up and over the levees. Compounding the problem is that homes and streets have been built next to the levees, leaving no margin for safety.

My father and many of the men who farmed the land around Lakeland were not well educated. But they were incredibly wise when it came to preparing their homes, the land, and their families for what spring rains or hurricane season might bring. Most people in that part of Louisiana built their houses on stilts of some sort, usually concrete or cinder blocks that raised the living area three or four feet off the ground. They knew that if the river flooded, the elevated houses would likely be spared. It was the same for hurricanes, which were primarily wind and rain events by the time they got that far inland. Any flooding from hurricane rains would never reach the first floor of the houses on stilts.

The old, antebellum plantation homes in the lower river valley often were built seven or eight feet off the ground. Many of the stately homes in that part of Louisiana still stand today because the builders planned ahead. They planned for the worst and built for the worst. They lived with a culture of preparedness. Now it is not uncommon to drive through the region and see brick houses in new subdivisions that are built on concrete slabs right on the ground.

New Orleans is much like that. When my family visited my aunts in the 7th and 9th wards there was always a flight of steps to walk up to get to the living area of their homes. Many of the houses were built off the ground two or three feet to factor in the possibility of floods. If those floods came, seldom was the living space violated. There were several occasions, though, when my relatives came to the country to escape a hurricane and the flooding got so bad in the city that the men went back first to clean up and get the houses ready to live in again. Sometimes they would have to rip out all the lower levels of the houses and it would be a week or two before their families could move back in.

But the flooding never was as bad as we would see years later in Katrina, when entire houses were under water. But as I said, many of those modern-era houses were built slab on grade, right on that low-lying dirt, with absolutely no forethought about flooding. During my occasional drives around the city in the years after Katrina to check on the pace of restoration and rebuilding, I would see a number of homes being built or rebuilt at ground level. The next flood will get them, too.

As was the case with Katrina and New Orleans, how well anyone survives a hurricane or disaster of any type is in direct correlation to where they were before the event occurred. When it gets hot the poor always seem to get a little hotter. When it gets cold the poor get a damn sight colder. And when it rains the poor are going to be a little wetter. We were forever trying to patch up our old house as best we could to make it more livable and more survivable. But when the storms came through and the wind ripped off the tin roof, we had to get up there with hammers and tar and put it back in place. When the weather turned cold it took an incredible amount of wood to keep the house warm. People who lived in more substantial houses did not have to do those sorts of things. The poor spend a great deal of energy doing maintenance just so they can live.

When it got hot on those long and steamy Louisiana summer nights in that little house on the gravel road outside Lakeland, the one small fan trying to pull a cool draft through all the rooms provided no relief. Years later, during the Katrina operations, seeing all those people at the Superdome sitting in the heat and humidity with no place to go and no means of getting away from the flooding was like a flashback for what my life used to be like.

The two hurricanes that made the biggest impression on me as a child were Betsy, a Category 3 storm in 1965 and the first to cause more than $1 billion in damages, and Audrey, a Category 4 in 1957. Both hit Louisiana hard, but Audrey was more memorable because I was only nine years old at the time and much more impressionable. During the height of Audrey the wind ripped at the tin roof on our house and drove rain through the cracks in the siding. Our house was not insulated so it was not unusual for wind-driven rain to find its way into the house. Audrey seemed to go on forever although it had lost most of its punch and was little more than a tropical storm by the time the winds got to Lakeland.

One of the biggest differences between hurricanes then and now is the access to information about the storm's strength and path. It is impossible in this age of instant and constant news to go more than a few minutes without receiving a radio, television, or e-mail update on a storm. For Audrey, our only sources of information came from our relatives near the coast or the radio. By the time Hurricane Betsy hit eight years later we had a small black-and-white television set. But there were no on-the-scene, minute-by-minute accounts of storm damage as there are now. There was one guy sitting at a desk in Baton Rouge reading news updates about the impact of the storm as it hit the coast. We had to use our imaginations and visualize in our minds what horrific things these storms were doing as they pushed their way inland.

My life underwent a significant and dramatic change when I was about twelve years old. Although it was not apparent to me at the time, it was a change that would teach me the virtues of hard work, the value of planning and thinking ahead, the importance of being prepared, and the necessity of teamwork. Those lessons followed me through high school and college and on into the Army and beyond.

One day my aunt Gertrude Fuselier and I were in the yard killing chickens for dinner when a local dairy farmer by the name of Grover Chustz stopped and asked if I wanted to come to work for him.

He needed help on his farm. My father knew and respected him and although we had plenty of work to do on our rented land, the chance to earn a few dollars appealed to me.

Chustz was not an educated man by any means, but he had the best-looking farm and the best-looking cattle in that part of the parish. He had built his farm on his own through stubborn persistence and by making sure everything was done well. He was creative and innovative. One day he might say, "I'm getting older and it's getting hard to move this hay to the second floor of the barn." And just like that he would decide to build something to make it easier to move that hay. He wouldn't buy it. He would go to town and come back with some gearboxes and some chain, and two or three days later, using only a drawing he had done and couple of guys he hired to weld and put things together, he would have a conveyor. He was always an inspiration because he provided for himself. Chustz took a liking to me and me to him because he was successful in the same environment where everybody was just surviving.

We would milk cows in the morning and evening. We normally milked sixty to sixty-five head of cattle. During the summers we would start at four in the morning and finish up around six-thirty or seven. Then we fed the calves. After that was maintenance work, like moving manure from one place to another. Once we finished with those chores Chustz would take me home and I would sleep a couple of hours, have lunch, go back to the farm, and start the milking all over again at about one in the afternoon.

During school the bus would drop me off at the farm and I would work until dark, when Chustz would drive me home. That was the rhythm of my life from my last year of elementary school until my junior year in college. Chustz paid me $3 a day to start. By high school the rate was up to $6 a day. By my freshman year in college the pay was $12 a day and it eventually peaked at $24 a day.

The money was important back then but it was only later that I realized Chustz had been teaching me many other life lessons. Watching how hard he worked and how he wanted everything done to a standard made a lasting impression on me. With him everything was a precision process: how far apart we planted the corn, how many seeds went into each hole, and how fast the tractor should be driven. All those were important to him. If we went faster we finished early but we knew there was a direct connection between the time and effort we put in and the results we would eventually get back.

Chustz also taught me the very important lesson of teamwork. After I had been working for him for several years he brought another boy in to help. The new boy was white and came from a farm right across the road from the dairy. He and I just did not get along. At thirteen or fourteen years old it's a big deal to drive the tractor and when Chustz wasn't there that was my job. But when this other boy, who was older and more experienced, came to the farm, driving the tractor became his job.

This guy really frustrated me. I went to Chustz and very emotionally told him straight out, "I can't work with that guy."

Chustz looked at me for a minute then said, "Look, let me tell you something. Regardless of what you do, you don't necessarily have to like people. But when you're given a job you have to learn to work as a team."

He took a single wooden match out of a box he kept in his pocket and broke it in two. Then he took out two matches and put them together and they were a little harder to break. Then he took four matches and put them together and said: "Now, you break that. That's the power of a team when you work together." That became one of the lessons I used many times in my thirty-seven years in the military when talking to people about the power of the team. It's about people working together to do what has to be done.

Despite the infighting among federal and state agencies in the aftermath of Hurricane Katrina, I repeatedly tried to stress to people that even if they did not like one another, pulling together for the common good would get things done quickly and more efficiently. But that was not a lesson that was well received in some quarters because of the constant friction between state and federal officials, a legacy of the Civil War that survives to this day in many parts of the South.

My work on the dairy farm brought me into contact with the 4-H club and the New Farmers of America, the black version of the Future Farmers of America during that segregated era. That, in turn, brought me into contact with the black parish agent, Tom Smith, who taught me how to show and judge dairy cattle. My father had a mixed-breed Guernsey-Jersey cow named Weezie that he had bought from the Chustz farm. Weezie became my first 4-H club project. She had beautiful conformation for a dairy animal. But to demonstrate how divided we were racially in that part of Louisiana in the 1950s and 1960s, the first year I took Weezie to the parish fair to show, she had to go in the back of the tent because she was a "colored" cow. She did not belong up front with the cows that had been raised by white farmboys. Not only were the people segregated, so were the cows, simply because of who had raised them and cared for them.

My agriculture teacher in my junior and senior years in high school was a man by the name of Roland Roberts. He was an Army veteran of World War II who had served in France. If he was teaching something that was hard, or something we were bored with, someone would ask: "Mr. Roberts, when you were in the war, what would you do if . . ." When that happened we knew the rest of the class would be about the war.

He used to tell us that when he was in France he could go into any restaurant he wanted and nobody would say anything to him. Those stories created something of a dilemma in our minds. If men of all races, creeds, and colors helped free France and were welcome everywhere over there, why couldn't we do that in America? I was never at the forefront of the civil rights movement but those kinds of stories certainly caused me to pause and question why it wasn't that way here. It made me think that maybe this guy Martin Luther King, Jr., we had been hearing about, despite the dislike many of the whites in Pointe Coupee Parish openly exhibited toward him, might be the guy to change things. And maybe I should not believe all the negative things being said about him. Maybe King was doing the right thing to help make America a better place and directly affect me in terms of opportunity and fairness.

In 1964, my sophomore year in high school, Roberts put together a group of New Farmers of America students to attend the organization's national convention in Atlanta. I had the twelve dollars needed to make the trip because of my work on Chustz's dairy farm. It was a trip that left me with lasting impressions of the segregation and prejudice that still gripped many parts of the South, but also left me with a great deal of hope after what I saw in Atlanta.

We boarded an old yellow school bus in the middle of the night to start the trip and someone asked why we were leaving at that hour. "Boys," our school sponsor said, "you have to understand that we have to drive through Mississippi and we don't want to drive through there at night." That was the time of violent attacks on the Freedom Riders and there was concern our school outing might be confused with them. We had to be careful about what roads we drove on and where we stopped. We wanted to get through Mississippi as quickly as possible so people would have less chance to become suspicious of a busload of young black men.

At one point we stopped at a gas station in Mississippi and the sponsor looked at me and said, "Honoré, you go in there and ask if we can use the bathroom."

He may have asked me to go in because I was taller than everybody else on the bus and lighter skinned. So I ran inside and asked if we could use the bathroom. The man behind the counter looked me over and said, "Who are you all?"

"We're from Louisiana and we're heading to Atlanta," I said proudly.

He walked out, looked on the bus, and shook his head. "Y'all just keep right on going," he said. We went on down the road until we found another place where we could use the bathroom.

For me, the most lasting memory of that trip was the startling differences between that part of the South, where prejudice and bigotry were so ingrained, and Atlanta, where blacks owned businesses all around the Clark, Spelman, and Morehouse college campus where we stayed. Blacks owned restaurants, movie theaters, and barbershops. That was not something we saw in the part of Louisiana our group came from. It was an incredible education for me and left me believing that one day it would all change for the better. Now I routinely fly in and out of Atlanta on military jets and nobody has a second thought about it.

My work with dairy cattle and ability to judge them opened a number of doors and put me on a path I thought eventually would lead to my own dairy farm. Raising and judging dairy cows became a passion. I was able to go on occasional trips to Southern University in Baton Rouge for 4-H conferences, where I began learning about leadership and being in the public eye. I also got a chance to go to Mexico with the 4-H, where I saw a much larger world out there waiting to be explored. I began to think that things could be different for me. For the first time in my life I could see a world beyond the boundaries of Pointe Coupee Parish.

For many people in that part of Louisiana the education target was to learn to read and write and finish elementary school before dropping out to go to work on the family farm. Finishing high school was a luxury for many folks. Several of my older brothers never finished high school, primarily because of tough economic conditions. They dropped out to learn a trade so they could go to work and survive.

My oldest brother, John, was among those who did not complete high school. He went to Baton Rouge and became a bricklayer. He moved to Los Angeles in the 1960s and became a master brick mason and a supervisor for the Los Angeles water department. Several other brothers followed much the same route: Baton Rouge to learn a trade and then on to Los Angeles where jobs were plentiful, the pay was better, and prejudice not so pronounced. My second brother, Clarence, after returning to the Baton Rouge area as a master carpenter and contractor, established himself in the housing industry. Only my third brother, Marshall, stayed in the Lakeland area. He spent all his adult life either working on the old family farm or was a local hire on farms or at the sugar mill in the winter during the sugarcane harvest.

Tony, my fourth-oldest brother, was a carpenter by trade who also took the Baton Rouge–Los Angeles route. He went on to own a major construction company that specialized in projects involving earthquake or fire damage in the Los Angeles area until his retirement. My fifth brother, Lloyd, Jr., was the first in the family to finish high school. He also became an electrician and followed my other brothers to Los Angeles. He owned his own electrical contracting business, was a licensed electrician, and taught many young apprentices the trade.

James, my sixth-oldest brother, also finished high school and went straight to the West Coast and decided to take a different path. He started working in the mailroom for a major movie studio and eventually became an apprentice film editor. He went on to become the vice president for postproduction at Sony/Columbia TriStar Studios. Alvin, the seventh brother, born just before me, didn't finish high school but went to Los Angeles, enlisted into the Army, and served in Germany. After returning to Los Angeles he received his GED and became an electrician. Later, he and a friend and business partner opened Harold and Belle's restaurant, which specializes in Creole cuisine in south-central Los Angeles.

All three of my sisters, Mary Joy and the twins, Loretta and Lorraine, chose careers in the health-care industry and became supervisors in their respective jobs. While the twins remained in the Baton Rouge area, Mary retired and lives in Dallas. Our youngest brother, Jude, also served a stint in the military as a Marine. He too spent time in Los Angeles learning the electrical trade from Lloyd, Jr., and Alvin before returning to the Baton Rouge area and becoming a supervisor for a major local power company.

How my parents, neither of whom finished elementary school, could raise such a large family and have every one of their children become so successful in their own fields is absolutely astonishing.

I was the first in my family to go to college. People ask why I chose

Southern University in Baton Rouge. There really wasn't much choice at the time. Southern was one of the historically black universities and colleges and my entire educational career had been in a segregated school system. All my teachers had gone to Southern. And I had visited Southern several times while in high school, was familiar with the campus, and felt comfortable there.

College was a struggle because I had to work my way through. Loans and part-time jobs paid for tuition and books. In addition to my work on the Chustz farm, I worked for the Department of Agriculture measuring quota crops like cotton and sugarcane on farms around Baton Rouge. It was pretty good pay and the work allowed me to use my head instead of my hands. The job brought in enough money to pay my first semester. I also earned money my freshman year when the annual livestock show came to campus. That was a show I had competed in during elementary school and high school, but once in college I could work as an assistant to the manager. School was second on my list of priorities that week the livestock show was in town. Sixteen to eighteen hours a day were not unusual for what then was big money, six to eight dollars an hour.

In the spring of my freshman year I started working for a cousin, Raymond Honoré, who owned a drive-in and a car wash. I would flip burgers and then go to work at the car wash. Study was something done after nine o'clock at night and sometimes until just before the first class in the morning. It was not unusual for me to be right on the edge of getting my reports done. But I was able to discipline myself to get them done despite the part-time jobs and other commitments, including Reserve Officer Training Corps. It was a discipline learned working on our farm and later on Chustz's dairy farm. It was a matter of improvising, overcoming, and adapting to find ways to get schoolwork finished in time.

By the fall of 1966, my freshman year, the Vietnam War was hitting its stride and choices for young men were rather limited. It was either be subject to the draft or go into ROTC. I had no real intention of making a career out of the Army. I set my sights on becoming a dairy farmer and having my own herd of cows and land on which to graze them. But joining ROTC and getting the draft waiver that would allow me to finish college was a big motivator. I wanted to be an officer. I wanted to be Lieutenant Honoré. My only previous exposure to a military officer was my cousin, J. F. St. Amant. He and his wife had come home to bury a child they had lost. He was a major at the time and looked absolutely striking in his uniform. People held him in the highest regard and when I heard what people were saying about him because he was a commissioned officer and saw how he looked, I thought, That's pretty cool. Maybe this is something I'll do.

Those years of ROTC, especially the last two, were hard. Other students would heckle us while we were marching. "Why do you want to be in the Army?" "Why do you want to be officers in a country that doesn't allow you to be free?" "Why do you want to go to Vietnam?" Those remarks made me think a lot but in the end it strengthened my resolve that this was a life learning experience and there always would be issues involving me that were not going to be popular with everyone. I had made a commitment to serve my country and while my country had not been all it could be to me, I was going to be all I could be to my country. I believed the opportunity would enable me to overcome.

One of the most valuable lessons I learned from ROTC was never to let anyone outwork me. I knew I was not the sharpest knife in the drawer. I also knew I would have to be better than the next guy to get what I wanted. That still drives me today but it also drives me up the wall. There were times when my kids were growing up when my wife, Beverly, would ask, "Why are you always the last one to get home? Why, as a colonel, are you working every weekend and most of these other colonels are not?" I wanted to earn the right to lead while others were content to follow.

ROTC taught me what it means to be a leader and all that implies. I had been president of my senior class in high school and became one of the leaders of the corps of cadets at Southern. But it was not until I was confronted with a particularly difficult ROTC class that leadership became a tangible thing. I had to give a block of instruction to other cadets and decided to teach map reading. I did not adequately prepare for the presentation. As a result, I failed that block of instruction. I failed on my technique. I failed on the technical aspects. I failed on my delivery. The instructor, an Army major, called me into his office. When we were alone he asked what had happened and I said I was joining the Army to be a soldier, not a teacher.

He almost jumped out of his chair. He glared at me and said, "If you come in the Army you are going to be a teacher. You're expected to teach because leaders teach. If you're going to be a good leader you're going to have to learn how to be a good teacher. The concept of leadership is teaching."

After he was finished chewing out my ass I pulled out the technical manual on map reading and learned it. I learned the language needed to get my points across, developed my demonstration charts, and eventually passed that block of instruction. But the lesson that major taught me has stuck with me to this day—If you're going to be a leader, you also have to be a teacher. Great leaders teach their ideas and get people to follow them.

It took me four and a half years to finish college even with several summer sessions. That last year was a living hell. For several years after graduating in January 1971, I had nightmares about college, often waking up in a sweat. Was the paper right? Was my grade-point average high enough? Would I embarrass my family by not graduating in a reasonable amount of time?

By the time I graduated with a degree in vocational agriculture the Army's involvement in Vietnam was starting to wind down and my initial choice of branches, Quartermaster, or supply, seemed more likely to be beneficial once my military obligation was completed and I returned to Louisiana. My ROTC advisor did not see it that way. He advised me in no uncertain terms that my future was in the infantry and ordered me to erase Quartermaster as my first choice and put down infantry. I did as he demanded and put down Quartermaster for my second choice. He made me erase that and put down infantry. He did the same with the third choice. That's how I ended up in the infantry. By February 1971, I was at Fort Benning, Georgia, embarking on a career in the uniform of the United States Army that would last thirty-seven years.

CHAPTER 2
Lessons Learned for Building a Culture of Preparedness

1. Red Cross debit cards should be issued to poor people in areas frequently hit by hurricanes, floods, or earthquakes. People should preregister with the Red Cross and in the event of an evacuation, money for food and gas can be put into their accounts.

2. State and local governments should establish strict building codes in hurricane-prone areas.

3. Counties and parishes should have simple, precise maps that show where people live in flood-prone areas.

4. Families should be Red Cross ready:

   A. Have a plan—know where you are going and when.

   B. Have a kit with three days' worth of food and an evacuation pack.

   C. Stay informed with a weather radio. (Details of Red Cross preparedness can be found on its website, www.redcross.org.)

5. Education systems should teach the Red Cross disaster preparation modules in elementary and middle schools.

6. National Preparedness Month should be in May, not September.

3

Learning the Zumwalt Rules

THERE MUST HAVE BEEN A CERTAIN AMOUNT OF DIVINE INTERVEN-tion that kept me off the farm and in uniform for all those years. In January 1971, I married Beverly, graduated from Southern University, and received my commission as a second lieutenant in the U.S. Army. My original plan was to serve a few years, then find a nice plot of land in Louisiana and return home to raise cattle. I requested a six-month deferment from reporting to the Infantry Officer Basic Course (IOBC) at Fort Benning, Georgia, to take a job with the Farmers Home Administration, a federal agency that provided loans to small farmers. The plan was to work with that agency for a few months, go into the Army for two or three years, then come back and resume work with the federal agency. Not only would that give me job insurance for my post-Army life, it would allow me to spend a few months with my new bride before reporting to the basic class.

All the necessary paperwork was submitted and it was just a matter of waiting for approval from the Department of the Army, which I thought was a mere formality. But two weeks after I was commissioned I went back to Southern University and ran into an ROTC instructor who seemed surprised to see me. He said he had received a message that I was due at Fort Benning the next week. There was no letter from the Department of the Army granting my deferment. I could not risk ignoring those orders to report to the basic class so I regretfully left my bride, hopped on a bus, and headed straight for Fort Benning and Columbus,

Georgia. I was there a week when the Department of the Army letter granting the six-month deferment was forwarded to me. The letter had passed me somewhere en route. I decided it was meant for me to turn down the deferment and complete the basic course. Call it fate or divine intervention, but I simply told myself, "Okay, I'll just get through the basic course and see what happens from there."

In February 1971, the Army was in its Vietnam withdrawal phase. Infantry officers were not as much in demand as they once had been, since more and more of the fighting was being turned over to the Vietnamese. The infantry officers of my class were among the first of a new crop of officers who were expected to be the vanguard of a new, post-Vietnam Army. At that time we had an Army that was demoralized and unsure of what it should be in the years to come. My classmates and I were to lead the next-generation Army. But in order to do that we had to learn the lessons our predecessors brought back from the battlefield while at the same time we looked down the road and tried to determine what the service would look like ten, twenty, or thirty years from that point.

My class at Fort Benning was the usual mixture of ROTC lieutenants commissioned right out of college and West Point graduates who had spent their entire four years of college in an atmosphere of strict military discipline and rigid military instruction. It was obvious they had something of an advantage militarily. But I had learned some valuable life lessons they had not because of how cloistered they had been during their four years in the military academy.

One of those lessons was to make the most of my abilities. In my senior year at Southern University I had heard an inspirational speech by an educator who used the biblical parable of throwing seed on barren ground and not watering or weeding it. That seed will not produce anything. If I did not take advantage of the skills at my disposal I was not going to produce anything in life. Knowing what to do and doing it are two different things. There were classmates of mine at Fort Benning who seemed to have it all. They came from good families. They had money. They had gone to first-rate schools. But they were not ready to tend the seed. They were not ready to make the best use of the skills they had.

One skill I did not possess was writing. Much of that had to do with how little time I spent developing my writing skills in college after coming out of a segregated school system where it was apparent that writing was not one of my strengths. I could communicate well with people just by speaking with them. But when it came to communicating via the written word, I really struggled. I wrote well enough to get by, but not good enough to ever feel comfortable with writing the required papers.

One part of the IOBC was an assessment of writing skills. Fail the initial writing test and the next step was a course called "Bonehead English." I did not pass, so remedial English became an extra class for me. A contract teacher made one of the first assessments of my writing. She wrote on the evaluation sheet, "This officer should never return to Fort Benning as an instructor." That hurt me to my heart. It still hurts and was one reason I avoided Fort Benning for years. Many of my buddies spent their whole careers trying to get back there because it's the home of airborne training, the infantry, and the Army Rangers. Fort Benning is a significant part of the Army's "Hooah" culture.

I had to return to Fort Benning three years later for the captain's course, but when that was over I told people, "The only way I'll come back to this place is if I can command it." About twenty years after that I went back as the deputy commander of the post. There was some sweetness in that, coming back in that capacity and remembering what that lady had written in my assessment. I was in charge of the school where my writing skills had been judged as inadequate. One of the officers who had held that position years before me was General Omar Bradley, who commanded First Army during the D-Day invasion. When I go back to Fort Benning now and see the wall with Bradley's picture and my picture up there with it, it is a testament to how the Army trained me to overcome my educational shortfalls.

My early assignments helped me learn how to interact with enlisted soldiers, some of whom, like me, had grown up poor and disadvantaged educationally. I spoke their language, a language that on occasion was quite profane, something which my wife, Beverly, has consistently chided me about throughout our marriage. But it was a language soldiers understood. The more straightforward and blunt my language, the less chance someone would misunderstand me. It was a practice that would often get me in trouble with my superiors, but it was often the only way to get the job done. Getting the mission accomplished, whatever that mission was, was always the primary goal. That bluntness reverberated throughout the country during my stint as commander of Joint Task Force–Katrina and is one thing that people still remember about me.

One of my first assignments was as the executive officer of E Troop, 9th Cavalry Regiment, at Fort Hunter Liggett, California, a unit that traces its lineage to the Buffalo Soldiers of frontier days, the black cavalry soldiers. As a bright young infantry officer, I thought I knew a lot about the infantry. I knew absolutely nothing about tanks, however, yet there I was assigned to a unit full of tankers who didn't think a lot of the infantry. I was occasionally the butt of jokes from veterans in the unit. When the jokes came at my expense I merely tried to roll with the punches and learn about dealing with soldiers and their tanks. Both learning experiences were to come in handy years later.

The Army was going through some difficult times in the early 1970s. Our troop became a temporary holding unit for soldiers coming back from Vietnam who had only a few months left to serve. Those soldiers, many of whom had seen difficult combat for months on end, did not give a damn about a garrison Army. Many were marijuana smokers and cared little about standing in formation, keeping their uniforms pressed, their boots shined, or their hair cut. It was a constant struggle between them, the young officers, and the senior noncommissioned officers, the "lifers" as they were called, to get things done. There was constant friction between them and us. It got to the point where when we pulled staff duty we carried loaded weapons to protect ourselves.

We did not realize it at the time but some of those soldiers were really struggling with emotional problems. They had been in some horrific battles. Today we call it post-traumatic stress disorder. But at that time we had no appreciation for what they were going through and we weren't doing anything to help them. A number of them just lost themselves in marijuana, which was plentiful in the nearby California mountains. They were self-medicating with pot and we were not addressing what they needed in any meaningful way.

The marijuana problem was just as bad in Korea in 1974, when I served first as a platoon leader and later as a company commander in the 23rd Infantry Regiment of the 2nd Infantry Division. At the time, the entire Army was struggling with the issue of marijuana use. In Korea it was so pervasive that it grew in the cracks of sidewalks in the company area. It was a big joke to all the soldiers. They knew what it was but the officers had to be sent to school to learn how to identify it. The leadership was ignorant to what it was seeing. And the leaders were not prepared for the impact it was having on performance and morale.

After the officers became more adept at spotting the plants the soldiers became more adept at hiding them. One day, while conducting a class on the side of a hill near our company area, I looked down on the tops of the barracks and saw neat rows of bright green plants in coffee cans. The soldiers had taken the cans from the mess hall and planted marijuana in them and tried to hide them on top of the barracks. Company First Sergeant Otis Wright of Alexandria, Louisiana, was dispatched with a detail of soldiers to pull down the marijuana.

Dealing with marijuana use among the troops during those years, when the Army morale was at particularly low ebb, seemed at times like a losing battle. But to me it was just a challenge to overcome. We had people like First Sergeant Wright who wanted to do the right thing for the country, the Army, and for the soldiers for whom he was responsible. He was one of those senior enlisted men who helped pull the Army through that post-Vietnam funk.

Despite the problems with marijuana use the soldiers always responded well when it came to the unannounced alerts that simulated an attack by the North Koreans. The Korean War was still very real throughout South Korea twenty years after the fact. The North Koreans made frequent incursions into the South and there were occasional shooting incidents along the Demilitarized Zone. We always thought the North Koreans would attack at night under the cover of darkness so when that horn went off at two or three in the morning we never knew if it was a drill or for real.

During those drills we had to meet certain standards by having the company formed and moving out of camp within two hours. It was a matter of preparation and practice in order to survive a North Korean attack. The better prepared we were before the attack, the better we would be after it. Living in Korea near the DMZ meant constantly maintaining and upgrading a culture of preparedness because of the potential danger from the other side of the wire.

One of the lasting impressions from that first tour in Korea was the crushing poverty. I thought I knew what poor was, growing up in Lakeland, Louisiana, in a family of twelve on a subsistence farm. Our Louisiana poor was nothing compared to the poor I saw in Mexico when I went there as a youngster in the 4-H club. But Korea took poor to yet another level. The things some families did to survive were unbelievable, such as positioning their daughters to marry American servicemen so they could get out of Korea and go to America where they would have a good life and send money home to the family. Some great marriages came of that, but I found it disturbing that some families encouraged their daughters to marry GIs so they could have a better life.

Stealing to survive was a part of the culture of the poor in Korea. When we went out to the rifle range or the mortar range we literally had to put guards on all our gear or it would be stolen in a heartbeat. The Koreans would often risk their lives to try to catch the brass from our guns as we were firing. They were not stealing just to steal, they were stealing to sell what they could to buy food. They were hungry. They were hungry enough to risk their lives.

That same sort of behavior surfaced in New Orleans in the aftermath of Hurricane Katrina. There comes a point when people who are poor enough and hungry enough will do whatever it takes to survive. After Katrina we saw people breaking into stores and taking out food and water so they could feed themselves and their families. Some people call that burglary. I call it survival. Some of those people did what they had to in order to stay alive. That does not justify what happened in New Orleans. But if that food is there, and you're hungry, and your family's hungry, the human instinct is to eat.

A good number of reporters in New Orleans were jumping up and down wondering what we were going to do to stop people from taking food out of stores and hotels. "They're probably just taking it to eat," I told them. "What's the big deal? They took mattresses as well. Are you going to let grandma lie on the ground when you've got mattresses right there you can use?"

In any disaster, when there is a lot of emotion involved, there's a fine line between whether the media are reporting what they are seeing, whether they are reporting what they are thinking about what they are seeing, or whether they are reporting what they feel about what they are seeing. A good story probably has a little bit of all of that, but when it comes out of balance, it can be problematic for a democracy. In New Orleans some of the reporting was out of balance because the networks seemed to be competing against one another to see who could get the most sensational story out to the world before that story was fully vetted or put into proper context. The poor were demonized and disparaged in some of the early, more sensational reporting. But all that many of those folks were trying to do was survive until help arrived.

There are those who say that the Army is always preparing to fight the last war, never the next war. But the fact is that the U.S. military in general is always preparing for what might be next. Among the many institutions in this country, the military over the years has created one of the best cultures of preparedness. We are constantly looking into the

future trying to perceive where the next threat will come from and how
we will best respond to that threat. Soldiers are put through repeated
battle drills and exercises to maintain certain standards of proficiency
so they are properly prepared for the next war or the next peacekeeping
mission or the next disaster. The military is among the most proactive
of all the institutions in this country when it comes to preparedness.
Too many other government agencies, from the federal level on down
through the state and local, are far too reactive. They wait until after a
problem occurs before they consider ways to solve it. Seldom do they
try to prevent a problem before it occurs. The military tends to look
ahead and tries to find solutions to problems it anticipates it will face.
That proactive approach can get expensive, but it is never as expensive
in terms of dollars or lives as the reactive response.

A perfect example of the military being proactive is the National
Training Center (NTC) at Fort Irwin, California. When the Army opened
that facility in the Mojave Desert west of Las Vegas in 1980, it was with
the intent of providing a world-class training facility for armor and
mechanized infantry units that would likely be called on to counter the
Soviet threat in central Europe should a war break out there. With more
than a thousand square miles of desert in which to train and restricted
airspace overhead, the Army was able to conduct large-scale exercises
against well-trained and well-equipped opposing forces, known as the
OPFOR, to sharpen the skills they would need if they came up against
Soviet units in an armor fight.

What no one realized at the time was that the NTC was the perfect
training ground for American forces that would later fight in the Iraqi
desert against Saddam Hussein's forces in Operation Desert Storm in
1991 and later in Operation Iraqi Freedom in 2003. The quick, initial
successes of both those campaigns were the result of the years of training and preparation at Fort Irwin. The Army had had the foresight to
create that culture of preparedness among its armor and mechanized
infantry forces and it paid dividends with very few American lives lost
initially.

The key to training at Fort Irwin is not just the opportunity for units
to learn the importance of synchronization among widely dispersed
armor and mechanized infantry units on the modern battlefield. It has
to do with how that training is conducted. When units go to the NTC
for a two-month rotation they are expected to lose virtually every fight.
The odds are stacked against them. The OPFOR, made up of the 11th

Armored Cavalry Regiment, pushes every unit beyond the breaking point. The NTC was never intended to be a friendly place. Battalions and brigades and their commanders are there to learn and the best way to learn is to be beaten soundly and frequently and then have after-action reviews to figure out what was done wrong and why.

The OPFOR presents and executes the worst-case scenarios for every unit it faces. What does a battalion commander do when one of his companies is wiped out? What does he do if his communications go out? Or his logistics train gets ambushed and he has no way to get ammunition, food, and water to his soldiers? Or he is taken out of the fight? How well do his junior leaders and senior noncommissioned officers step into the breach and rally the troops?

Training at the NTC is tough and realistic. I served there as the senior mechanized task force trainer from 1992 to 1994 and had been there on exercises with various units prior to that. In 1979, before the facility had been approved as the NTC, I was with a unit from the 194th Armored Brigade that did a run-through.

It was frustrating to be an officer in a unit going there to train and knowing we were going to get our butts whipped the whole time we were in the field. But we learned from those simulated defeats so we would not have to learn when lives were at stake. As a trainer, I knew how important it was to push commanders and soldiers beyond what they had ever experienced so if they were ever again faced with similar situations in real combat they would know how to react.

Government agencies, from federal to local, would do well to look at the training model of the National Training Center when it comes to preparing for disasters. Too often disaster preparedness exercises are well-scripted simulations. Those involved sit in comfortable chairs in air-conditioned rooms and play out the exercise. All their communications systems work. The lights and computers are all on. They don't have to fight through downed trees and flooded streets to get to the command center. All the gas stations are open and operating so they don't have to worry about fuel. It's a nice, neat package in which they say they are planning how to manage the worst-case scenario.

That's not the worst-case scenario. That's not even a disaster exercise. A true disaster is when nothing works; not telephones or electricity or computers. A true disaster is when the infrastructure is devastated and first responders and key city and state workers can't get from their homes to their workplace. A true disaster is one that wrecks everything and sets technology back several generations. Hurricane Katrina was a true disaster. Those who had planned for it did not plan for a disaster; they planned for minor inconveniences in an atmosphere that came nowhere near to replicating what actually happened in the aftermath of the storm.

The Army model of combat preparedness worked well for those units initially sent to Iraq and Afghanistan. They had seen in training what they might have to one day face in combat. As a result, they were adaptive and innovative and were quickly able to overcome any set-backs, which they considered minor obstacles, on their way to liberating Kuwait and later taking down Saddam Hussein.

Just as the Army sometimes received unintended advantages from its training facilities and methods, so too did I receive unexpected benefits from some unique assignments during my career. One of those came shortly after the captain's course at Fort Benning in 1976. Instead of being sent to an infantry unit I was sent to Fort Ord, California, for a twenty-two-week course in something called Organization Effective-ness, which paralleled what was going on in American industry, Organi-zation Development. It was a new program the Army designed to help it learn to function more like corporations in the business world.

The Army is much like any other organization in that it is a system of systems and of people. The chief of staff of the Army at the time was General Bernard Rogers, and it was his opinion that we were not functioning as well as we should as an institution because we were not taking care of the people in our institution, our soldiers. The systems within the larger Army system were not in synch. He said the reason we were having so much trouble with the troops was that we were not communicating with them. He said we, the officers, did not listen to them and did not meet their expectations. He said there was too much distance between the top of the chain of command and the troops. So he created this thing called Organization Development, and those who were responsible for utilizing it were known as Organization Effective-ness Officers.

Those of us who completed the course were to make ourselves avail-able to Army commanders who wanted to conduct assessments of their units. The assessment essentially consisted of a survey of the troops, their likes and dislikes, their morale, and what they would like to see improved. We would give that assessment to the commander and it would be up to him to bring his chain of command in to figure out how to address what needed to be sustained and what needed to be changed or implemented.

The concept worked for a little while but then became subject to the whims of the chain of command. Things that individual commanders thought would work were retained or implemented. Those they did not like were trashed. The program lasted three or four years until someone figured out that the Army cannot be run like a corporation and so the program was abandoned.

Despite its short life, that course taught me some valuable lessons. Foremost among them was the concept of dealing with perceptions and nonverbal communications. I learned how to get information from people that they might not want to divulge, by asking leading questions. I also learned interpersonal skills, such as how to avoid arguments, how to communicate ideas, and how to get people to willingly accept those ideas.

By the time I got to the Army's Command and General Staff College at Fort Leavenworth, Kansas, in 1982, I had decided to stay in the Army to see how far my career would go. I had discovered my skills as a trainer and as a leader of soldiers. I could communicate well with them although I still struggled with writing. I was not at the writing level of my peers so another round of "Bonehead English" gave me a chance to catch up to them.

The tactics examination at Fort Leavenworth is the most important exam for an infantry officer. A part of my exam was to visualize a fight between a U.S. unit and a Soviet unit and write about it. The exam had to be written in longhand and was as much about the command of the English language as it was about the substance of the fight.

I failed that exam on two counts. I failed to account for all of my companies and I misspelled some words. I was told to take the exam again. Here I was, a major who had been to Europe as the aide-de-camp to the commander of allied forces in central Europe and had seen the big picture. I had commanded two infantry companies. Yet I was being taken to task again because of my lack of writing skills.

I could do the job in the field and had already proven that. But the exam had nothing to do with what we could do in the field. This was a cognitive tool to determine if I could visualize a fight in my head and write a complete and understandable narrative about it. Unlike college, when the blame for my lack of focus on writing papers could be shifted to all my part-time jobs, there was nothing here to blame but myself.

I was supposed to be a fast-rising major destined for brigade and perhaps division command. Yet I had flunked the tactics exam. It was embarrassing. Still, I pressed on, focused on my writing, and eventually passed the test. Three years later I went back to Fort Leavenworth as the tactics instructor at the Command and General Staff College.

Young majors at Fort Leavenworth also are given media training that consists primarily of how to do an interview. The media were not as pervasive back in the early 1980s as they are now, and the 24/7 news cycle and the instant news on the Internet had not yet become a part of the culture. The Army wanted to make sure, however, that we were properly prepared to do media interviews if we were called on to do so. I have never had a problem talking. Sometimes I have been a bit too blunt about things and left my superiors cringing. But that is just a part of who I am. I speak my mind, even when it is not politically correct.

During the media training we were taught how to stand and where to look for television interviews and how to interact with print reporters. We were also told to read the book *On Watch: A Memoir,* by Admiral Elmo Zumwalt, Jr., as an example of how to be an effective leader. Zumwalt had three basic rules when it came to being interviewed. Rule one is that no matter what question is asked, respond with the most important thing you want to pass on to the public. Rule two is that when the second question is asked, respond with the second-most important piece of information you want to get out. Rule three follows the same pattern. Essentially, no matter the question asked, respond with what information you think is most important to get out.

After Hurricane Katrina there were many interviews in which the answer I gave had no relation to the question that was asked, particularly when there was gang reporting. My standard operating procedure for press briefings was to decide beforehand three key pieces of information either the media or the American public needed to know, and then, no matter what questions were asked, I would rattle off that critical information. It served the American public, Katrina survivors, and me quite well, even if it did not necessarily give the media what they wanted.

A lot of loaded questions were tossed at me after Katrina and I decided to sidestep them. That's why my answers were usually very short and focused on the mission, not in defense of or critical of anything. That was not an environment where a yes or a no answer was the best answer to any questions. Somebody would ask a question like "Wouldn't you agree that the city was not prepared for the storm?" I was not going to answer that with a yes or no. I just followed the Zumwalt Rules. I gave them the message I wanted to get out, regardless of the question and we drove on from there.

Despite my being an infantry officer and commanding infantry units at every level, none of the units I commanded ever saw direct combat. During Operation Desert Shield in late 1990 and early 1991, I commanded the 1st Infantry Division's 4th Battalion, 16th Infantry Regiment, which was based in Germany. We were sent to Saudi Arabia to serve as the security detail for the Port of Dammam, where much of the U.S. and coalition equipment was being unloaded before it was sent out into the desert. My understanding was that my unit would become the VII Corps reserve force after we did the port duty. That was the rose at the end of that less-than-glamorous mission. Unfortunately, after we had done our jobs and everybody left the port, the commander of U.S. Army Europe asked that my battalion be sent home because he wanted to demobilize it as part of the drawdown of American forces there.

I felt cheated. I felt I had been lied to. My battalion never got a chance to fight and was pulled out of Saudi Arabia. We knew we had made a contribution because things were really screwed up when we got there and we helped straighten them out and got them running smoothly. But it was a major disappointment to have to go back to Germany just as the ground war was starting. The only thing that helped was that it wasn't a long ground war and I didn't have to see my friends and my peers get killed while I was sitting in Germany.

In 1994, after being promoted to full colonel, I took command of the 3rd Infantry Division's 1st Brigade in Kuwait when Saddam Hussein once again threatened to move south against the Saudis or Kuwaitis. However, our mere presence and the memory of what had happened to his elite forces just a few years earlier were apparently enough to make him back off. I spent two years commanding that brigade and as part of what was known then as the Army's Rapid Deployment Force, we were constantly preparing for war and constantly getting ourselves ready for whatever world disaster might crop up. The better prepared we were before the disaster, the better shape we would be on the other side of it. With deployment anywhere in the world at any time a real possibility, preparedness was an integral part of our culture.

CHAPTER 3

Lessons Learned for Building a Culture of Preparedness

1. Plans at the state and local level must be based on worst-case scenarios; for example, levees will be overtopped, or the eye of the storm will score a direct hit.

2. Assume the worst-case scenario for communications—the cell towers are broken. There must be a backup satellite system.

3. Telephone companies should develop a means of pulling down cell towers before the hurricane hits and then raising them back up after the storm passes.

Residents of New Orleans arriving at the Louisiana Superdome

Pentagon correspondent for CNN, Barbara Starr,
interviewing Lt. Gen. Honoré

Katrina survivors huddled inside the Ernest N. Morial
Convention Center

COURTESY OF MAJOR SCOTT TRAHAN, U.S. ARMY

Lt. Gen. Honoré with a map of the Gulf behind him

COURTESY OF MAJOR SCOTT TRAHAN, U.S. ARMY

USS *Iwo Jima* docked at the port of New Orleans

LEADING THE MISSION ANDERSON COOPER 360°

COURTESY OF MAJOR SCOTT TRAHAN, U.S. ARMY

Command Sgt. Major Marvin Hill (far left), Lt. Gen. Honoré,
and unknown soldier rescue mother and twin babies near
Harrah's casino at the corner of Convention Center
Boulevard and Poydras Street

The power and awe of Hurricane Katrina

Vice Admiral Thad Allen (center), Vice Admiral (retired)
Jim Hull (left), Lt. Gen. Honoré

Lt. Gen. Honoré

Lt. Gen. Honoré and his son, Sgt. Michael Honoré

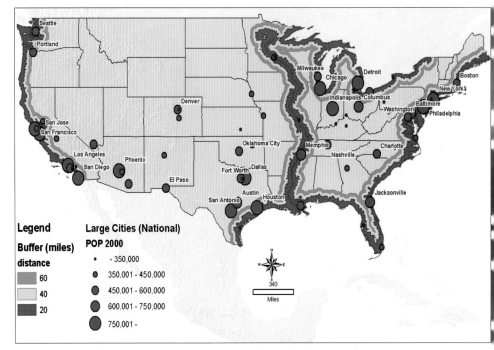

Concentrations of U.S. population in flood-prone areas

4

Command, Control,
and Occasional Chaos

AS A YOUNG MAJOR AT THE COMMAND AND GENERAL STAFF COLLEGE
at Fort Leavenworth in 1982, my focus was on doing my job and perhaps being promoted one more notch. Some of my classmates already
were talking about becoming general officers even though this was long
before they had gotten the necessary experience to even consider rising
to that rank. They seemed to be focusing more on their own promotions
than on what was best for the Army. The idea of becoming a general
seemed so out of reach that it never entered my thoughts. When my
promotion to brigadier—or one-star—general was approved in 1996, it
was a quantum leap for someone who had grown up in rural Louisiana
in a family of twelve children that depended on subsistence farming to
survive. I had overcome my humble beginnings and academic shortcomings. It was a great honor to reach that level because only a select
few officers are privileged to wear generals' stars.

The fact that I had competed in the same arena with colonels from Ivy
League schools and the U.S. Military Academy and had been selected to
become a general officer made me feel that all my hard work as a junior
officer had paid off. I always tried to be the hardest-working officer no
matter what the job was. But this new rank brought with it a whole new
set of responsibilities and the knowledge that the work would be even
more difficult. The bar was about to be raised higher than it had ever

53

been for me. More would be expected of me. My work habits had to set an example for those under me and my conduct and bearing also had to be exemplary.

The Army has a saying that promotions are made in part because of past performance. But selection for the next higher rank also is based on potential and the Army's future needs. My edge was connecting with the troops and inspiring them to perform. Troops generally responded to my leadership style, which was a take-no-prisoners approach to get the mission accomplished. Other officers got noticed because they were profoundly smart and wrote books or theses and got quoted in national magazines. The units I commanded were known for their readiness and performance and the fact that soldiers responded to my leadership. I was not as book smart as some of my peers but was street smart and knew how to motivate people.

The Army once had a mold for its top generals and often looked to West Point for officers to fit into that mold. But by 1996 the Army had changed the mold. No longer was it necessary to be a West Point gradu- ate to make general officer. Some of the top four-star generals of the last twenty years have been graduates of ROTC programs, including Colin Powell, Hugh Shelton, Johnnie Wilson, Larry Ellis, Dan McNeill, and George Casey, several of whom were my bosses at one time or another. Those of us who came from ROTC programs were not shut out of the process as some of our predecessors had been. It was gratifying person- ally but it also spoke well of the Army that ROTC graduates were able to fill many top jobs and take on the responsibilities that often had gone to West Pointers.

My first assignment as a one-star general might have been my last because of my habit of speaking my mind when people least expected it, especially my superior officers. My troops respected me for it because I spoke in their vernacular, the earthy language of the streets and the barracks. Some may have thought it was not fitting for a general offi- cer to speak that way, but that was the way I talked then and still talk today when trying to get a point across. During the Hurricane Katrina operations my approach with the media was to be open and blunt and to the best of my knowledge the soldiers working for me and the gen- eral public we were serving appreciated my candor and lack of political correctness.

In 1998 I was the assistant division commander for support of the 1st Cavalry Division at Fort Hood, Texas. At that time the Army was modernizing the division with a number of new systems, including the AH-64 Apache Longbow helicopter, the M1A2 Abrams main battle tank, M88A2 Hercules heavy recovery vehicle, the M2A2 ODS (Operation Desert Storm) Bradley Fighting Vehicle, plus a new generation of cargo trucks. The division was the first to field many of these systems. One of my jobs was to see what might work best in combat. It was just another example of the Army's culture of preparedness; we were planning ahead by field-testing the new equipment and seeing whether it met our needs.

Some of the new equipment worked fine. But some was worthless and a waste of taxpayers' money. I let my superiors know exactly what the soldiers told me did not work. The division commander at the time, Major General Kevin Byrnes, supported me and my numerous memos seeking fixes in some of the equipment.

That March I was invited to be part of a panel discussion with four other generals at the Redstone Arsenal in Huntsville, Alabama, put on by the Army Materiel Command. We were to provide feedback to the Army Acquisition Corps on the equipment it was sending us. It was supposed to be a closed conference. The media were not invited. It was like an after-action report when everybody speaks their mind without fear of being taken to task for what they say.

When it was my turn to speak I pulled no punches. One of my first remarks was "You are fielding pieces of crap. Is that clear enough for you?"

I talked for about fifteen or twenty minutes and everybody thanked me for my assessment, including the panel moderator, Lieutenant General Dennis Benchoff, who was the deputy commander of Army Materiel Command. He said, "Russ, thank you for your honest assessment." I thought nothing more about it and went home to Louisiana for a few days vacation before returning to Fort Hood.

On the way back to Fort Hood while on a layover at the Dallas airport, I picked up a copy of the *Wall Street Journal*. There was a story on the front page with a headline that said, in so many words, "General Says Army Fields Crap." Just then my telephone rang. It was my brother, James, who was working for Sony Pictures. He was in New York and had seen the story.

"Hey," he said, "I see you really shot your mouth off. You're in the *Wall Street Journal*."

"Wait a minute," I replied. "I'll call you back."

I quickly read through the story and discovered my remarks from the conference were now public. The gist of the story was that a relatively unknown one-star general, me, had told the Army Acquisition Corps it was fielding a lot of useless equipment. By the time I got back to Fort Hood the whole world seemed to be whipping down on my ass. The Forces Command deputy commander called my boss and asked why I was shooting off my mouth and bad-mouthing the Army. Even the commander of III Corps, who was one of my bosses at the time, came to me and said, "Russ, you're in a heap of shit. We'll stand by you on this as much as we can."

The story quickly got legs. The next morning it was in the *Killeen* (Texas) *Daily Herald*. Shortly after that it made the front page of the *Army Times*. In that story I was quoted as saying, in so many words, "We've got a tank now that cost $5 million and a guy who's the gunner on the tank who has a wife and three children and they're on the [federal] WIC [Women, Infants, and Children] program because he doesn't make enough money to keep them fed. We've got a problem here. That's a very complicated tank and the soldiers who are operating it are not being paid for what we are asking them to do."

I identified with the underpaid soldiers. I grew up poor and identified with young soldiers struggling to make ends meet. That was my strength. My strength was not in writing papers describing what twenty-first century warfare was going to be like. My strength was working with the troops and if something had a negative impact on them or was not up to standard, I would raise holy hell to get it fixed. I frequently complained about the dining facilities at Fort Hood. When troops go in there they should get a first-class meal. When we field equipment it should be the best we can buy and soldiers should be paid according to the skills it takes to run that equipment.

One officer under me once wrote something that got a lot of play on the Internet. He wrote that "Honoré speaks like an uneducated person. But he has great effect inside the unit." That was kind of hurtful because my degree of comfort was speaking to the troops and motivating them.

One of my friends once told me, "Honoré, you're not very good at writing."

"I know," I replied, "but I can communicate."

I was not sorry for what I had said about the equipment. But I was curious about how this information from a closed-door meeting had been leaked to the media. General Johnnie Wilson, the head of Army

Materiel Command, started an investigation to find out how it had gotten out of that room. It turned out that one of the officers in attendance had a tape recorder and passed on the tape of my remarks to the media. As the story picked up steam it eventually made its way to Congress. "I've got to get away from this," I eventually told myself. The division had a brigade at the National Training Center at the time so I took off for the desert and holed up in a trailer there until things cooled down.

That story and my comments about equipment followed me through my career. A few years before I retired, a friend who was going to the acquisitions course told me my remarks were required reading there. One of my mentors, General Tom Schwartz, who commanded Forces Command in Atlanta in 1998 and 1999 and then was instrumental in getting me to Korea as commander of the 2nd Infantry Division, once told me, "Honoré, you're a good general, but you're somewhat controversial. One day that will be a limiting factor for you unless you change your ways. But I like you because you speak your mind."

My outspokenness has always been my Achilles heel. Some people like that and some are uncomfortable with it. When General Dan McNeill was commanding Forces Command and I was at First Army, he called me in to counsel me after the Katrina operation. He told me people had called him about some of the things I said. "I never called you about it because you were getting the effect we needed for the nation," he told me. "But there were some people who were very upset with your outspokenness. That's what I admire about you, though, your outspokenness and I never really talked to you about it because you get the job done."

There is a part of the old Army guard, the retired generals, many of whom had served with distinction through the Cold War and who came up in that West Point side of the Army, who really took exception to Honoréspeak. It would have been unconscionable for them to say "bullshit" to the media. It would have been just as unconscionable for them to say something like "stuck on stupid." Some people in the Army wrote very derogatory things about my language during JTF-Katrina. And there were some who said the only reason I got away with it was that I was a black officer and there was no way a white officer could speak to the press like that.

That's a lot of nonsense, although color has always been an issue for the Army, dating back to 1948, when President Harry Truman ordered the full integration of the services. My career was neither hindered nor aided by the fact that I am considered African-American Creole. A number of black officers were at Fort Leavenworth the year I was there as a major. That class produced one black four-star general, Kip Ward, and two three-stars, Mike Rochelle and me. Several other black officers from that class made brigadier or major general.

Not long before my retirement I was asked by someone in Louisiana if my promotions had been because of affirmative action. I was really hurt by that insinuation. The Army promotions system is extremely competitive and I was comfortable with the system and what it took to become a lieutenant general. Still, there is a sense, and always has been in the consciousness of the Army, that while it wants to promote the best, the senior levels of the Army have to look like the rest of the Army and the rest of society. To a great degree, it is. For the guy who doesn't get promoted, though, the viewpoint on that likely is much different.

After leaving Fort Hood in 1998 I went to Fort Benning as the deputy commander for the Army Infantry Center and School. I was there about eleven months before receiving a call that my name was on the list for promotion to major general and possibly division command. That prospect excited me because there is nothing more fulfilling to an infantry officer than being able to command a division of about eighteen thousand soldiers.

But not long after that first call there was another that informed me I was being looked at for a job on the joint staff at the Pentagon. The initial indication was that the job was as the deputy for operations. I was not sure I was up to that. It sounded like a job that required a lot of academics. That's also a job that usually goes to someone who has already commanded a division. But the Army is adamant about its general officers doing time on a joint staff and that was the assignment that came my way. As it turned out, it was another of those opportunities that better prepared me for my time as commander of JTF-Katrina.

General officers usually have served at least one tour at the Pentagon as a lieutenant colonel or colonel. Yet there I was, a brigadier general in my twenty-seventh year in the Army and about to embark on my first tour at the nerve center of America's military might. I was so ignorant of the place I had to have somebody pick me up at my quarters and show me how to get there and what door to go in. It took another two weeks with an escort to learn how to go from Point A to Point B inside the building.

At the time, Army General Hugh Shelton was the chairman of the

Joint Chiefs of Staff. I had never worked for him before but knew of his reputation. He was one of the most impressive soldiers I had ever seen. He was tall and ramrod straight, an Airborne Ranger who had spent time in the Special Operations forces. To my way of thinking, Shelton was the very model of a soldier.

That first morning before reporting to the Pentagon I spent a great deal of time making sure my uniform was perfect and my grooming was meticulous. For years I had worn a small, neatly trimmed mustache. In an effort to make sure my mustache was very neat I was a bit too meticulous and ending up whacking off part of it. There was no way to repair the damage so the whole thing came off and I reported for duty with a naked upper lip for the first time in years.

An Air Force master sergeant was showing me around the Pentagon that morning when Shelton approached us from the other direction. He was walking straight as a picket, his aide in tow, when he said, "Good morning, Russ. Welcome to the Pentagon. You're going to love the shit out of this place."

Then he paused for a second, looked directly at me, and said, "I'm glad to see you got rid of that facial hair."

That set the tone for my fourteen months in the Pentagon. The mustache did not reappear for another year.

The learning curve was steep in my new job. I supervised the National Military Command Center, which essentially monitors the heartbeat of the Department of Defense (DOD) throughout the world. If something happened to a ship, or Saddam Hussein did something, or a soldier got into trouble in a foreign country, it went through the National Military Command Center. It was also my first staff job in several years and my first in a joint-service environment. To add to the stress, this was 1999, the year before the millennium year. No one knew what would happen when all the clocks and computers went to 2000, so we were busily planning for a possible doomsday scenario.

Another part of my job was to serve on a working group for counter-terrorism with Marine Brigadier General John Sattler, a subject matter expert. We regularly went to the White House for meetings with representatives from the State Department, the National Security Council, the Central Intelligence Agency, and the Federal Bureau of Investigation, among other federal agencies. This was heady company so I simply took notes, tried to keep my mouth shut, and stayed out of the line of fire.

I learned an invaluable lesson from that job and it came in handy years later during the Katrina operations. I learned how the interagency process worked and how at times it did not work because of bureaucratic infighting. The big issue back then was trying to find Osama bin Laden. The second most troubling problem was that we had these sporadic actions by Saddam Hussein against the ethnic Kurds in northern Iraq. And then we had operations going on in the Kosovo-Bosnia area where we were trying to find Radovan Karadzic, the fugitive president of Yugoslavia, and his henchmen because of the war crimes they had committed.

Some of the issues my staff dealt with in that job will forever remain a secret. But one of which I'm particularly proud is the contribution we made to a House committee report on homeland defense that started a dialogue about the American government's ability to deal with weapons of mass destruction. This was right in the middle of the millennium planning and we had to come up with a plan to respond to a weapon of mass destruction. We developed what became known as Weapons of Mass Destruction–Civil Support Teams. The idea was to integrate Department of Defense support with various state and federal agencies to manage the consequences of a nuclear, biological, chemical, or radiological attack. It started with a few regional teams and now is a very robust operation in every state.

We also started working on the National Response Plan, now known as the National Response Framework, for homeland defense, particularly the role in which the Department of Defense could best be utilized. At that same time there were rumblings from Congress that the military was the best organized and best equipped to do the homeland defense mission. In one think tank discussion led by former Senator Gary Hart, a number of senior officials from various federal agencies said they were of the opinion that the military should be put in charge of homeland defense.

That gave me some pause because the role of the military is to play the away game. The home game is up to law enforcement and federal agencies. Inside individual states it is the responsibility of that state's governor and the National Guard to respond. The whole notion of putting the military in charge of homeland defense was a bit frightening. People were looking for an easy answer and the military seemed to provide it. But how do you take a federal force and use it within the United States without violating the Posse Comitatus Act? The question was,

How much leeway should be given to the military in a domestic crisis?

Working on the joint staff gave me a sense of how complex this democracy really is. This subject of the use of the military for homeland defense would rear its ugly head in the aftermath of Hurricane Katrina, but my education on what the active military could and could not do was greatly enhanced by my time on the joint staff and helped me make better decisions after the storm.

In my fourteen months on the joint staff we also dealt with significant flooding in Venezuela, Hurricane Floyd in North Carolina, and floods in Mozambique. But we didn't have a catastrophic or near-disaster experience. There had been some talk about what would happen if a Category 5 storm hit New Orleans. But that talk had been around for a while. When we talked about hurricanes the issue was always who would be in charge after one hit. It was clear to me that in the event of a hurricane, everyone on the federal side would work in support of the governors in the affected states. There was no question in my mind, as there apparently was for some in the federal government, as to who would run the show after a disaster. Control of any situation, whether federal, state, or local, is always the source of friction among competing government agencies.

After my stint on the joint staff I was sent to Korea to command the 2nd Infantry Division, the unit in which I had served as a young lieutenant. I knew the Korean people and the territory and getting back with the troops would be a welcome change from the political infighting in Washington, D.C. I was getting back to the real Army where the boots were on the ground and there was a stark reality about life, not the theoretical mumbo-jumbo with which Washington and the Pentagon seemed to deal daily.

My command in Korea was nearly thrown off by an unexpected bout with prostate cancer. A routine predeployment physical exam discovered the disease. My PSA test the year before had been normal. The cancer just hit me in a heartbeat. I was in a dilemma. Should I reveal the cancer and risking losing division command? Or should I take command and then come home for the surgery and pray for the best?

Doctor David McLeod, my physician at Walter Reed Army Medical Center in Washington, D.C., told me, "You don't have to get this operation and you can go command that division. But it's the last thing you'll ever do because that prostate will kill you." He suggested I go to Korea, take command, and then come home in a few months for the surgery.

I followed his suggestion, had the surgery over Christmas, and within a few weeks was back in the Far East.

The Army was really struggling for money at that time. We had problems getting spare parts, especially engines for our tanks. We also were struggling to keep enough soldiers in Korea to maintain troop levels of at least 90 percent of what we were authorized. The 2nd Infantry Division was a burden on the Army because in order to get a soldier forward-deployed there for a year it takes three soldiers. One is in-country, one has just left and is going elsewhere, and one is preparing to come to Korea. People at the Pentagon were constantly whining about the impact the 2nd Infantry Division was having on the rest of the Army because of the struggle to keep those eighteen thousand troops in Korea. The division was continually fighting for more money, more spare parts, and more sensible troop rotation policies so we could maintain that front-line presence against the North Koreans. If the U.S. Army is about a culture of preparedness, the U.S. Army in Korea is about the ultimate culture of preparedness because of the threat just north of the DMZ.

Our culture of preparedness in Korea was not only military, though. We also had to make special preparations each monsoon season to ensure that the heavy rains washing down the steep hillsides did not back up behind debris that collected in the gullies. That created a flood hazard for the military camps and civilian villages downstream. We sent out working parties just before the monsoons started to clear brush that had grown up over the previous year and pick up trash that had been dumped there. We did not have to worry about federal or state environmental restrictions on clearing brush. It was considered good management on the part of the military to keep the gullies clean so the runoff water would flow smoothly and not create dangerous walls of water that could inundate entire villages in an instant.

That is a lesson that California would do well to heed, especially homeowners who build in areas prone to wildfires. There are prohibitions in some areas of Southern California against clearing underbrush because they protect certain endangered species. But if state and local officials are going to allow homes to be built in those areas, it would be to the benefit of homeowners and fire officials to ease the restrictions and allow brush clearing to remove potential fuel, no matter what species are endangered by it.

The restrictions on brush clearing in Southern California can sometimes be contradictory and frequently are confusing for homeowners.

One example comes from the city of San Diego's brush management guide. It states that natural vegetation within one hundred feet of houses "must be thinned and pruned regularly to reduce vegetation by 50% without harming native plants, soil, or habitats." The problem is that the vegetation is all native, the soil is all native, and the natural habitat is all native. It is the ultimate catch-22. Homeowners must thin and prune brush around their homes as long as they don't thin or prune any native brush. It makes absolutely no sense. As long as people are allowed to build in areas with regulations such as these, their homes will continue to burn when the Santa Ana winds start to blow and fires erupt.

My command in Korea was gratifying despite the frequent battles over money, but I left there in 2002 with a heavy heart. I thought I knew the Korean people. I always respected their culture and traditions. In June of that year, however, two of my soldiers were involved in the accidental deaths of two Korean girls. It quickly escalated into an international incident and had some anti-American Koreans calling me a murderer and suggesting that I be tried for what they were calling war crimes against the Korean people.

On June 13, 2002, Shim Mi-son and Shin Hyo-sun, both thirteen-year-old schoolgirls, were walking on a narrow road in rural Kyonggi Province when they were struck and killed by an armored vehicle that was part of a 2nd Infantry Division convoy. It was a tragic accident in which everything that could go wrong did. The road was too narrow. The girls were walking on the road. The vehicle the soldiers were in had a blind spot to one side. It was the worst of circumstances at the worst of times.

Korea was in the international spotlight that June because of soccer's World Cup tournament. In addition, the country was transitioning from a culture in which many of the old politicians who had lived through the Korean War and were anti-North were giving way to younger politicians who were more anti-American and pro-North. The younger group wanted to expand the economy by establishing friendly relations with their countrymen on the other side of the DMZ. The accident and the tragic deaths of those two young girls became kindling for anti-American forces to try to make a political point. They wanted to get out from under what they perceived as the onerous presence of the United States military.

After the accident I did the same dumb thing that many senior leaders do in a crisis situation. I put my Public Affairs Officer (PAO) out in front. I let a young major be the face and voice of the 2nd Infantry Division's response to the tragedy. He was a good PAO but it was the worst possible move in that culture. It was completely counter to the culture of Korea. There, if you or someone you are responsible for does something wrong you should profusely apologize. It doesn't matter if you were to blame or not. You should be in the apologizing mode. My young PAO was in the explaining mode. That sent the wrong message to the Korean people, which played into the hands of the anti-American minority party and the result was riots and demonstrations throughout the country. By the time I realized my mistake it was too late to make amends. I vowed never to let that happen again.

In any crisis situation it should be the leader who is out front speaking. The leader should speak from the heart, not from a printed statement. I never read a statement during Katrina operations. It is more important for a leader to say what he knows, not what he feels or thinks. In New Orleans, leaders were saying what they thought happened or what they felt happened, as opposed to what they knew happened. From that lesson in Korea I decided never again to give up the voice of my command to my public affairs team. They would give me talking points on important issues but as the leader of JTF-Katrina it was my responsibility to speak to the public.

It is the Army model to put the PAO out front. The Army has created this pool of officers to speak to the media and in turn to the general public. Having a team of PAOs work a particular issue is fine for a long-term event such as Iraq. But in a short-term crisis, such as we had in Korea in 2002 and in Louisiana in 2005, people ought to be listening to the leader.

At my change of command at Camp Casey in July 2002 it was raining so hard I could barely read my notes. We had four thousand troops on the field for the ceremony but about half again as many Koreans were at the front gate protesting the deaths of the two girls and the American presence in the country. We heard them shouting slogans and as I spoke they started trying to get onto the base. I shortened my speech and the assistant division commander had to lead the troops down there to keep the protestors at bay because there were not enough Korean police to control the crowd. That's a country with thousands of police and only a few were at the front gate of Camp Casey that day.

It was disappointing and hurtful to leave Korea that way, being literally shouted out of the country and reading signs that read "Honoré

Murderer." I thought the Army's relationship with South Korea was better than that. We had been there fifty years. We had suffered 33,000 dead and more than 103,000 wounded during the Korean War. Our soldiers made a lot of sacrifices to serve a year's tour in Korea. It's such a different culture that Americans almost become isolated inside the country. We share the same space but there's very little cultural exchange between us and the Koreans. After all these years and all we've done for that country and all those people who haven gotten rich off the Americans, I don't remember a single one standing up in our defense.

After Korea, my next two years were spent as commander of Standing Joint Force Headquarters–Homeland Security in Norfolk, Virginia. A new command, Northern Command (NORTHCOM), was being created to deal with issues of military support to civilian agencies and defense of the United States, and I eventually transferred many of the duties in my command to NORTHCOM in Colorado Springs, Colorado.

During the two years in that job, my staff and I reviewed the National Response Plan for disasters and terrorist attacks in the wake of 9/11, dealt with at least a half dozen hurricanes, provided military support to work the shuttle *Columbia* tragedy, and did some work on the D.C. sniper case, although our hands were tied as active forces because of the Posse Comitatus Act.

During that time we also did a number of studies about better preparing ourselves for potential disasters that were either natural or man-created. We did a border study with Joint Task Force 6 looking at how to deal with the immigration issue. We did a bridge study, a hazardous materials movement study, and a study on the security of nuclear power plants.

The joint-service environment gave me an education once again on how various branches of the military interact with one another and with the numerous federal agencies. That knowledge was invaluable during the Hurricane Katrina operations. Despite the frequent bureaucratic infighting and interagency friction that accompany any disaster, a lot of good people were working hard to try to make things right. It became clear that if ever I found myself in the middle of a genuine disaster, my needs would be priority one. If I asked for something I would get it. That made it incumbent on me to be particularly careful about my requests because I was likely to get what was requested, whether it was needed or not.

CHAPTER 4

Lessons Learned for Building a Culture of Preparedness

1. Mayors and governors need to participate with Northern Command, the Department of Homeland Security, and FEMA in extensive tabletop exercises that depict worst-case scenarios.

2. States should conduct quality training events to practice emergency response plans.

3. Each city should have a grid-based search-and-rescue plan so military helicopters can more easily find specific addresses.

4. Coastal airports need to improve their infrastructure so they can reopen and evacuate people quickly after a disaster.

5. The Transportation Security Administration needs to waive requirements to search evacuees from a disaster area. These people are victims, not terrorists.

6. Airports need efficient generators and fuel on hand to run the airport for up to five days after a disaster.

7. Airport staff should be evacuated to a prearranged area so that they can be brought back in immediately to open the airport.

8. Port and levee clearance equipment should be taken upriver then brought back immediately to reopen ports and rivers.

9. States should develop decision points that would allow for the evacuation of the most vulnerable people earlier from retirement homes, hospitals, and assisted-living facilities. They should not wait until the general population starts moving to begin moving people who cannot move themselves.

10. There should be evacuation plans for pets and livestock. Families should not have to abandon their pets. Livestock should be removed from hurricane landfall areas days before the storm hits. It is "cruelty to animals" to leave them to fend for themselves.

11. Weather radios should be required, just as smoke alarms are, in rental property, including apartments, houses, and mobile homes. Insurance companies should give weather radios to their customers or provide a rate break for those families that have them in their homes.

12. Businesses that can assist in recovery efforts and debris removal should move their trucks away from the area where the eye of the storm is heading.

13. Automobile dealers should allow people who do not have cars to drive their cars out of town so that they can evacuate rather than leave the cars to be caught in the floods.

14. The Federal Aviation Administration should not allow airlines to bring vacationers to cities that have started to evacuate. Airlines were bringing visitors to New Orleans on Saturday before Hurricane Katrina hit and on Sunday the visitors were told they had to leave.

15. Mayors and the airlines need to agree on a plan so mayors will know when the airlines will stop flying and when planes will be evacuated.

5

Theater Immersion Training for War and Disaster

MY ASSIGNMENT AS THE COMMANDER OF STANDING JOINT FORCE Headquarters–Homeland Security in Norfolk, Virginia, in 2002 seemed like a major step backward after Korea. I was going from commanding 17,000 troops to commanding 165. It was as if someone were sending a message that my career would stop short of the four-star rank. Peers with less operational experience than me had gone to division and corps commands in the run-up to the war in Iraq. I was given another staff job in a joint command and had to watch the war on television. Still, by then I was among the less than one-half of one percent of all commissioned officers who ever reach the rank of major general or above and that was some consolation.

I was considered for several jobs while waiting for promotion to lieutenant general. One was as deputy commander of Forces Command at Fort McPherson in Atlanta to oversee training and mobilization for active Army forces. My name also was among those on the short list to go to Iraq to straighten out the mess at Abu Ghraib prison. The scandal was unfolding quickly and the Army wanted a central, high-profile figure to go over there to run the prisons. When I asked how long it would take the response was "Maybe three or four months." Back then everybody thought the war would be over quickly and all the troops would be home in a few months. I was ready to go if that was what the Army wanted me to do. I was in good shape after twice-daily physical training but was bored beyond belief waiting for a decision.

When my name went to the joint staff for the Abu Ghraib job it was rejected because I was in line to get a three-star command in the summer of 2004. At the same time, Major General Geoffrey Miller, who was running the detention facility at Guantanamo Bay, Cuba, raised his hand and volunteered for the job in Iraq. He had the background in prisons and seemed the best candidate for the job. Miller went over there and saw his career fall apart because of continuing problems at the prison and some of the decisions he made regarding treatment of prisoners. To this day I wonder what would have happened to my career had that job been handed to me.

The three-star job I wanted was commander of Third Army, which also has its headquarters at Fort McPherson. Third Army is the active Army component of U.S. Central Command, which controls all military forces in the Middle East. It was where all the action was at that time. But I was told neither the Third Army job nor anything in Iraq was available. I was not in the select group for any of the top jobs. They were going to the three-star generals who the senior leadership of the Army thought were on track to become full generals.

The idea of taking command of First Army, which is headquartered at Fort Gillem, in a suburb of Atlanta just a few miles southeast of Fort McPherson, eventually was tossed my way. Initially, it did not excite me. First Army had a reputation for many years as a place where three-star generals went to retire. It was a headquarters unit with only a few hundred staff. The commander was a general without any soldiers. Whenever First Army needed forces for a mission it had to make a request to Forces Command. Then Forces Command would go searching for who might be available for that mission.

First Army's primary role at that time was training all Army National Guard and Reserve forces east of the Mississippi River. Units west of the river were assigned to Fifth Army, which had its headquarters at Fort Sam Houston in San Antonio, Texas. These last two remaining continental armies also had the dual task of providing military support to civil authorities for emergencies and natural disasters in their respective regions. I had been doing homeland security and was a good trainer, so there was no question First Army command was well within my capabilities.

The wars in Iraq and Afghanistan and the threats of terrorist attacks within the United States changed the roles of First Army and Fifth Army significantly. With the smaller active Army relying more and more on National Guard and Reserve soldiers to fill the gaps in troop requirements, the postmobilization training for what had been part-time soldiers had to be more realistic than ever before.

In the summer of 2004, First Army was making a transition in its training focus. My predecessor, Lieutenant General Joe Inge, had started more intense postmobilization training for National Guard and Reserve soldiers before he went on to be the deputy commander of Northern Command in Colorado Springs, Colorado. But after his departure things began changing quickly in the war zones and our training needed to keep pace with what the soldiers there were seeing. The feedback we were getting from returning troops and from special trainers we sent over there to observe the situation was that our training was not keeping pace with changing requirements. We needed to make a shift in how we trained so we adapted the concept of "train them like they are going to fight."

The First Army staff developed what we eventually called Theater Immersion Training. From the moment soldiers arrived at the training sites they were put in situations and environments similar to what they would find overseas. They had to carry their weapons at all times. They were subject to random attacks by role-playing terrorists. They had to be constantly on alert. We were implementing lessons learned from Iraq and Afghanistan as quickly as we received them.

But the more realistic training meant the end of some of the perks many of the National Guard and Reserve soldiers had gotten used to over the years, like having their own cars during training and being able to drink when they were finished for the day. They didn't have cars in Iraq or Afghanistan so why should they have their personal vehicles during training? They were not supposed to drink while they were overseas so why let them drink during training? It doesn't do anyone any good for a soldier to be carrying an M-4 carbine in one hand and a Bud longneck in the other at the end of the working day. In Iraq and Afghanistan the working day never ends.

National Guard and Reserve officials and some members of Congress gave me hell for taking away the cars and the booze. But we had only ninety days to get those soldiers ready for war and they did not need those distractions. We were trying to create a culture of preparedness for life-or-death situations once the soldiers got into the war zone. Our training was far more realistic with those restrictions in place.

We started Theater Immersion Training with the 155th Armored Brigade of the Mississippi Army National Guard at Camp Shelby, Mississippi, in late 2004. We did not have all the money or the facilities we needed at first, and the no-cars, no-alcohol edict had not yet been imposed. We took away the cars and booze after several soldiers died in automobile accidents trying to race home or back to base during breaks in training. I did not want to lose soldiers to accidents or alcohol and the best way to avoid those losses was to sequester them on post for the duration of the training.

Old habits die hard, though, especially in Mississippi. The state has something called "Mississippi Monday," an unofficial holiday especially popular during fishing season in the summer and hunting season in the fall. I would ask somebody a question like "Did the parts come in and that truck get fixed?"

Back would come this slow drawl: "Well, no sir. We think it got hung up in Mississippi Monday."

It turns out a certain number of state employees would take a Monday off if they worked extra hours the week before. If something didn't get done when it was supposed to, "Mississippi Monday" would usually get the blame.

Our peak time for training the National Guard and Reserves was July to September when we often would have 19,000–21,000 soldiers in camps. That also was the peak hurricane season. The remainder of the year we would have anywhere from 7,000 to 8,000 at a time. In 2005 four of every ten soldiers in Iraq were from the National Guard or Reserves, so the importance of what we were doing was obvious throughout the military.

Among the soldiers we trained were many National Guard brigade commanders. I spent a lot of time at the training sites and had the opportunity to get to know them and the adjutants general of the various states. Come Katrina, those personal relationships served me well. Instead of going through elaborate requests for equipment or personnel in the wake of the storm, all I had to do was pick up the phone and make a few calls. Red tape could be cut in minutes whereas following the proper protocol and filling out all the paperwork might take days. It was invaluable to have cultivated those relationships.

When I began to look at First Army's role in providing military support to civilian authorities after disasters, the process looked entirely too reactive. It was not at all proactive. The system was designed to respond to emergencies, not to be prepared to deal with them before the fact or on the left side of the disaster. The right side of the disaster is after the fact and is purely a reaction to what has happened. The left side of the disaster is anticipating and preparing for the event. The better prepared you are before a disaster, the better off you will be after it.

It was extremely unwieldy to have to wait for requests from areas damaged by hurricanes or tornadoes or floods before sending in liaisons from our headquarters to make assessments and send back reports and requests for assistance. Why not lean forward? Why not send liaisons in before the storm? Why not create that culture of preparedness among our staff and those who would respond to disasters in various states?

This concept flirts with the Posse Comitatus Act to some degree. In addition, lawyers for First Army told me that under the provisions of the Stafford Act and the Helms-Biden Act we would not be reimbursed if these liaisons, which were called Defense Coordinating Officers (DCO), were sent into an area and the storm did not actually hit there.

That was fine with me. If my staff saw a hurricane brewing in the Atlantic or the Gulf of Mexico or some other natural disaster was looming we would send in the DCOs ahead of the disaster. If the disaster hit, we would get reimbursed through the Stafford Act. If there was no disaster we would call it a training exercise and the money would be taken out of our training budget.

Having someone on the ground before a disaster such as a hurricane hit would give First Army a leg up on preparations prior to the event and enable us to get immediate assessments after it occurred. We would not have to wait for days to get someone into the affected areas, which could be difficult after a hurricane because of infrastructure damage. The idea was unorthodox and not at all in keeping with standard protocol but it was a way of beating the disaster to the punch by making necessary preparations on the left side of it. It was sort of like standing on the railroad tracks watching a train come at you. You don't stand there and wait until it hits you and then try to figure out what happened.

First Army headquarters had a good, functional staff when I took command from Joe Inge in the summer of 2004. It was doing the nation's work. But that work was being done according to the book and long-established protocols that needed to be updated because of the changing world situation. It was a staff-centric headquarters. My objective was to change it to a commander-centric headquarters. The way it was, problems would come in and get bounced around among staff officers at various levels and by the time I found out about them, they had been solved without any input from me. My job was to make decisions. I kept going to meetings and hearing about issues that had never crossed my desk but should have. I was there to make the decisions and take the responsibility for them, not delegate that authority to the staff.

First Army's motto from World War I to World War II was "First in Deed." It was the first modern Army, formed in France under "Black Jack" Pershing. That's the same motto First Army used on the beaches of Normandy when General Omar Bradley commanded it. After Desert Storm someone came up with another slogan: "Leave it better than you found it." In other words, you're not getting all the money, you're not getting all the time you need, but leave the soldiers better than you found them.

That latter slogan did not really fit what we were doing as a continental army headquarters so we put out a bumper sticker that read: "See First. Understand First. Act First." That was the concept I wanted to stress throughout the headquarters and among the soldiers we trained for Iraq and Afghanistan and the civilian authorities with whom we dealt on disaster preparedness.

The summer of 2004 was an especially difficult hurricane season for First Army. Four hurricanes—Charley, Frances, Ivan, and Jeanne—and one tropical storm—Bonnie—hit Florida, the first time that had ever happened. In addition, other hurricanes hit Alabama, North Carolina, and South Carolina, all in our area of operations.

For each of those storms we had First Army headquarters fully activated. We colocated the DCOs with state officials at the Emergency Operations Center in Florida before the storms hit. The protocol in these situations had been to send in the DCO when FEMA asked because FEMA triggers the Department of Defense response. The request is supposed to go from the state to FEMA and then from FEMA to the Office of the Secretary of Defense. My two years in Standing Joint Force Headquarters–Homeland Security convinced me that we needed to get those DCOs in ahead of the storms instead of after. I was breaking established protocol.

To get around the complaints I decided to call each of these "Exercise Ivan." The staff at Northern Command wanted to know why we were calling them exercises. "We are training," I told them. "We are getting ready." The concept just blew people's minds. People were really upset with me. They accused me of overstepping my authority. But I really did not care.

One particular incident during that storm season of 2004 demonstrates how the best post-storm intentions can get snarled in the bureaucracy that is supposed to respond to emergencies.

We had a DCO in Florida who told us that some areas needed bottled water. The water was at Fort Gillem in Atlanta, where FEMA stores some of its supplies. We trucked cases of water to Dobbins Air Reserve Base northwest of the city then flew it on military transport to Florida. I argued against that because Interstate 75, which runs right through Atlanta and down to Florida, never closed and we could have driven that water down there in seven or eight hours at much less cost. But the state of Florida and FEMA insisted on using Air Force transports to get the water down there.

I discovered after going to Florida that the Army Corps of Engineers, which does much of the purchasing for FEMA, was in the process of buying water to replace what had been sent from Fort Gillem. When I asked where the water was coming from the response was that it would probably be bought from a company in Ocala, Florida. Here they had the water they needed within a few miles of the storm but instead of using that water they wanted water shipped from Atlanta. Then they wanted to buy replacement water in Florida and ship it back to Atlanta. I just had to shake my head over the waste of time and money on that deal.

There is a culture in Florida that because they have so many hurricanes and because it has been so long since they have had one like Hurricane Andrew, which devastated the southern part of the state in 1992, it is pretty hard to get residents to evacuate. Prior to Katrina more than 80 percent of the people in New Orleans evacuated the city. Not so in Florida. Those people stubbornly cling to their homes and condos thinking the big blow will miss them.

The five storms of 2004 were a bit of a wake-up call for some. But they were not really what anyone would call major disasters. People suffered minor inconveniences for the most part. We did not have entire cities flooded and communications were restored relatively quickly. People were frightened and uncomfortable for a while but things got back to some semblance of normalcy within days of the storm.

I spent much of the 2004 hurricane season and the months after it infusing in the First Army staff the lessons learned at Standing Joint Force Headquarters–Homeland Security. The primary lesson was to be more proactive. That was a seismic shift because First Army, like most other federal response units, is typically in a wait-and-see mode; wait for the disaster to hit, see what happens, then respond. The staff was following what had been done previously. It was not that it was wrong, but the staff was strictly following the protocol and that protocol was that you wait to move until you get a request. I wanted to change that so that we were leaning forward. You can see the storm coming so you want to be in position before the storm hits. You can see the train coming down the tracks so you get out of the way.

Through the winter of 2004–2005 and on into the spring the First Army staff conducted a series of tabletop exercises in each FEMA region east of the Mississippi River. Depending on whether the scenario was a natural disaster or a man-made catastrophe, we looked at options not only for how to deal with the situation after the fact, but also what could we do to mitigate damage before the fact.

People had gotten very comfortable after the terrorist attacks of September 11, 2001, had receded, and many thought we had good plans. But as the old Army saying goes, a plan seldom survives first contact with the enemy. A plan is basically good intentions. The key question is not "Do you have a plan?" The question is "Are you executing that plan? Can you take the plan and adapt it to the situation on the ground, no matter the situation?" We thought we could, even though we knew things happen in real life that cannot be replicated in a tabletop exercise. Stuff happens that more often than not is totally unexpected. The good intentions of a plan often go right out the window.

In New Orleans some people said we had a failure of the plan. But it wasn't a failure. It was that the plan was not designed to work in that environment. The conditions were different. The biggest thing we had done before Katrina was Hurricane Andrew and that was about ten generations of officers removed from where we were in 2004 and 2005.

That same summer of 2004, when First Army was wrestling with hurricanes and tropical storms throughout the South, especially in hard-hit Florida, Fifth Army was faced with its own disaster—Hurricane Pam.

The *New Orleans Times-Picayune* described the storm this way on July 20, 2004:

> A hurricane packing winds of 120 mph and a storm surge that tops 17-foot levees slams into New Orleans, killing an untold number of people and trapping half the area's residents in attics, on rooftops and in makeshift refuges in a variety of

public and office buildings. Parts of the city are
flooded with up to 20 feet of water, and 80 percent
of the buildings in the area are severely damaged
from water and winds.

It was an eerie turn of phrase that described virtually word-for-word
what would happen in the city little more than a year later. Fortunately for the city of New Orleans and its residents, Hurricane Pam was a
tabletop exercise. Over eight days, more than 250 planners from more
than fifty federal, state, and local agencies played with this catastrophic
scenario and tried to figure out what to do if a Category 4 or 5 storm
actually hit the city.

Unfortunately for the city of New Orleans and its residents, all anyone did about it was congratulate one another on what they had just
been through. "We made great progress this week in our preparedness
efforts," Ron Castleman, FEMA's regional director, was quoted as saying
in a news release from the Governor's Office of Homeland Security &
Emergency Preparedness.

First Army did not participate in the exercise because it was not in
our area of operations. Louisiana belonged to Fifth Army. Come Katrina
we would be starting at ground zero with virtually no knowledge of
what preparations, if any, had been taken, and who were the key players with whom we would have to deal. It was no way to jump into the
middle of one of the largest disasters this country has ever seen.

CHAPTER 5
Lessons Learned for Building a Culture of Preparedness

1. When I was commanding First Army, we had a saying: "Train like
   you're going to fight." Local, state, and federal officers need to train
   together. You don't want to exchange business cards after a disaster.

2. In hurricane-prone states, state and federal officials need to share
   the burden of planning and training together. This needs to be
   directed by the president. There should be an in-state team of
   leaders, "men and women of consequence," who work together
   year round, not just during hurricane season. We need national
   standards.

3. There needs to be an equivalent of the federal Stafford Act that would be approved by Congress and provides money to states when a hurricane warning is issued.

4. FEMA and the states should turn water requisition and distribution over to Wal-Mart, Home Depot, Lowe's, or trucking companies, to mention a few, and get out of the business of trying to write and execute contracts after a storm. Let people who know logistics and have the equipment available handle the distribution of water. That way the states can tell the companies what they want and where.

5. FEMA needs to give money to states so they can execute basic contracts—that is, water, ice, trucks, generators, and buses. FEMA needs to be more into looking at books and how money is spent, rather than watching where a truckload of water is or whether a mayor's request for a generator is approved.

6. When a disaster is declared, state and federal workers should be exempt from overtime pay. People in public service should not be paid overtime for helping to save lives. The Army does not pay overtime. Public service workers can be given a bonus if they do their jobs well.

6

First Army's Storm Surge

CREATING A TRUE CULTURE OF PREPAREDNESS IS NOT SOMETHING
that can be done overnight. Nor can it be created by only occasionally
paying attention to the major issues that affect individuals, communities, businesses, and government agencies after a disaster. It is something that has to be worked at constantly. It has to be examined and
reexamined to ensure that not only is the big picture taken into consideration but so too are those small details that often mean the difference
between success and failure, life and death.

A perfect example of that occurred not long after I took command of
First Army in July 2004. Members of my staff picked me up in a Dodge
Caravan after the change-of-command ceremony and drove me to my
office. When I asked what kind of vehicle was available for me to move
around in I was told it would be that same Dodge Caravan, a soccer
mom's car.

"No," I said, "what kind of vehicle do I move around in if we have
an event?"

Again the answer was the Dodge Caravan. The plan for dealing with
a major event or a disaster included moving my headquarters forward
to the scene and me being driven there in a soccer mom's van. The only
communications available would be my cell phone and an Iridium satellite phone. That was not going to cut it. There was no way I could deal
with a hurricane or flood or tornado without adequate communications
or the ability to drive through flooded streets or across uneven terrain.

That minivan would crap out at the first obstacle. Something more substantial than that was needed, something with a decent communications system.

I told my chief of staff that we needed a vehicle that would allow us to communicate on the move during a disaster. He told me that the year before they had gone through the regulations and the only vehicle authorized for the First Army commander was no more substantial than a Dodge Caravan.

"You're not asking the right question," I told him. "I want a C2V, a command-and-control vehicle, and I want two of them, one for me and one for my deputy. I want to be able to talk on the move and have Internet connections on the move and have video teleconferences on the move."

"We can't do that," he said.

"No," I replied, "we can do that."

We sent an authorization request up to Forces Command for two well-equipped Chevrolet Suburbans. There was a lot of wailing and gnashing of teeth from the FORSCOM staff about my budget and our request eventually went all the way up to the Forces Command boss, General Dan McNeill. He immediately saw the importance of what we were trying to do and approved the request. We paid less than sixty-five thousand dollars for those two vehicles and they proved their worth several times over in the aftermath of Katrina.

The lesson there was that creating a culture of preparedness means looking down the road and anticipating what may happen and then being willing to spend the money to make the necessary preparations. We never could have done what we needed to do after Katrina and Rita had we been forced to drive around in a minivan without adequate communications. A little foresight and the willingness to spend a few extra dollars to take that next step for preparation is a key to creating the culture of preparedness, whether it's the Army or in a family of two or three.

On August 8, 2005, the staff at First Army began tracking a tropical wave off the west coast of Africa. It seemed no more unusual or ominous than any of the other nine tropical waves the staff had already tracked that summer. After the unusually active 2004 hurricane season we felt well prepared for 2005. The National Hurricane Center was predicting twelve to fifteen tropical storms that season, with seven to nine becoming hurricanes. It also predicted that as many as five could become major hurricanes.

We watched every tropical wave. If one became a full-fledged hurricane we would go to around-the-clock staffing at our headquarters. As
each storm approached land we created decision points so that once a
hurricane got to a certain point it would trigger specific responses regarding asset requests or deployment of our DCOs. Once the hurricane made
landfall and our DCO on the ground assessed the damage, we would
send in the appropriate-size headquarters within twenty-four to thirty-
six hours to do whatever was needed. If the storm did not come ashore
we used it as a training opportunity. To my knowledge no one else in the
government worked hurricanes and tropical storms like that.

On August 13, as the tropical wave continued to move west, it was
designated Tropical Depression 10 and was forecast to head for Puerto
Rico. Three days later, as it approached the Bahamas, Tropical Depression 10 dissipated as a result of unfavorable weather conditions. But the
staff at First Army continued to watch the disturbance because computer
models indicated that a low-pressure system could redevelop from the
remnants of the tropical depression.

Sure enough, on Tuesday, August 23, the National Hurricane Center
issued an advisory at 5 P.M. that a low-pressure system had developed
over the southern Bahamas from the remnants of Tropical Depression
10 and was organized enough to be classified as Tropical Depression
12. The NHC advisory predicted that the storm would move "westward
across Southern Florida in 60–72 hours . . . and then into the Eastern
Gulf of Mexico by 96 hours . . ."

We knew from past experience that no matter what size the storm,
once it hit the superwarm waters of the Gulf of Mexico that late in the
year it would only increase in size, strength, and speed. And depending
on how capricious nature wanted to be, the storm could be relatively
mild or it could be a killer. Daily staff updates from our Crisis Action
Team focused on the storm as it got close to Florida. We also started
updating our decision points.

At 11 A.M. on August 24, the National Hurricane Center upgraded the
tropical depression into a tropical storm and gave it the name next in
line in the alphabetical listing of storm names for 2005—Katrina. It was
the twelfth storm of the season.

Late in the afternoon of the 25th, Katrina made landfall between
Hallandale Beach and North Miami Beach as a Category 1 storm with
winds of eighty miles per hour. Katrina quickly lost much of its energy
once it hit land and was mostly a wind and rain event for South Florida.

Still, I was a bit uneasy about the storm. My wife, Beverly, was sched-uled to fly to Tampa the next morning to visit our daughter Stefanie, her husband, Jimmy, and our first grandchild, James Russel Acosta, who had been born just two weeks earlier. In addition, our daughter Kimberly was flying in from New Orleans for the visit.

All the forecasts were predicting the storm would take a southerly dip once it hit land. After crossing the southern end of the Florida pen-insula it would emerge into the Gulf of Mexico and strengthen before turning north. I told my wife and daughter I did not think the storm would move into the Tampa–St. Petersburg area but knowing the unpre-dictability of hurricanes, it was impossible to be sure.

Just how much Katrina would strengthen and where it would hit after it entered the Gulf was anybody's guess. The computer model on the 25th showed the storm tracking a bit to the northwest before turn-ing due north and making a second landfall in the panhandle of Florida. Each day the storm track was pushed a little farther west. The predicted track on the 25th had it hitting around Apalachicola, Florida. By the 26th the morning prediction was for landfall around Panama City, Flor-ida. At 5 P.M. the storm appeared to be heading for Mobile, Alabama.

The real unknown, and the great concern, was New Orleans. As early as Friday, August 26, there was a lot of chatter in our headquarters about the storm scoring a direct hit on the city. At the rate Katrina was growing, it had the potential to be the real-life version of the fictional Pam from a year earlier. Every storm has a vote about where it goes and it doesn't tell us how it is voting until it starts to move. New Orleans, Houston, Biloxi, Mississippi, and Pensacola, Florida, were potential targets.

There is always a great deal of concern about a major storm hitting areas with large populations. If it hits land and gets sucked up in the swamp it's not that big a deal. It's the major population areas that every-one frets over and rightly so. As the storm track kept moving west, Loui-siana Governor Kathleen Blanco and New Orleans Mayor Ray Nagin started talking about a mandatory evacuation of the city. Max May-field of the National Hurricane Center was keeping a close watch on the storm and was especially concerned about New Orleans. He personally called Blanco and Nagin on Saturday the 27th urging them to evacuate the city. Blanco had issued a state-of-emergency declaration for Louisi-ana on Friday the 26th but it was not until Sunday morning, less than twenty-four hours before the storm hit, that Nagin and Blanco actually ordered the evacuation of New Orleans.

On Thursday and Friday that week, I received Katrina updates several times a day. The briefings usually would start with a weather report and potential storm tracks. Assessments of each state's preparations for the storm in our area of operations would be given as well as what decision points we had reached or were approaching. The staff also provided guidance we were receiving from Northern Command and Forces Command, plus any orders we were sending out telling various units to be prepared to move on our command.

One of the issues we concentrated on that Friday was the preparation of Camp Shelby, Mississippi. We had about three thousand troops from Minnesota and Wisconsin training there and very few, if any, had been through a hurricane. We put a lot of energy into making sure we dropped the tents those troops were staying in so the tents would not be damaged or destroyed. Then we pulled the troops into garrison on Friday evening because of the potential for hurricane-force winds and tornadoes. The brick and cement-block buildings at Camp Shelby were built to withstand one-hundred-mile-per-hour winds. Flooding is not a major issue because of the terrain.

We also wrestled with whether we should displace those National Guard troops before the storm hit. Camp Shelby occasionally had been used as an evacuation center for civilians coming from the Gulf Coast since it was only about sixty miles away. But no troops had been training there during those previous evacuations. In this case, with more than three thousand troops, we likely would not have enough room for everybody if we started taking in civilians.

The question for me was whether to send those National Guard soldiers to Fort Stewart, Georgia, to get them out of harm's way and make room for displaced civilians. We were concerned about the safety of the soldiers and the potential disruption of their training. I decided to leave them at Shelby but if the firing ranges took a significant hit from high winds or tornadoes we would bus the soldiers to Fort Stewart so they could complete their training there. They still had more than seventy of their hundred days of training to complete.

There was another reason to keep the soldiers at Camp Shelby: once the storm passed we would have that much more manpower to clean up the roads and get the post operating quickly again. Those troops eventually played a major role in opening roads and clearing debris after the storm, and within two days we were back training. We had been through this in 2004 when Ivan came through and the personnel at

Camp Shelby are used to it. It is part of the culture there because it is a controlled environment and we can practice doing the things we need to do before and during a storm. And the camp is in tornado alley so our staff there is very sensitive to the lethality of tornadoes and the safety of the soldiers.

By Saturday the 27th we had the DCOs in position. One was in Florida and others were in Alabama and Mississippi. As Katrina pushed farther to the west, Fifth Army moved into action. On the 28th it put two representatives from its staff in Baton Rouge and nine in Houston.

That morning, as my wife and daughter visited my grandson in St. Petersburg and Katrina churned her way northwestward through the Gulf, gaining strength and size every hour, I attended an early morning briefing at my headquarters. The storm looked like it was moving closer to a Mississippi-Louisiana landfall, putting it right on the border between the areas of responsibility for First and Fifth armies. That concerned me a bit because the interoperability between the two headquarters was not what it should have been for an event as potentially dangerous as Katrina.

Those thoughts were whirling around in my head as I returned to my quarters on Staff Row at Fort McPherson. My plan was to relax a bit and do a little gardening late that morning. I kept a small vegetable garden on post near my quarters where I grew potatoes, tomatoes, cabbage, onions, sweet potatoes, and pumpkins. Some generals play golf for relaxation. I tended my garden.

That morning I pulled my aging Ford F-150 pickup truck close to the vegetable patch and turned on the XM radio that one of my children had given me for Christmas. I kept my eyes on the vegetables while weeding but my ears were tuned to news reports about Katrina's approach. Mississippi Governor Haley Barbour declared a state of emergency that morning to go along with Blanco's state of emergency from the day before, further confirming the feeling that Katrina would be a dangerous storm.

With the DCOs in place in our region, my staff and I began to consider moving my forward headquarters to Camp Shelby to direct rescue and relief efforts from there. That's always a dilemma for a commander involved in disaster response. Should we move forward and be there when the storm hits? Or should we wait until after it hits so we would not have to go through the drama of the storm and the potential damage to our communications systems?

The question I wrestled with was whether I could make better decisions in Atlanta or Mississippi. If my staff and I went forward and Camp Shelby took a major hit, would we be part of the problem or part of the solution? If there were concerns about evacuating me and the staff, we would be part of the problem. We had not gotten the order to do anything yet. But the call was mine to make. I did not have to wait for an order or a request to move into position ahead of the storm. An old lesson is that we can *deploy* wherever we want anywhere in the United States. The decision to *employ* comes from the chain of command. My staff and I went through a couple of contested discussions about that and we eventually decided to wait until after the storm hit before moving the headquarters.

That Saturday afternoon I called the staff back together for another update. The track of Katrina was moving more toward New Orleans. We sent a request to Northern Command for a list of military assets we might be able to get, including aircraft and ships. Later, I had a conversation with Major General Rich Rowe, the director of operations for Northern Command, and suggested that since it appeared the storm would hit somewhere between Mississippi and Louisiana, it would be advisable to create a JOA, or Joint Operations Area. The JOA would focus on where the storm hit as opposed to recognizing the boundary between First and Fifth armies. My recommendation was to put one of the army headquarters in charge rather than splitting the duties. My suggestion was to give Fifth Army the lead because it was more familiar with New Orleans. I did a video teleconference with Northern Command officials on Sunday afternoon and another on Monday over whether there would be a JOA or a single individual in charge of the Department of Defense response but there was no decision at that point.

That weekend saw a lot of moving parts throughout the South in response to Katrina's movements. The Department of Defense reset many of its aviation assets in Florida, Alabama, Mississippi, and Louisiana. Those aircraft were moved north. Navy ships put out to sea to ride out the storm in deep water. It was almost as if a major invading force were descending on the South and nobody wanted to stay and fight. But in the case of hurricanes, discretion is the best option and saving the expensive equipment is a well-established priority. What we did not know was that by moving many of those assets north our ability to use them after the storm would be greatly reduced.

In addition to the movement of military equipment, there was a mass exodus of people out of New Orleans and from along the Gulf Coast of Mississippi and Alabama. The culture among the people who live in hurricane country is to track the eye of the storm. If they think the eye is going to New Orleans and they are in Biloxi or Pascagoula they are probably not going to move too soon. They sit and watch what that eye is doing and then make a decision to move at the last minute. When it appeared the eye was going to New Orleans people headed for Baton Rouge or Jackson, Mississippi, and took up most of the hotel space. Later, when it appeared that the eye might hit Mississippi, people from the coast went north to Hattiesburg and Jackson and found most of the motel rooms filled.

Then there was the issue of those who could not move themselves. Evacuation is easy for people who have cars and money. But during that last week of the month, when the welfare money is running low, evacuation is hard for those who are dependent on government subsidies. On the Gulf Coast of Mississippi and Louisiana a lot of people are dependent on state and federal government subsidies. On the 28th and 29th of the month the next check has not hit the bank yet nor has it showed up in the mailbox. Most people don't have a preparedness kit with money in it so they are unable to call a hotel and reserve a room. So we get stuck in this conundrum of what preparations can actually be done when there are financial and health constraints as there are in New Orleans.

Those New Orleans residents who could not leave when Blanco and Nagin ordered the evacuation of the city were told to go to the Louisiana Superdome, which had been designated a "shelter of last resort." The thinking was that those who were physically or economically unable to evacuate would go to the Superdome, ride out the storm, and then return home. The plan was good in its intentions, and would have worked fine had Katrina been a normal storm, had the roof not been ripped off the Superdome, had the levees not broken, and had disaster preparedness planners taken a hard look at the lessons learned from Hurricane Pam the year before and implemented some of the necessary fixes.

The mandatory evacuation order was right and necessary for the majority of the people. But such an order always has second-and third-order effects that are never dealt with in any of the training exercises. When that order is issued much of the governmental and institutional capacity in the city follows the order and gets out of town. It's a mandatory order, right? But what about the city transit workers? Are they supposed to stay or go? If they go, how do you get them back if all the telephone lines and cell phone towers are down? What does mandatory evacuation mean for public servants? Do they stay or do they go?

If you are a bus driver is there enough detail in your job description so that if there is a mandatory evacuation you know enough to go and grab your bus because the bus becomes a tool for saving lives? That's the level of detail you never see in most of these evacuation plans and training exercises. After Katrina we saw hundreds of yellow school buses that served the lower parishes sitting in the water. They were flooded out because no one had thought to move them to high ground before the storm. But even if they had been moved, the bus drivers were under mandatory evacuation orders and most could not be found.

Even the Louisiana Army National Guard found itself a victim of these types of planning assumptions that follow tradition and protocol and waits until after the fact to respond. The Louisiana Guard had a tradition of setting up at Jackson Barracks right next to a bend in the Mississippi River a few miles east of the city. Much of the equipment used by its first responders is based there. But when the levees broke and flooded St. Bernard Parish that equipment was inundated by twelve feet of water and was useless.

At 7:30 A.M. on Sunday, August 28, the First Army Operations Center at Fort Gillem went to category red, the highest status, with full staff on duty around the clock. We had upgraded from green to amber two days earlier, bringing in additional staff to prepare for what we believed would shortly be a move to red. We learned from the year before that if we waited until after the storm hit before going to category red we did not have the situational awareness and the staff had not gotten into a routine of briefing and tracking and talking to the right people. Once we went to category red that Sunday morning we were fully functional as a staff headquarters.

The more we watched the projected track of Katrina the more it appeared it would likely hit New Orleans. It had made a turn to the north and slowed its forward progress to little more than five or six miles per hour. But as it slowed it fed off the warm Gulf waters and continued to grow until it was approximately 120 miles off the coast. Then, without warning, it started to move at twelve miles per hour. What had been a poorly organized low pressure system only a few days earlier was rapidly exploding into a monster storm. Even if it hit New Orleans we knew that the First Army area of operations would be affected. No matter which way it went, it looked like it was going to be ugly. Little did anyone realize just how ugly.

CHAPTER 6
Lessons Learned for Building a Culture of Preparedness

1. In disasters, leaders should focus on doing the right things and not just trying to do things right. Doing things right is from the plans drawn up by people who do not have to look poor people in the eye.

2. States and cities need a plan to evacuate their workers to a predesignated location so that they can be quickly recalled.

3. State, city, and federal agencies should have an agreement to share facilities in the event a disaster occurs.

4. Each state should have its own defense coordination team. The current plan is to put DCOs at FEMA regional headquarters. The DCO must have trust and confidence of the state team. If DCOs can't be funded, then put them in states along the east, south, and west coasts that are more prone to weather effects, terrorist attacks, or earthquakes.

7

Running Against the Wind

PRESIDENT GEORGE W. BUSH DECLARED A STATE OF EMERGENCY IN Louisiana on Saturday, August 27, two days before the storm came ashore. He made similar disaster declarations for Alabama and Mississippi on Sunday the 28th. It was the first time in history that a president had signed a disaster declaration before a storm hit land. Those declarations triggered the Stafford Act and gave FEMA the authority to begin moving personnel and supplies into the region and enabled the governors of those three states to request assistance. The myth about the federal government failing to prepare for Katrina just does not pass muster.

The problem with the federal response was not so much the speed but the nature of it. The entire federal government response was based on practices and protocol FEMA used during the 2004 hurricane season in Florida and for most storms in previous years. They had worked then. There was no reason to believe they would not work for Katrina. No reason, except that no one—not Bush or FEMA officials or me or the First Army staff—fully realized the destructive power contained in that huge mass of swirling winds that carried the deceptively pleasant name of Katrina.

There were some, though, who were more proactive and were able to look down the road and see what Katrina might do. General Dan McNeill, the commander at Forces Command and my immediate boss, was one of them. He is always leaning forward in the foxhole, as they like to say in the Army, meaning he believes in being ready for any event. He had given a brigade of the 82nd Airborne Division at Fort Bragg, North Carolina, a warning order on Thursday the 25th to be prepared to move to New Orleans to assist in search-and-rescue efforts and whatever else those soldiers might be needed to do. On Saturday the 27th, McNeill sent a similar warning order to a brigade of the 1st Cavalry Division at Fort Hood, Texas. With those brigades on standby we could bring active forces in from the east or the west with just a few hours' notice. However, we had to wait for a governor to make the request of FEMA, which then had to send the request to the Department of Defense. Only then could the orders be issued to send active-duty troops into the region.

The dilemma for the active military in situations such as this is that while we know we will likely be sent in because of the size of the storm and the amount of damage it has the potential to inflict on people and property, we cannot guess for how long we will be there or how many resources we should commit. People now speak emphatically of what should have or what could have been done but the question is, How do we put enough in there so if this storm creates significant damage we are ready to start assisting rescue and relief efforts immediately?

We had learned from previous storms that if we did what we could on the left side of the event we would all be better off on the right side of it. We had people in place, but not equipment. The equipment needed in the immediate aftermath of the storm is usually for search and rescue, such as helicopters and small boats. But the lead agencies for those sorts of things, other than the U.S. Coast Guard, come from the affected states and those governments often jealously guard that turf. There is still a great deal of friction between state and federal government agencies, especially in the South.

States have a tendency to try to handle things on their own before requesting federal resources. Then, if we respond and that response is not instantaneous or state officials do not consider it robust enough, they complain that the feds did not do enough. As a result, the civilian federal agencies have a tendency to sit back and wait to see where the storm hits and what damage has been done before moving in resources. For the active military, the constraints are rooted in law, although they are also a result of following that same federal protocol of wait and see. However, a DOD policy allows commanders to help local communities save lives without having to wait for an order from the Pentagon.

First Army's requests for assets to deal with the aftermath of Katrina went first to Northern Command, then to Joint Forces Command in Norfolk, Virginia, and finally to the Pentagon. Once those requests hit the Pentagon they were looked at through a much wider lens. This is personal to us because it's our mission in our area of responsibility. But at the Pentagon it is looked at from a national and international perspective without being filtered through that culture of preparedness. These requests were being looked at in Washington as they had always been looked at, and officials there were waiting for a request from FEMA before moving anything into position. Pentagon officials were following protocol and not being proactive. They had not adapted to the culture of preparedness.

For those of us on the active military side, this issue of dealing with state governments during disasters is almost like a dance. Do we lead or follow? In this sense the feds, especially the active military, are always the junior partner. So the conventional wisdom of a lot of people in the military and the federal government was that we were going to dance but we were going to have to follow, not lead. Until the storm arrived there was only so much we could do.

At first light on Monday the 29th I was in my headquarters at Fort Gillem monitoring the radios, watching news reports of the storm's progress, and continuing to second-guess myself about the decision on Saturday not to move my headquarters to Camp Shelby. A move then would have enabled us to beat the storm to Mississippi. By Sunday it was too late to get in there and establish the headquarters and our communications system. By Monday morning the storm was between me and Camp Shelby and there was no way to get in there via helicopter or airplane without risking the lives of everyone on board.

Hurricane Katrina had been a Category 5 storm shortly before it plowed through Plaquemines Parish at 6:10 A.M. (CDT) on Monday. It was the sixth most powerful storm in the recorded history of hurricanes. But by landfall it had dropped to a Category 4 and even though it fell another notch to Category 3 before coming ashore on the Mississippi coast near Biloxi and Gulfport, it carried 135-mile-per-hour winds and pushed a thirty-foot storm surge ahead of it.

Our efforts at First Army through the weekend and on into Monday were focused on Mississippi and Alabama and the damage we would have to deal with in those two states. Louisiana was not in our area of operations and although Northern Command was considering my request to appoint an overall commander for the Joint Operations Area, it was my belief it would be someone from the Fifth Army. We watched on television as the situation at the Superdome continued to deteriorate throughout the day on Monday but at that point we were not asked to assist in any way and believed we would have our hands full in Mississippi.

The area hardest hit by Hurricane Katrina appeared to be in the First Army area of operations. Mississippi, Alabama, Tennessee, and to some extent Georgia had been hit by high winds, tornadoes, and heavy rains. From a technical standpoint only a small portion of Louisiana suffered significant damage before the New Orleans levees broke.

Katrina was not only massive in size, it was unpredictable in its movements and, if human characteristics can be ascribed to an inanimate object, it could have been characterized as an evil force. What else would fit the description of a storm that had the ability to send a thirty-foot wall of water into the Gulf Coast of Mississippi, wiping out virtually everything within a few hundred yards of the beachfront and tossing boats and massive casinos across the highway as if they were a child's toys before sending a seventeen-foot storm surge up the Mississippi River and into Lake Pontchartrain?

Those storm surges were what made Katrina so dangerous and its aftermath so difficult to deal with. When that surge hit the levees, water not only went over the top but also undermined the foundation in several places. It was like punching a hole in the side of a bathtub and letting the water run out onto the floor. Only in this case the floor was the city of New Orleans, most of which is below the level of the nearby rivers and lakes. The water poured out of the lake and into the streets. It was not like a tidal wave but rather more like a steady flow that enabled some people to get out of their homes and find high ground while others headed for the upper floors of their houses and, in some cases, their roofs.

In the past, when hurricanes came near New Orleans and dumped a lot of rain, there might have been a couple of feet of water in the streets. The city was able to pump the water into Lake Pontchartrain so the flooding usually was little more than an inconvenience for many. But when the level of Lake Pontchartrain rises by seventeen feet it breaks any plan the city or the state has to deal with flooding. There was no adequate blueprint for dealing with failed levees. Even the best of schemes likely would have been no match for this storm. Katrina seemed intent on breaking all the rules and making a mockery of any plans anyone might have considered adequate before August 29, 2005.

Late Monday morning we received confirmation that the levees had been breached and water was slowly but steadily pouring into New Orleans. Hardest hit were the lowest points in the city in the 7th and 9th wards, which were also home to many of the city's poor African-American residents.

Our primary concern that day at First Army was Mississippi. We were getting word that food, water, and medical supplies were the primary needs but those were well within the capabilities of the state National Guard. Some search and rescue assets were needed in Waveland but the sense we got was that while Mississippi was badly wounded by the storm, it was not a critical situation. It did not have thousands of people trapped by floodwaters. The water came in and went back out or was absorbed into the sandy soil along the coast.

In the weeks and months after Katrina there was this sense among some state officials in Mississippi that their efforts were far superior to those of officials in New Orleans. They tried to convince everyone they had their act together while the people in Louisiana were incompetent. Some even tried to put a political spin on it—the governor of Louisiana and the mayor of New Orleans were Democrats; the governor of Mississippi was a Republican.

Politics had absolutely nothing to do with anything related to the storm, despite the best efforts of many people to make it seem so. The one significant difference between what happened in Mississippi and Louisiana was that New Orleans had thousands of people who had become homeless and were trapped by rising waters; Mississippi did not.

I decided Monday afternoon to move my headquarters to Camp Shelby because of the amount of damage being shown on televised news reports coming out of Mississippi. But the storm had turned north-easterly and blocked our route. It was also spinning off tornadoes as it headed our way, killing two people in western Georgia. In addition, the Gulfport-Biloxi airport was closed because the navigation aids were down and there was debris on the runways. It was not yet safe for fixed-wing aircraft. The only other option was driving to Mississippi. It was more than a little frustrating but once again was an object lesson in making decisions on the left side of the disaster to mitigate the effects on the right side.

We pushed back our departure to later Monday night to allow a satellite communications unit out of Fort Gordon near Augusta in east Georgia to link up with us in Atlanta. We needed that unit because it would supply telephone lines and computer access for my headquarters. But those Fort Gordon soldiers could not travel because Interstate 20 between Augusta and Atlanta was closed due to high winds. So we pushed back our departure again, this time until early Tuesday morning, August 30.

The decision to move my headquarters forward was my own. I received no orders to make the move. Nor did I request permission to move. I just moved. Some on my staff and others at the Pentagon thought I should have waited for an order from Forces Command before departing for Mississippi. The hell with that. This was my area of operations and it was my job to be at the right place at the right time. We have an ethos in the Army to take initiative; don't wait for someone to tell you to do what you are supposed to do on your own.

That culture of waiting until somebody gives an order before doing anything had become commonplace in DOD disaster response. Nobody wants to take the initiative on something and risk making a mistake that could be career-ending. The Army I knew valued taking initiative. And within the confines of ability and authority to make decisions, make them. Don't wait for somebody else to make the decision for you.

What was driving me that Monday was the welfare of the three thousand troops on the ground at Shelby. They were my responsibility. The governor of Mississippi had no authority over me and could not prevent me from going into his state to perform my duties as First Army commander.

Some Army officials have been critical of me for not remaining in Atlanta to provide overall direction and for not running my headquarters from Baton Rouge, where the Louisiana governor and FEMA officials were located. In a war, having a general at the front is not the best idea because he has to be able to command and control broad areas of the battlefield. That is a nonpermissive environment. Katrina was different. It was a permissive environment. We were dealing with American citizens, not an enemy. It was better for me to be on the ground assessing the situation and making rational decisions rather than having them filtered through staff officers and federal bureaucrats.

Besides, my deputy commander, Major General Jay Yingling, and Colonel Jim Hickey, my chief of staff, were at First Army headquarters

back in Atlanta and I had the utmost confidence in both of them to handle anything that popped up. We communicated either by text message,
e-mail, or telephone almost hourly.

My experience in Korea when the two little girls were accidentally
killed had taught me that during a disaster those in charge should be
the public face of the response. It would have done no good, and likely
would have been detrimental, had a junior Public Affairs Officer been
sent to Mississippi and then to New Orleans while I stayed behind in my
headquarters cocoon in Atlanta. In a permissive environment people
want to see the leaders at the front.

At 5:40 A.M. on August 30, one Chevrolet Suburban command-and-
control vehicle we had purchased a few months earlier turned west on
I-20 out of downtown Atlanta, and headed for Camp Shelby. I sat in the
backseat with my operations officer, Lieutenant Colonel Ron Rose. In
front were Major Lee Gutierrez and my aide, Captain Scott Trahan, who
was driving.

Command Sergeant Major Marvin Hill, my senior enlisted soldier
and a man on whom I depended heavily before and during Katrina, followed us a bit later just ahead of the communications convoy out of
Fort Gordon.

Several hours later we were just outside Birmingham, Alabama, hitting
about eighty miles per hour when I called McNeill at Forces Command.

"Hey, dude," he said cheerily. "Where are you?"

"We're pressing on Birmingham and pushing toward Shelby," I
replied.

"What are you talking on?" he said. He had heard that much of the
telephone service in the area we were heading into was down.

"It's the phone in my C2V."

"That was a pretty good idea for you to buy that wasn't it?"

"Well, sir," I said, "you approved it."

For the next twenty-four hours the satellite communications in that
C2V and my hand-held Iridium satellite phone were my primary sources
of communication. That communications system saved my butt because
I was able to have conference calls with Admiral Timothy Keating, my
boss at Northern Command, and many of his staff while on the move.
Once we got past Birmingham, cell phone and BlackBerry service disappeared into the blackness that surrounded us.

As we drove on through the early morning light, chasing the darkness into winds that were rocking the heavy vehicle, we started running into areas south and west of Birmingham that had completely lost power. By the time we got to Mississippi there was a great deal of debris on the road and occasionally we had to stop to clear tree limbs out of the way.

The Interstate Highway System is a wonderful thing. But in an effort to make driving it more pleasant state officials often allow trees to grow in the medians and close to the shoulder. The trees look nice but hurricanes and high winds have a way of flattening those trees and those trees can block the road. Along much of Interstate 59 heading south into Hattiesburg from Meridian, trees blocked the outside lanes of the four-lane highway and impeded traffic trying to get into or out of the area. That could be especially critical in an emergency situation and states need to consider cutting back some of those trees close to the roadway.

During the drive we were getting a lot of reports from my headquarters about what they were seeing on CNN. The situation sounded bad in Mississippi and worse in New Orleans. We were able to track news reports through the XM radio I had brought along. At that time we did not have a satellite radio in the C2V but news reports we were receiving from CNN and Fox via the XM radio kept us tuned into the situation as it was unfolding in the wake of Katrina.

We arrived at Camp Shelby shortly after 11 A.M. on Tuesday. It was obvious a storm had been through there. Pine trees were down all over the place and debris was scattered everywhere. There was no electricity, no cell phone service, and no landline services save for a single DSN (Defense Switched Network) line that was a left over from the old culture of preparedness during the Cold War. It was the only damned phone still working anywhere on Camp Shelby.

When the communications package from Fort Gordon arrived, the soldiers quickly went to work trying to establish a high-speed, computer-based satellite phone system through which we could also use our computers. They did one heck of a job and within twelve hours had the system set up and nearly ready to go. But when they flipped the switch to get the phones working and get us online, nothing happened. We had nothing but blank computer screens and dead phone lines.

I asked what the hell was going on and the soldiers scratched their heads and said they had no idea. They said they had a good shot to the satellite but the program would just not come on. They told me they had upgraded the computer system just a few weeks earlier with a commercial vendor and everything worked fine then. So why wouldn't this high-speed program come on? Well, as we soon learned, the civilian company that runs the satellite had not been paid to activate the link. The Army had not paid its bill.

It was sometime after midnight when I started making telephone calls raising all kinds of hell about this. One call was to the Army Chief Information Officer, Lieutenant General Steve Boutelle, and within an hour we had the satellite link. The only good thing that came out of that experience was that once we found the right person to authorize the money the problem was solved. Because of the importance of what we were doing, people were paying attention to us, and when I made a request for something it was usually delivered quickly. That little piece of knowledge was tucked away for future use and it came in handy on numerous occasions over the next six weeks.

The Mississippi National Guard, under the leadership of Air National Guard Major General H. A. "Hac" Cross, was on the job in the most heavily damaged areas along the coast long before we hit Camp Shelby. No sooner had the storm passed than scavengers and looters in boats followed it in and began rummaging through the damaged and destroyed homes in the area. The National Guard soldiers went in to chase them away while also doing some search and rescue.

Later that afternoon my staff and I drove the roughly forty-five miles from Camp Shelby to the Gulfport-Biloxi airport where I met with Governor Haley Barbour and Cross. They gave me a quick briefing on the situation before we jumped into a Huey helicopter for a flyover of the hardest-hit areas.

For years military officials have speculated about what ground zero of a nuclear attack might look like. That's what the Mississippi coast reminded me of that day. The scope of the damage was almost beyond comprehension. Even with my appreciation for the power of hurricanes dating back to my childhood, I was amazed at the scene below. Huge barges and floating casinos had been lifted out of the water, shoved across the coastal highway, and tossed on top of hotels and houses. Houses were sheared off their foundations, leaving only a few stilts or a concrete slab. Trash and debris were everywhere. The destruction the storm had brought to coastal Mississippi was difficult to comprehend even for hurricane veterans.

Earlier that day we had received a warning order from Northern Command that First Army should be prepared to establish Joint Task Force–Katrina. We had received a similar order late Monday night but at the time it seemed little more than chatter among the headquarters staffs. I started sorting out possible scenarios for what we might do if we were sent to New Orleans but my focus on Tuesday was Mississippi and the damage there. Besides, I was still trying to deal with getting my headquarters set up at Camp Shelby and wrestling with the problems of the communications system.

Finally, at 10 P.M., the order came down from Northern Command that First Army had been officially designated JTF-Katrina and I was to be its commander. The order made it clear that that the majority of effort for the task force needed to be in New Orleans because of the number of people trapped in the city and the amount of search and rescue that needed to be done. My staff informed me that the situation in the city was grim and getting worse by the hour. Tens of thousands of people were trapped and needed to be rescued or evacuated.

No sooner had the order been issued than Northern Command and people at the Pentagon began pushing me to go to New Orleans immediately. I briefly considered it but thought it a bridge too far at that hour. It was late. It was dark. I was still trying to get my headquarters and communications system set up. My opportunities for getting anything done that late at night in a city that was slowly drowning, a city without electrical power or telephone communications, a city that to some seemed on the verge of disintegration, was highly unlikely. Besides, we would be operating in an information vacuum. My staff and I would be going in cold and would have to learn everything on the fly. As great as the crisis was at that moment, there was little chance that JTF-Katrina could make any difference before first light on Wednesday.

CHAPTER 7

Lessons Learned for Building a Culture of Preparedness

1. President Bush signed the disaster declaration for Louisiana on Saturday, August 27, 2005. Future presidents need to continue to be proactive when dealing with potential disasters. Governors and mayors need to be given authority to spend money before the storm hits.

2. Federal troops should be sent in before the storm hits so that they can be in position to respond quickly. If they are not needed they can go home.

3. Congress should reconsider what federal troops are permitted to do in domestic situations. The current law was designed to prevent the federal government from undermining the authority of a governor. Federal troops should be able to stop people from breaking into houses and prevent property from being destroyed after a disaster.

4. The federal government should push assets and capabilities to a state and not wait for the governor to ask for help. The military has the capability to deploy to any state at any time. The decision to employ the military should be made through a request from the governor to the president with decision makers between the two.

5. FEMA should be a separate agency and not part of the Department of Homeland Security. Other federal agencies sent to disaster areas with the exception of law enforcement should be under the command of FEMA. Currently the Principal Federal Officer has to ask other agency representatives to do something, and they have to request approval from their headquarters in Washington, D.C., before anything can be done.

6. States should create programs that will train schoolteachers to be Red Cross workers. That way, local folks are taking care of local folks after a disaster.

8

Sorting Out the Super Mess at the Superdome

THE NUMBER-ONE PRIORITY IN ANY NATURAL OR MAN-MADE DISAS-
ter is saving lives. The number-two priority is evacuating people from
the disaster area whose lives might be at risk. But in order to do either,
the capacity to do them must first be there. That is, the tools and resources must be available to pluck people out of harm's way or to move
those who might be in danger into a safer area. That Wednesday morning, August 31, after I landed at the Superdome, it was abundantly clear
to me that both needed to be done simultaneously.

Thousands of people were stranded in their attics or on their roofs
by the floodwaters and needed to be taken to high ground. The water
had stopped rising and helicopter crews were working nonstop to get
those most at risk out of danger. We also had upwards of 16,000 people
at the Superdome and, unknown to me that morning, a similar number at few blocks away at the Ernest N. Morial Convention Center by
the river. All of them needed to be evacuated because their homes were
flooded. Most had lost everything of value except their lives. They had
no extra clothes, no money, no important papers, and no way to get out
of the city.

We had the capacity to accomplish the first task—saving lives. We
had helicopters from the Coast Guard, the Louisiana National Guard,
and the Navy ship USS *Bataan* working around the clock to find and save

people who were stranded in low-lying areas. We also had the Louisiana Department of Wildlife and Fisheries and the "Cajun Navy," local residents in small boats who were slowly patrolling the watery streets of the 7th and 9th wards looking for those who needed and wanted help.

What we did not have was the capacity to transport more than 30,000 people from the Superdome and the convention center. That is not the type of capacity that can be built immediately. It takes time. Five hundred buses do not magically appear after just a few phone calls. Since the local school and city transit buses were flooded, other buses had to be rounded up from around the country and driven to New Orleans. Even then, getting them into position to rescue these people was a tricky proposition, because the water was blocking portions of Interstate 10 that ran through the city.

By late Wednesday morning, my staff and I no longer were working off decision points. We had not tabletopped this scenario. The more we saw of what the storm had done the more capacity we knew we had to build quickly. Coast Guard Rear Admiral Robert Duncan had evacuated all his people out of the city to St. Louis before the storm and some had not yet returned. The Marine Corps Reserve headquarters in New Orleans also had been evacuated. The Louisiana Army National Guard was on the ground but much of its equipment was underwater at Jackson Barracks, several miles downriver. Even if that equipment had not been flooded it would have been impossible to drive it into the city from where it was staged because of the high water in St. Bernard Parish.

One of my first calls after being named commander of Joint Task Force–Katrina was to my good friend and head of the Louisiana National Guard, Major General Bennie Landreneau. We had known each other for years and my son, Sergeant Michael Honoré, was serving in Iraq with the Louisiana Guard's 256th Brigade Combat Team. Landreneau is a top-notch soldier and a first-rate Guard commander but it was evident in his voice that he was under a lot of pressure. He also was in charge of the state's homeland security disaster relief operation. He was, as they say in the military, "dual-hatted." The idea behind giving one man both jobs was to streamline the decision-making process in times of emergency. But trying to do both those jobs after a major disaster was too much for anyone. The problems inherent in such a system were evident during Katrina and it was changed shortly after so there is now a separate homeland security official for the state.

I asked Bennie what he needed.

"Send everything you got," he said.

He told me the National Guard Bureau in Washington, D.C., was sending in troops from Arkansas, Kansas, and Oklahoma to assist his efforts. Bennie's strength was down about 2,500 troops to a total of about 8,000 Army and Air National Guard because of the combat brigade in Iraq. The situation was similar in Mississippi, where the 155th Combat Brigade also was in Iraq. Both states were missing some of their most experienced and battled-tested Guard members.

The relationship between National Guard forces and active forces in disaster relief is one that confuses a great many people, particularly those in the media. Many think because we wear the same uniforms we are part of the same chain of command. But there are distinct and unique differences between active forces and the National Guard. As the active-duty commander of Joint Task Force–Katrina I had no say over what the Guard Soldiers could do or where they could go. They were under control of their TAG, The Adjutant General, who is the commander of a state's National Guard. In Louisiana it was Landreneau. In Mississippi it was Cross. They in turn were under the command of their respective governors.

My job was to assist them and coordinate our efforts as best we could. I had no authority to tell Bennie or Hac or any of their soldiers what to do. But what I could do was use my friendship with them and back-channel communications with other longtime friends in uniform to make sure we got the assets we needed, when we needed them. Except for one minor incident a few days later, Bennie and Hac and their staffs worked with me and my staff as if we were a team. And, in a sense, we were, because the goal of all of us was to save lives, get people evacuated from the city, and help establish order so the recovery could begin.

After I surveyed the situation that Wednesday and discussed it with Blanco, Nagin, and Landreneau, it was obvious that if we were going to bring in any additional assets it would have to be through the connectivity I had with my headquarters in Atlanta and the staff of Northern Command in Colorado Springs. The priorities for the active forces would be set by Blanco and Nagin. Despite stories to the contrary, those two were on the same sheet of music when it came to priorities for New Orleans: continue the search and rescue and start the evacuation of the Superdome.

The absence of telephone communications and the impact of that was a major issue in New Orleans, though, and led some to believe that

Blanco and Nagin were not talking to each other. In a sense they were not, because there was no physical way of communicating in the first few days after the storm. They relied on cell phones before the storm but after it hit there was no cell phone capacity anywhere in this part of Louisiana. The few people who could get a line into Baton Rouge were going through a system run by the Louisiana Emergency Operations Center.

Just getting the governor on the phone at the Baton Rouge EOC was a very competitive event. The call had to hit at just the right time, when she wasn't talking to someone else. That's one reason I flew to Baton Rouge twice on Wednesday. Getting her on the telephone was extremely difficult and we needed to be sure of her priorities for us.

Going into downtown New Orleans on the heels of Katrina gave me a much better feel for what we were dealing with there. That personal view, one that was not filtered through staff officers or the amplified emotions of the television reports, put into context the number and severity of the problems we were facing, especially how much the people who had been stranded were suffering. There was no electricity, no water, no cell phone or landline services, no Internet. The challenges the first responders were having just talking to one another, whether it was the police, fire officials, emergency medical services, or other city workers, were astronomical. It took only a few hours on the ground to realize why there was such a gap between Baton Rouge and New Orleans. In Baton Rouge the disaster was something they were watching on TV. They could keep an emotional distance because television to a degree filtered out the smells and the sounds and the magnitude of the disaster. In New Orleans the disaster was real and in our faces every second.

It is difficult for those who were not in New Orleans after Katrina to fully understand the impact on the people of not having the basic conveniences. That only compounded their misery after losing their homes and belongings. There was no ability to talk long-distance, to move freely about the city, to drink fresh water, or to go to the bathroom and have the waste flushed away when you wanted. Those are basic human functions and the people stranded in New Orleans had none of them. I used to say that Katrina set back technology sixty years, but it was more like eighty years. It certainly set technology back to a time when most people did not have any of those conveniences.

For months after my first view of the Superdome that Wednesday morning, I tried to find words to describe it. I always came up short. But the scene on the plaza was as breathtaking and as appalling in human terms as had been the physical damage along the Mississippi coast. The damage on the coast was primarily property damage, though. Houses and businesses could be rebuilt. At the Superdome we were dealing with human beings, some of whom were literally forced to stand in their own waste because of how crowded it was. After seeing and smelling that, I knew we had to get those people out of there as quickly as possible.

The situation at the Superdome was a classic example of officials thinking about the worst-case scenario but providing only enough resources for the best-case scenario. In the culture of preparedness, planning worst-case and resourcing worst-case go hand in hand. There is never one without the other. The Superdome had been used as an emergency evacuation center in the past. It was actually a good idea. Although it was built for 70,000 people to go there on a Sunday afternoon, have a few drinks, and watch the Saints play football, it could be used short-term to house people during an emergency.

In the best-case scenario the hurricane comes in, dumps some water, does some damage, and people walk back home the next day. In New Orleans there is a generation or two of people whose response to the storm is to wait until the last minute to see where the eye goes and then if things get too bad, find a public building and wait it out. Then they go home. Most of those people are poor and black.

City and state emergency preparedness officials considered the worst-case scenario when they did the Hurricane Pam exercise the year before. But for Katrina they provided only enough resources for the best-case scenario. Katrina proved to be the worst-case scenario come true and the resources were not there to deal with it. The roof of the Superdome was ripped off during the storm. The inside, what had been the sanctuary for the poor, was soaked with storm water. Then the power went out. The bathrooms stopped working. There was no drinking water. When all these dynamics are working, even if there are only 16,000 or 17,000 people in a place designed to hold 70,000, life goes downhill in a big hurry.

Portable toilets that were desperately needed at the Superdome were ordered but showed up five days late, hundreds of them, long after everyone had been evacuated. No one gave any thought to having those toilets on hand before the storm because it would have cost money and it was not in keeping with the protocol that had been followed for previous storms. The culture of preparedness in New Orleans went only so far and no further. People who had come to the Superdome, some as early as Saturday night, suffered as a result. And even as late as Wednesday and Thursday, people who abandoned their homes were trudging through the storm waters to the Superdome because that was supposed to be a place of refuge, a safe place for them and their families. But inside, the building was a foul-smelling, rain-soaked, uninhabitable hellhole.

My first contact with the media covering Katrina came on Wednesday. It was quite a contentious introduction. The big question from everyone was why the people stranded at the Superdome had not been evacuated yet and who was to blame for this. Many in the media and even some government officials already were looking for somebody to blame for what was being perceived and reported as a slow and ineffective response to the disaster. I tried to put this in context for people, especially the media, some of whom were letting their emotions get in the way of reporting the story. I had checked my emotions at the state line. I had to think objectively about what needed to be done and how best to do it. For me, emotions were a distraction at a time like this, even though several relatives living in the 7th and 9th wards were still unaccounted for.

The magnitude of this event was such that the media were continuously reporting on what they were seeing, but too often they were reporting on their *feelings* about what they were seeing and not on the *reasons* behind what they were seeing. The media had opened a one-way dialogue with the American public that was not focused on the significance of the storm but rather on who was to blame, how this happened, and why it happened. Within twenty-four hours we even had people in the entertainment industry shooting their mouths off about who was to blame. People with absolutely no knowledge of the situation were focusing on how bad the government was handling it and not on how bad the storm had been.

Many in the media knew little about disaster relief and the laws that govern it. They did not know about the Stafford Act or the Helms-Biden Act or the Posse Comitatus Act. Many were merely bodies on the scene who were giving the American public impressions and feelings rather than news.

I was not answerable to anyone but my chain of command but I still took the assault on the government personally. I had been a part of it for more than thirty-four years. I could not understand why the media did not see the amount of preparation before the storm. They did not see how we had pulled our equipment out of the danger zone so it could survive. They did not see us leaning forward, waiting for the request to move in assets. What is the counterattack for that? How can they be made to understand that we flew the helicopters north to keep them out of the storm even though people were waiting to be evacuated?

Much of the media focus was on the government officials and institutions responsible for disaster preparedness and response. But what struck me most about the situation in New Orleans was the cumulative effect of the infrastructure failure caused by the storm. That failure radiated out, like a pebble thrown into a lake. The infrastructure failure had second- and third-order effects that only compounded the numerous problems New Orleans was dealing with before the storm, not the least of which were poverty and crime. If the storm had not destroyed the infrastructure, assets would have been available to evacuate those people. But the fact that the city was flooded, and the challenges that that created, reinforced in some people's minds what they saw as a failure of leadership.

Effective leadership takes capability and capacity to get things done. New Orleans after Katrina was not unlike inviting a few people over for dinner and having more than 16,000 show up. Ray Nagin was under the media gun almost from the moment the storm hit. He was the most visible government leader available on the scene. But he, like so many other government officials in that city, was a victim of the storm. He had lost his home. His city was drowning. People were dying. He knew what needed to be done. In our first conversation he kept saying, "We've got to get a flow started. We've got to start flowing people out of the city." But he had neither the resources nor the authority to get that done. He had to rely on others, yet he was taking most of the heat.

A great deal of time was spent those first few days in scheduled and unscheduled news conferences, partly to take the heat off Nagin and partly to try to put into context what we were doing, how we were doing it, who was responsible for doing it, and why it was that the storm was to blame, not the leadership. Still, as early as Wednesday afternoon the media were hammering me, trying to get me to place blame on someone. They wanted to know if the Corps of Engineers did not build the levees right or if the mayor and the governor didn't act quickly enough. I didn't have time to deal with blame at that point. I was still working on saving lives, trying to get food and water to people who were trapped, and then trying to get those people out of the city. If the media wanted to spend their time trying to blame somebody there wasn't much I could do about it. I was focused on moving forward and saving lives.

The rescue operation was primarily a Coast Guard mission, although the Army, Navy, Air Force, Marines, and National Guard also supplied helicopters. The sound of helicopters around the Superdome was continuous that Wednesday morning. They were running search-and-rescue missions throughout the city and occasionally dropped down into the Superdome parking lot to pick up the most critically ill people because ambulances could not drive through the high water surrounding us. At the same time we were getting reports that the two nearby hospitals, Tulane Medical Center and Charity Hospital, were being evacuated by private air ambulance services.

The more pressing task for me and my staff was to coordinate enough assets to get people evacuated from the Superdome. We did not have option of using the airport. We knew it would take a couple of days to build the capacity we needed there. As ludicrous as it may sound, we were told we would have to wait until the Transportation Security Administration got enough people out there to do the screening of people getting on the planes, even though all those people had been screened before they were allowed into the Superdome.

Brigadier General Mark Graham, the deputy commander of Fifth Army, was assigned to Joint Task Force–Katrina, and I placed him along with a planning cell of about twenty people at the EOC in Baton Rouge. Graham was my liaison with Governor Blanco and was in charge of making sure the empty buses got into New Orleans and the full buses got out again and on their way to Houston.

Our initial plan was to set up rest stops on the highway because some of those small towns along the route were already full of people from New Orleans who had evacuated earlier. We also planned to have fuel trucks from the Louisiana National Guard for the buses along with water and Meals Ready to Eat (MREs) in place for the passengers at various stops along I-10.

The Louisiana National Guard had moved its headquarters to the Superdome and the community of Carville after Jackson Barracks was flooded. That was a good news / bad news situation for Bennie Landreneau and his troops. It was bad news because much of their equipment was under more than twelve feet of water. It was good news because with them at the Superdome I could talk to Guard officials face-to-face rather than trying to catch them on the telephone, which was nearly impossible at that point.

Staying at the point of the problem as much as possible and being a collaborator between the mayor and the governor was one of my priorities. Both were under an enormous amount of pressure from the national media, federal officials, and their own constituents. I wanted to be perfectly clear about the priority of work Nagin wanted done, since he was the senior elected official on the ground. Normally that information and any requests would have gone from the mayor to the senior FEMA representative but I became a conduit for the mayor because I had freedom of movement and backup communications that enabled me to talk to state headquarters. Neither the mayor nor the FEMA folks had that.

One of the criticisms of First Army and me is that I did not take thousands of troops to New Orleans. Blanco later complained about that, as did others. But what they did not realize is that I did not command thousands of troops. I had to request troops for specific missions or have them assigned to me by higher headquarters. The National Guard had about 2,500 soldiers on the ground at that point and more were on the way.

A major concern of mine on Wednesday was what the trigger for more ground troops should be. We had a brigade from the 82nd Airborne at Fort Bragg and another from the 1st Cavalry Division at Fort Hood prepped and ready to respond in just a few hours. But if a request to use them went out Wednesday or Thursday, a place needed to be found for them to stage. They would need truckloads of MREs and water. There was no easy way to get them into a city that was unable to provide any of the basic services for its own citizens. Extra troops would have created an entirely different logistics issue, complicating an already extremely difficult logistics puzzle we were trying to solve.

My sense in those first two or three days was that we did not need those active troops for the evacuation because we had thousands of National Guard troops flowing in from other states. We would need those additional troops when we started going into houses to search for survivors and the dead. The priorities were to rescue the people we could and evacuate those trapped at the Superdome and the convention center before we started doing a house-by-house, building-by-building search. We're not talking about a few houses here. We're talking more than 250,000 structures in the affected areas. That was how many addresses my staff in Atlanta came up with that had to be checked.

Bennie Landreneau had about 2,000 of his National Guard soldiers scattered between Jackson Barracks, the Superdome, and the convention center. His forces were stretched thin. The remainder were spread all across the state, especially in the hard-hit areas. Some of his forces were sheriff's deputies and policemen in civilian life who were released from their Guard duties to go home to do their primary jobs. That's a dilemma that occurs whenever the Guard tries to handle a local disaster: those people are needed both as members of the Guard and as local first responders. It's a situation that has to be addressed if the country is going to have a true culture of preparedness.

Landreneau also was dealing with the issue of members of the Guard who were from New Orleans. In some instances soldiers had no idea what had happened to their families or their homes. He tried to keep some of the Guard members who were New Orleans residents out of the city so they did not immediately start looking to the welfare of their families and homes. Had they done that, it would have gotten personal for them, just as it got personal for members of the New Orleans Police Department. That's why we ended up with the National Guard brigades from Oklahoma and Oregon in New Orleans instead of a large contingent from the Louisiana National Guard.

It is interesting to note that when the Pentagon began looking at which National Guard units to send to Iraq there was no discussion about which ones from hurricane-prone states would be in Iraq during the storm season. The Army's point of reference on that issue was not Katrina. The point of reference was storms from the past. Katrina changed the equation. If the city had not flooded and suffered only minor damage we would have used the same equation we had been using for years. And most likely we would still be using it today. Nowhere in the calculations of available forces was a catastrophe the magnitude of Katrina factored in, but that must now be taken into consideration whenever the National Guard Bureau considers what forces to make available for overseas duty during hurricane season.

The Louisiana Guard's 256th Brigade Combat Team, under the command of Brigadier General John "Bo" Basilica, got back from Iraq just before Rita struck a few weeks later. The 256th soldiers did not even have time to unpack and barely had time to kiss their wives and pat their kids on the head before they rushed out for storm duty. They made a tremendously positive contribution to the preparations and quick recovery from that storm.

But the key question that Wednesday after Katrina hit, the question no one seemed capable of answering, was just when the buses would arrive. Nagin had neither buses nor drivers. Neither did FEMA. It was FEMA's responsibility, though, to get the buses there. But it had to contract for them. During that first meeting Wednesday morning with Nagin, Landreneau, and the FEMA officials, the mayor kept asking the question "When is FEMA going to get the buses here?" Nagin was very direct at times and was on the verge of losing his patience with federal authorities. "You guys said the buses were going to be here. Where are they?"

When I met with Blanco and some of her advisors in Baton Rouge shortly after 6 P.M. on Wednesday I told her FEMA officials had assured me they were pushing the buses but we had not seen any yet and did not know how many were coming. I asked if she could put out a call to all the parishes and have them send school buses so we could get the evacuation started. There are a lot of school buses in Louisiana because it's so rural. Why not use them? The situation at the Superdome was deteriorating rapidly, and riding a school bus to Houston was better than standing around in filth.

Even if we had to drop those people off in Baton Rouge, which already was overflowing with Katrina evacuees, more good could be done for them there than we could do at the Superdome. And using the school buses was consistent with Nagin's desire to get a flow going out of the city, no matter to where or with what.

Blanco put out the call for school buses and the next day dozens showed up in Baton Rouge. But the drivers, apparently spooked by news coverage of what they perceived to be chaos in the city, simply parked the buses at a shopping center and found their way back home. We had school buses but they were seventy miles from where we needed them. And we had no drivers.

By late Wednesday night my patience with FEMA was running as short as Nagin's. That evening I had put in a call to Mike Brown, the FEMA director who was running the federal response from Baton Rouge. If anyone could tell me where the buses were, it would be the guy at the top of the federal food chain closest to the disaster. I wanted to try to pass along that information to the Louisiana National Guard and others around the Superdome so it could start circulating through the crowd and provide some hope for those thousands of people.

When I called Brown's office, however, I was told he was out to dinner and could not be reached. Baton Rouge was crowded and the lines at the restaurants were long and Brown would be tied up for a while. I was stunned. Here we had a major disaster on our hands. The people at the Superdome had little to eat or drink. Some who had been without their medication for days were starting to have health problems. But Brown apparently thought nothing of taking time to go to a restaurant. I told his assistant I needed to talk to him ASAP. He eventually called me back.

Had the people at the Superdome heard that Brown was out having dinner we more than likely would have had a riot on our hands. It was no wonder the federal response to Katrina was being so soundly condemned by so many. I still marvel at the infinite patience of all those people standing and waiting on the plaza at the Superdome, some in their own excrement, unwashed, underfed, and many with only a few hours of sleep over the previous four nights. Yet when I looked at them I could see a glimmer of hope that something would happen soon and the nightmare they had been living would be over.

Later that evening I learned several hundred buses contracted by FEMA would finally be arriving the next day to take out those stranded at the Superdome. I had one final conversation with Nagin before returning to Camp Shelby for the night. We briefly went over the walk-out plan to make sure it met his approval. The plan, developed by Louisiana National Guard officials, was to walk the evacuees through the Hyatt Regency hotel to the buses, which would be waiting on Loyola Street.

Nagin's eyes were red-rimmed and there was a growth of stubble on his chin. He looked like the weight of the world was on his shoulders. "You know," he said wearily, "we've got another large group down at the convention center that we're going to have to evacuate as well."

CHAPTER 8
Lessons Learned for Building a Culture of Preparedness

1. The National Guard needs the same quality equipment as federal troops. The Army keeps buying equipment for ten divisions when it has eighteen. The Congress needs to fully fund the National Guard to have the latest equipment.

2. Every state National Guard should have a military police battalion, an engineer battalion, a satellite-capable signals battalion, a decontamination platoon, a DMORT platoon, an infantry battalion

trained in crowd control, and a battalion trained in fighting fires where applicable. Engineer battalions need IBBs (itty-bitty boats).

3. Cities need to review mandatory evacuation orders with state officials before the next hurricane hits. Who has authority? Do public workers get paid if told to evacuate? If so, how long is it before they have to report back to work?

4. Elected officials need media training. Being glib enough to get elected does not qualify anyone to deal with the media after a disaster. Elected officials need to stay focused on the people and the disaster, not on who is at fault. Put information out about priority of work and do not read any prepared statements. Tell folks what you know. Note: don't cry in front of the media.

5. Hospitals in the path of hurricanes cannot be allowed to provide shelter in place of those who are ill.

6. The Adjutant General of a state's National Guard should not be in charge of the homeland security operations. He or she could be in control of thousands of troops from other states. One person cannot do both jobs. It looks good on paper but does not work.

7. DOD needs a plan to bring troops back from a war zone as soon as possible if their families have lost their homes.

8. Power lines need to be underground or trees should be cut if during a storm their fall would bring down overhead lines.

9. Trees cannot be allowed close enough to interstate and state highway evacuation routes that they pose a danger of blocking the roads if they are downed during a storm.

10. Before a storm hits, police need to evacuate patrol cars that are not needed and have backup gasoline tanker trucks on hand.

11. Cities must have emergency medications available for the police, firefighters, and EMS workers. During Katrina, emergency medications had to be rushed to New Orleans for first responders because many lost their homes and their medications.

12. Cities should rethink the requirement that all their employees live within the city limits. It makes sense for morale, but if the city gets hit, so do all the workers, their families, and their homes.

9

"You're Looking at a Calendar and I'm Looking at My Watch"

ON THURSDAY, SEPTEMBER 1, WHILE WAITING FOR THOSE WHO HAD been stranded at the Superdome to load the buses for the trip to Houston, I got into a conversation with one of the men about to be evacuated. He had been trapped since Saturday and was dirty, hungry, and dispirited.

"Why did God do this to us?" he asked plaintively.

His question made me think of what my mother might have said had she found herself in a similar situation. She was one of the most optimistic people I have ever known despite the hardships she endured throughout her life. "Always look on the bright side," she would say when things looked especially bleak. She always found something to smile about, something in which she could take hope.

"You know, sir," I said to the man, "that storm came right to the mouth of the Mississippi River and turned right. Mississippi took the hardest hit. Gulfport and Biloxi didn't have that many people in town. They had some deaths but they did a good job of evacuating people. Think what would have happened if the strength of that storm had hit New Orleans. So how can you say God wasn't involved with it? Maybe He was. Maybe He turned that storm."

The man thought for a moment and then walked off. Maybe he was convinced God had turned that storm. I don't know. I never saw him again. But I knew that as bad as things were in New Orleans, they could have been far worse. Many more lives would have been lost had Katrina hit the city with the strength with which it hit Mississippi. A thirty-foot wall of water coming into Lake Pontchartrain instead of the seventeen-foot surge would have been devastating and the death toll astronomical.

The Katrina death toll was a source of much speculation those first few days. We were still doing search-and-rescue operations from dawn to dark and there was no way we could estimate what the eventual death toll would be. Those who did the Hurricane Pam exercise the year before had been careful to avoid sounding like doomsayers when asked about casualty estimates. A spokesman for FEMA said after the exercise, "We would see casualties not seen in the United States in the last century" if a storm as strong as Pam actually hit the city. The *New Orleans Times-Picayune* noted in a story about the exercise that two years earlier an American Red Cross official predicted 25,000–100,000 could die if a "catastrophic hurricane" hit the area. Mayor Ray Nagin mentioned the Pam figure of 10,000 possible deaths soon after Katrina and it stuck in the minds of many.

As early as that Thursday, September 1, the media were repeatedly asking for my opinion about whether that estimate of 10,000 was close to being correct. I was extremely hesitant to speculate about the death toll without some knowledge of how many people had been evacuated, how many had stayed behind, and just how the levees had been breached.

One story making the rounds about the levee breaching came secondhand from a soldier who had talked to a man who lived near the 17th Street Canal. That levee failed on Monday and, according to the story, this man heard something on the radio about water coming into the city. He gathered up his family, ran downstairs, got into his pickup, and as he drove away he looked back and saw a wall of water coming down the street. The way the story was told and retold it sounded like the Red Sea closing in on the Egyptians after Moses had led his people safely through. That story left me with the impression that a lot of people could have died if the water came in that quickly and with that much force. It would have trapped thousands in their homes.

That story just did not make sense, though. If there had been a catastrophic failure of the levees and portions gave way suddenly, a wall of water would have had the power to flatten buildings in its path. We were not seeing that. We were seeing numerous buildings awash in water to the second floor but none damaged by a powerful surge of water. We were also seeing hundreds and hundreds of people stranded on rooftops, leading me to believe that the water came in quickly but at a measured pace, not with a tidal wave–like surge. Still, it was the following week before I felt confident enough to tell people that the estimate of 10,000 dead in New Orleans was way too high.

The challenge on Thursday once we started getting buses into downtown New Orleans and moving people away from the Superdome was trying to determine how many other problems we were facing. Looking at it from the outside the city, the situation may have appeared chaotic. That is partly a function of the news media and the 24/7 news cycle and partly a result of victims of the storm being overwhelmed emotionally and physically and adding to that perception of chaos.

The Army trains not only to prevent chaos, but to deal with it. Without those skills the Army would just have a bunch of MBAs running it. The situation in New Orleans after Katrina was nothing compared to conquering Baghdad. While this was emotionally charged and people were sick and dying, it was not on the scale of a combat operation. It was a permissive environment in the sense that no one was out there trying to kill us. All we had to do was deal with the water and the people. When dealing with food, water, and movement of people, it's a matter of logistics, not tactics. There is an old axiom in the Army that if logistics was easy it would be called tactics. Joint Task Force–Katrina was a function of, and a lesson in, logistics.

Three major problems were evident that Thursday. There was the continuing problem of trying to rescue people from the flooded areas. There was the problem of evacuating people from the hospitals and the Superdome. And there was the problem of evacuating thousands more people who had gathered at the Morial Convention Center. Getting coordinated responses to all these problems while trying to deal with numerous federal, state, and local civilian agencies plus the state National Guard and active-duty military in the middle of a major disaster was not something that had been done on a routine basis. We could define the major problems facing us but we always had to be on the alert for second- and third-order effects of those major problems.

It was obvious Nagin knew as early as Monday or Tuesday that a large number of people were gathering at the convention center who also needed to be evacuated. The convention center was on dry ground and people could easily walk there from those parts of the city that were not flooded. The convention center stretches for more than a half mile along the Mississippi River, but due to the topography of the area it was high and dry. It was not clear when FEMA officials learned of that second group but it may not have been until Thursday. There was a total breakdown in communications, because the New Orleans Police Department and the mayor knew those people were there.

In any disaster there is an incredible absence of information because the system for sending and receiving information is broken. Those in the middle of a disaster often find it difficult to determine what is fact, what is politically motivated opinion, and what is rumor. Nothing is easy in the middle of a disaster. The simplest things that are taken for granted when there is no disaster became extremely hard to do after Katrina. The ability to communicate was the cornerstone for everything we were trying to accomplish, but that capability was almost nonexistent the first few days.

Delays in getting rescue and relief services into downtown New Orleans were inevitable because of the communications and logistics issues we were facing. But, in my mind, they were not acceptable delays. Everything needed to be done at once and there was considerable pressure to move more quickly than it appeared we were. Whenever anyone on my staff talked about delays in getting things done, my typical response was "You're looking at a calendar and I'm looking at my watch." It was my way of trying to impress on them the extreme urgency of the situation.

On Thursday I briefly considered moving my headquarters from Camp Shelby into downtown New Orleans, but after reviewing the options it was apparent that such a move might create more problems than it would solve. The primary tasks were getting the buses in, getting the people out, and continuing search-and-rescue operations. It would have been a waste of time, energy, and manpower to move my headquarters because we had just set it up at Camp Shelby. We had a good base of operations there and a solid infrastructure with communications, food, water, and generator power. The telephone lines were operational, as were the computers, and we could do video teleconferences from there. Displacing my headquarters while doing the evacuation would not be an added value for the mission. The headquarters *was* an added value at Camp Shelby because my staff officers could more easily and efficiently work tasks from there with the staffs at First Army and Northern Command.

A leader in a crisis situation does not create communications problems. A leader is accessible to those he is there to help in order to deal with problems as they arise. Displacing the headquarters would have created short-term communications problems at a critical juncture of the evacuation operation. Still, I needed an enhanced communications capability that would enable me to stay in the city. The Belle Chasse Naval Air Station in Plaquemines Parish was considered, but that was thirty minutes by car from downtown New Orleans. The USS *Bataan*, an amphibious assault ship, was also looked at, but it was about eighty miles offshore at the time, too far from where things were happening.

We discussed bringing the *Bataan* upriver and docking it next to the convention center to give the active military forces a visible and distinct presence in the city. Captain Nora Tyson, the skipper of the *Bataan*, had worked with me on the joint staff at the Pentagon and if anyone could get that ship upriver she could. But the Coast Guard had closed the Mississippi River south of New Orleans because of sunken barges in the main channel and it was not navigable, especially for a ship the size of the *Bataan*.

My primary means of communication those first few days was through satellite telephones set up at the Superdome by the Louisiana National Guard's Weapons of Mass Destruction–Civil Support Team (WMD-CST). I could talk on classified and unclassified lines through that system. I also had my Iridium satellite phone and BlackBerry. Although there was no cell phone service to speak of in the area, there was one spot at the Superdome, discovered quite by accident, where my BlackBerry could send and receive messages. It was right next to a light pole on the parking deck overlooking the corner of Stadium Drive and Girod Street on the southwest side of the building. I had to stand in just the right position to be able to send and receive. Any movement away from that spot and the signal was lost.

Shortly after our arrival in New Orleans, my headquarters in Atlanta began receiving text messages from people trapped in their homes by the floodwaters. These people would send a text message to a friend who would forward it to the *Times-Picayune*, which would then send the message on to First Army headquarters. The message would be sent from there to the Coast Guard search-and-rescue officials with information about where these people were and what sort of condition they were in.

One such message came from a niece of mine, Melissa Delahoussaye, an operations manager with Smith Barney in Los Angeles. She had gotten a text message from a friend at Xavier University that as many as five hundred people were trapped without food or water in the administration building not far from downtown. Melissa sent the message to First Army headquarters in Atlanta and the message was relayed to me. We immediately dispatched a rescue team but by the time we got there some buses had arrived to evacuate the students along with the president of the school, Norman Francis.

Text messages were still working for many people even though the cell towers were down. There were a few cell towers out there somewhere with just a hint of life in them. They had enough power to enable people to send text messages. Anyone who has a cell phone needs to know how to send text messages in the event of an emergency. A text message is a burst transmission and uses only a fraction of a signal whereas a voice call will eat up a lot of the bandwidth. It is especially important for the elderly or the disabled who live in areas prone to hurricanes, floods, earthquakes, or wildfires to have a cell phone and be able to send text messages. Learning that simple skill could mean the difference between life and death.

Much of that Thursday was spent dashing from meeting to meeting with various state officials in Mississippi and Louisiana. Before 8 A.M. I met with Hac Cross in Gulfport to get an assessment of his situation. It was important to ensure that Mississippi was getting the federal assistance it needed even though much of the media and public attention was focused on New Orleans. I ordered the *Bataan* repositioned to support efforts along the Mississippi Gulf Coast.

I flew from Gulfport to the Superdome and from there to Baton Rouge to meet with Mike Brown and other FEMA officials and discuss the evacuation plan. We reiterated that plan in a midafternoon video teleconference with Secretary of Defense Donald Rumsfeld and Admiral Tim Keating, the commander of Northern Command. There was another meeting with Brown and Blanco in Baton Rouge at the EOC followed by a late afternoon news conference in which many of the early questions about why we did not get to New Orleans sooner and why it was taking so long to evacuate people were dealt with. I had to remind the media this was a true disaster. It was not a matter of someone's competence or incompetence or who was to blame. If this was easy it would have already been done. None of what we were doing was easy.

One of the major issues that occupied a great deal of time that day concerned reports of snipers targeting police and rescue helicopters. The story originated with police superintendent Eddie Compass. He mentioned to a reporter that a "sniper" had fired at a helicopter in which he was riding. To anyone in the military, the word *sniper* has a specific meaning. It means a trained marksman, usually with a high-powered weapon, deliberately targeting individuals. It does not mean someone with a handgun popping off a few rounds or firing wildly in the direction of a helicopter. A true sniper means the threat level is elevated significantly. I pressed Compass not to use the word *sniper* unless he was absolutely sure he or the helicopter had been targeted.

In a meeting with Nagin I told him, "We've got a problem here because your police chief told some news reporter there was are snipers operating in the city. Why would snipers be here?" If there had been a sniper he certainly could have hit a low-flying helicopter. I asked that the helicopter be checked for bullet holes. There were none.

"We're not communicating to the public," I went on. "There are people in Washington, D.C., watching these reports, and there are people with the state government in Baton Rouge watching these reports, and you've got volunteers on the way here to help who are watching this and they start to think maybe these people are running around taking over the city and that the city is out of control."

What apparently happened was a bad selection of words by a police superintendent under a lot of stress. Yet the story had legs and stayed alive throughout the day. Thursday evening we had helicopters coming in to pick up the seriously ill from the Superdome and someone heard what sounded like a shot. Somebody yelled "Sniper!" The invalid patients, some of whom were on oxygen, were just rolled right back into the urgent care center at the edge of the Superdome. We turned off the helicopters at that point because the patients stopped coming out. The helicopters did not return until the next day.

Our "sniper" in that incident apparently was nothing more than a water bottle popping when a truck ran over it. It sounded like a gunshot and with everyone already on edge, it was no wonder people scurried for cover.

In addition to the sniper issue we also had to deal with a number of unsubstantiated reports of rapes and murders at the Superdome and convention center. The stories were being broadcast or printed as fact with little effort to determine if there was any truth to them. Video of looters ran repeatedly on network television, playing into the public's fears of a city out of control with the lawbreakers free to roam at will and no police force or other law enforcement agency available to stop them.

Were thugs trying to break into gun stores? Yes, there were. There is always that criminal element that will try to take advantage of any disaster or crisis situation.

Were fires burning in New Orleans? Yes, there were. But there were only a few of them. The problem at that time was that the fire department either could not get to those fires or had no water pressure to extinguish them. Yet news reports kept showing those same fires over and over so it looked like much of downtown New Orleans was burning.

Were people breaking into grocery stores and taking food and water? Yes, they were. We also had thieves hauling off flat-screen TVs and other merchandise. They were taking advantage of the situation just as criminals do after every disaster. Thugs and thieves are always waiting on society's fringes to take advantage of weakness, real or perceived. The police were undermanned and could not be everywhere to deal with many of these situations. But some of those people who were breaking into stores were in survival mode and were just trying to feed their families.

The fires and looting were a small part of the bigger story of what Katrina had done to New Orleans and the Mississippi coast. The majority of people in New Orleans who had not already left just wanted to be evacuated. They didn't want to take over the city. They didn't want to burn the city. We had a common objective with the people, to get them the hell out of there. Unfortunately, those seamier elements are what ended up being the news of the hour. What should have been minor distractions became a major part of the story. The scavengers come out whenever there is a disaster, but it was being reported as something unique to New Orleans.

The noise level about crime and rapes and death far exceeded what actually was happening. Anyone who listens too long to that noise will end up making bad decisions. That Thursday the noise was unbelievable.

CNN aired a telephone interview shortly after 8 P.M. with a woman who said she was at the convention center. How she got a telephone to work from there is something of a mystery, since no one else was able to do that. There was no live video so it was impossible to tell whether she was actually there. But she sounded as if she was near hysteria when asked to describe the situation.

"We have six dead bodies in the freezer. People are dying," she said. "There is [*sic*] no lights, no water. There is no food. They are killing people ... They are looking for a thirteen-year-old child, but they just—they think she's been raped. They can't find her. There's a child downstairs that's ten years old that they attempted to rape this morning. And they broke both of her—they broke both of her ankles."

Not a single one of her claims ever was substantiated by police or medical officials. She appeared to be passing on rumors that got magnified with each retelling. With unverified reports such as that sandwiched between video of looters and fires it was no surprise that those watching and listening to events unfold thought New Orleans was on the verge of total collapse.

One of the unique things about the culture of Louisiana is the tendency to overexaggerate. Whether it is accomplishments or problems, in our culture it is not unusual for things to be magnified beyond what they really are. It is not a matter of outright lying. It's the way Louisianans view things and express themselves. I am well aware of that tendency and that is why I was not ready to jump to the same conclusions as Compass when he started talking about a sniper while others, including police, breathlessly talked about problems at the Superdome and convention center. My Louisiana logic told me that many of those stories were being overplayed and overhyped by the media but were largely a product of the culture of overexaggeration.

The security situation in New Orleans was not nearly as bad as it was being portrayed. Weeks later, after things calmed down a bit, it was revealed that only six people died at the Superdome: four from natural causes, one from a drug overdose, and one an apparent suicide. It was much the same at the convention center. Four bodies were found there despite initial reports of dozens of deaths, gangs running wild, and women and girls being sexually assaulted. Three of the deaths were attributed to natural causes and just one to an apparent gunshot wound. The alleged rapes and molestations were never verified. In fact, in the week after Katrina, only four murders were reported in New Orleans, a city that averages more than two hundred homicides every year. Crime was actually down in the storm's wake.

One of the problems with these stories was that the police were hearing them secondhand and then repeating them to the media as fact. I first heard from police about the alleged violence at the Superdome and convention center on Wednesday and Thursday, and those stories were in the news the next day. But what I was seeing on the ground did not match what was being reported on television and in newspapers around the world.

Sergeant First Class Jason Lachney of the Louisiana National Guard was on duty at the Superdome the entire time and was quoted in the *Seattle Times* as saying that 99 percent of the reporting about shootings and rapes inside the building "is bullshit. Don't get me wrong—bad things happened. But I didn't see any killing and raping and cutting of throats or anything . . . 99 percent of the people in the Dome were very well-behaved."

That was the same sense I had Wednesday after walking among the people at the Superdome waiting to be evacuated. They were, as anyone in that situation would be, quite frustrated. But they were also unbelievably patient. All they wanted was to be evacuated to where they could get some cold water, warm food, a hot shower, and a soft bed so they could begin the terribly difficult job of trying to reconstruct their lives.

I felt it was my responsibility to publicly dispute many of those more sensational but unverified reports. If we didn't tamp down those stories the situation was just going to get worse and there was no reason for things to get any worse than they were. False information would just feed on itself the longer the people were trapped. All we needed to do was move them out of the city.

The rank-and-file police who reported for duty were trying their best. But they were exhausted. They had started working the previous Saturday and on Thursday were still on duty. Many had taken rooms in the French Quarter because it was not flooded and did not close. They could go there and get a few hours of sleep. Those police officers in the French Quarter also provided a deterrent to looters and other criminals who might have thought about going into the crown jewel of the city and raising havoc.

The police were functional, but many were still wearing the same clothes they had on when they came on duty Saturday. The houses of many of them had flooded Monday morning, so they could not retrieve their clothes or any of their belongings, including medications they needed. New Orleans had a policy that its police officers had to live in the city. The department thought it would promote better community relations for a force that has had a history of corruption. Katrina hit New Orleans police with a double whammy, first personally and then professionally. Thursday night we got an extensive list from police of things they needed, including clothing, vehicles, radios, weapons, ammunition, and medications.

The police were stretched thin and we could not use the National Guard for law enforcement because while they have the authority to do it, most are not trained for it. They are trained for combat. There is an overemphasis on the business of law enforcement in the National Guard and it's a mission most guardsmen do not train to. Frequently the Guard will confuse authority with capability. The active soldiers can't do law enforcement because of the Posse Comitatus Act, which prohibits active-duty military from performing police functions within the continental United States. So, while we had all these soldiers in uniform with weapons, only a handful were trained and authorized to do law enforcement.

As we began working plans that Thursday for getting food, water, and buses to the convention center, deputy police superintendent Steven Nicholas got very upset with me in one meeting. "Where are the soldiers?" he demanded. He was so angry he could barely speak. He said people were being raped and killed at the convention center and the soldiers were doing nothing to assist the police. He said he needed more soldiers down there that night because he was expecting riots. I told him we had more than enough National Guard soldiers to deal with the situation. I had no sense there would be riots because if the people at the convention center were anything like those at the Superdome, all they wanted was a chance to get out of the city.

The way all this was playing out on television forced a question that was asked by many in the federal government: Could the New Orleans Police Department and National Guard handle the situation? Or should the federal government step in and invoke the Insurrection Act, putting the city under martial law and federalizing all military and police assets?

My chain of command kept asking me for my assessment of the situation. We still had to complete the evacuation of the Superdome and the convention center. We were still doing search and rescue. We had not yet started the process of trying to find the dead. And we were now trying to deal with the numerous media reports of rampant crime and numerous deaths at the Superdome and the convention center and of people looting and burglarizing buildings throughout the city.

Unbeknownst to me at the time, there had already been substantive discussions between Governor Blanco and White House officials about

President Bush stepping in and imposing federal control in and around New Orleans. That would have tossed responsibility for the whole operation right into the lap of the federal government. It was a decision, and a responsibility, not to be taken lightly, considering what was at stake for the city of New Orleans, the state of Louisiana, and the nation.

CHAPTER 9

Lessons Learned for Building a Culture of Preparedness

1. In a disaster, leaders must remember that this too shall pass; play the hand you are dealt.

2. The first report is usually wrong. But at the time you still go with what you know and start things moving as quickly as possible. Don't overstudy the problem. Things may be much worse than reported or much better but there is a group of people out there who know some part of the real situation. The question is how to get what they know.

3. Ignorance can be fixed, but stupidity is for life. A disaster can make you look ignorant and stupid. The press will let everyone know which squad you are in: the "I" squad or the "S" squad.

4. A real disaster will cause confusion and information gaps and will challenge you to catch up on what you don't know about what you should know about. Real disasters will break the communication system.

10

"Get Those Damn
Weapons Down!"

SHORTLY AFTER 5:30 A.M. ON FRIDAY, SEPTEMBER 2, THE FIRST RAYS
of sunlight were starting to sift through the pine trees at Camp Shelby,
Mississippi. It was already hot and muggy as my aide, Captain Scott Trahan, and operations officer, Lieutenant Colonel Ron Rose, and I drove
down Lee Avenue to the communications tent that had been set up behind Paxton Hall, the dun-colored two-story building that is the camp's
headquarters.

My day was already more than an hour old. It started with several
telephone calls and a quick briefing of overnight news developments
from my staff. Now we were preparing for the first major event of the
day, a video teleconference with top officials from the White House, Pentagon, and Northern Command. That teleconference would not only set
the tone for what would become an unusually hectic and stressful day,
but also would establish the ground rules for how the remainder of the
post-Katrina operations would be handled.

By that morning, little more than two full days into the existence
of JTF-Katrina, we had established a good flow of evacuations from the
Superdome and were starting to focus on getting food, water, and buses
to the people stranded at the convention center. The dire predictions
of New Orleans police officials from the day before had not played out.
There were no riots overnight at the convention center. My morning

briefing indicated that except for some scattered looting, things were relatively quiet throughout the city. Nothing indicated that riots or a citywide insurrection were imminent.

But the news reports from New Orleans provided an around-the-clock drumbeat of near hysteria. The television networks kept reporting on the few scattered fires and nonexistent snipers. They kept showing video of several bodies in the water we had been forced to bypass in order to focus our efforts on the living. To those watching and listening to those reports, however, especially the policy makers in Washington who had not been to the city, it appeared and sounded as if civil authority had totally broken down and New Orleans was on the verge of collapsing into anarchy. The heat on the federal government, especially the White House, to bring order to the city was becoming more intense by the hour.

High-level discussions had already been held about the possibility of President Bush invoking the Insurrection Act and putting the New Orleans area under federal control. He could do it unilaterally or he could do it if requested by Governor Kathleen Blanco. News reports and documents released in the years since Katrina suggest Blanco was under a great deal of pressure from the White House to make that request. I do not know if that was the case since I was never part of those early discussions. It was not until Friday morning that I was brought into what was a politically sensitive issue.

Blanco was a first-term female Democrat governor. If the White House simply stepped in and took over, the feminists and Democrats would have complained loudly that Bush, a Republican, was trying to push her around and look like he was a strong, decisive chief executive at a time when he was under fire for his decisions about the war in Iraq and the slow federal response to Katrina.

In addition, ever since the Civil War and Reconstruction there has been an inordinate amount of friction between federal and state governments. Sending federal troops into a Deep South state without the request of the governor would seem to those who championed the rights of states to make most of their own decisions, a usurpation of those rights by the federal government. This is something that cropped up again a few weeks later in Florida during preparations for Hurricane Wilma. And it is something that has to be addressed and solved in order for the federal government and individual states to develop a true culture of preparedness. Friction between state and federal agencies and bureaucratic infighting wastes time and money and can cost lives.

Adding still more confusion was the National Guard Bureau in Washington, D.C, whose commanders jealously protect their turf from incursions by the active military. Lieutenant General Steven Blum, commander of the National Guard Bureau, is especially watchful on these matters and, according to documents from Blanco's aides, played a key role in convincing her not to bow to administration pressure and give up control of her National Guard forces.

Handwritten notes from Blanco's executive counsel, Terry Ryder, indicate that on Thursday night, September 1, while Blanco was contemplating whether to request federalization of all forces in New Orleans, Blum told her, "You don't want to do that. You lose control, and you don't get one more boot on the ground."

Blanco appeared to be comfortable with my role in the operations and with the plans we had for the evacuations. Her big disappointment with me was that I did not arrive with 15,000–20,000 federal troops. But we did not need a large contingent of federal troops during those first few days. We needed the capacity to rescue those trapped in their homes. We needed the capacity to evacuate people stranded at the Superdome and the convention center. We did not need federal troops to do any of those missions.

We had to focus on getting people out, not bringing them in. We already had several thousand National Guard troops on their way to New Orleans and more federal troops were not needed at that moment. Brigades from the 82nd Airborne Division and the 1st Cavalry Division were standing by and ready move at a moment's notice, but at that moment they would have created more confusion and logistical problems than we were able to handle.

It was clear early in the video teleconference that morning that federal control of the New Orleans area was the key issue on everyone's mind, especially for President Bush, who was among those participating. He asked me point-blank if I thought there was civil order in the city and whether in my opinion it was necessary for him to impose martial law. I hesitated only briefly before answering.

My relationship with Bennie Landreneau, the head of the Louisiana National Guard, and most of his subordinate commanders was excellent. I had worked with many other Guard units flowing into the city when they were preparing to go to Iraq or Afghanistan and knew those soldiers and their capabilities. I didn't feel it was necessary for me to be in charge of them in order to get things done. Their commanders could get the mission accomplished. The active forces—Army, Marines, Air Force, and Navy—would handle the humanitarian side of the disaster. The National Guard would handle the security and supplement federal, state, and local law enforcement officials to help keep order.

"No, sir," I finally replied. "We can handle the situation as we have it."

"Can you make that work?" I was asked.

I explained that the federal troops would work in support of FEMA and the governor to save lives and do whatever other missions were necessary. We would do it through coordination and collaboration with state and local authorities, not in command of them.

"I can make that work," I said.

It might have looked cleaner and the command structure might have been simpler if the National Guard had been federalized. But Blanco wanted control of the National Guard to remain with the state and was reluctant to give it up to federal authorities. Plus, it would not necessarily have been any more effective had the forces been federalized at that point. Putting a single federal official in charge would have changed everything dramatically and not necessarily for the better.

Invoking the Insurrection Act would have introduced a number of federal laws into the equation, and some lawyer from the Justice Department would have showed up to tell us how to run things. We did not need that on top of everything else we were dealing with. The medicine might be worse than the disease. Federalization would change the scenario from us helping New Orleans and Louisiana lift the basket to being solely responsible for lifting the basket. I never heard another word about my suggestion to avoid federalization from the president or any of his aides. From that point on they left us to do the job we had started.

Bush made his first visit to New Orleans that Friday, September 2, but I was committed to dealing with the situation at the convention center and did not meet with him. The people at the convention center were closing in on a week without adequate shelter, food, water, sanitary facilities, or medical care. With the number of media we had on the scene—I was being shadowed by Barbara Starr and a crew from CNN that day—and the frustration of the people that was being transmitted to me by New Orleans police officials, I needed to get eyes on the situation. If something bad happened, as people were telling me it would once the food and water started arriving, I wanted to be there with my staff in order to deal with it personally.

Most of the thousands of people were sitting outside the convention center trying to find shade under the building overhangs or sprawled in the grassy median that divides the four-lane boulevard. The primary concern of the police and my staff was that unlike the people at the Superdome, who had been searched for weapons and drugs before they were allowed to enter the building, those at the convention center had not been vetted. They just showed up and took up temporary residence either in the lobby of the building—most of the rest of the complex was locked and uninhabited—or on the street out front.

Despite misgivings anyone may have had, we decided to venture four blocks down the street from the police command center under the driveway awning of Harrah's Casino at the corner of Poydras Street and Convention Center Boulevard to get some sense of what we were dealing with. My first reaction was that there appeared to be no significant differences between the convention center crowd and the Superdome crowd. The stories police were relaying to the media about people being out of control and ready to riot, of thugs with guns running around inside the building killing people and raping women and girls, just did not add up.

What could one or two thugs with handguns do in a crowd of 15,000–18,000 people? Who were they going to intimidate? These people were frustrated and impatient already and they were not going to put up with somebody threatening their families. The picture being painted by overworked and overstressed police was that these people were out of control. But if that many people get out of control it doesn't matter how many police are around them; they are still going to be out of control. A crowd that large will take whatever actions it wants to take. That did not happen. All they wanted was to get the hell out of there.

Someone once wrote that when rich people lose their money they jump off buildings. Poor people are used to not having money. Poor people learn to have patience. Poor people learn to wait. Poor people learn to do without. These people, like those at the Superdome, were poor and were simply waiting for a chance to escape the city and the Katrina nightmare they were living.

This convention center crowd was a bit more boisterous, though, because people could walk around and had access to the shops, restaurants, and hotels that line the west side of Convention Center Boulevard. There was much more food and water in this crowd than at the Superdome. There also was alcohol at the convention center. How much of the food, water, and alcohol people brought with them and how much they took out of nearby businesses was unclear. The owner of one nearby restaurant told me several years after the storm that his business had suffered more than $350,000 in damage from people who broke in and took alcohol and furniture.

The other thing that struck me about the people at the convention center was that they had somehow managed to acquire dozens of mattresses and had laid them out on the sidewalk and street for the many elderly in the crowd. There is a tradition in the poor community of keeping Granny at home instead of sending her to a nursing home, either because they can't afford it or Granny does not want to leave the home she has lived in for seventy or eighty years. At the Superdome the Louisiana National Guard did an exceptional job of separating those people and their families from the rest of the crowd because FEMA set up a care center for them.

That was not the case at the convention center. Granny had to either lie on the sidewalk, the grass, or on a mattress that had been taken from a nearby hotel. I could not criticize anyone for trying to ease the suffering. The hotels were right there. They had been abandoned. The storms had blown out the windows. So it did not take a genius to figure out that people were going to do what they needed to do to survive and make a bad situation better for the members of their family, whether it was taking a mattress or some food and water.

A number of well-educated people, including television and radio commentators, condemned these people for what they did. But what would the average, law-abiding citizen do when faced with the same situation? Is that stealing? Or is it survival? I looked at it as survival. It was a trade-off because of what Katrina had done to them and the city. It was not a breakdown in civil order. Yet that was what was being reported. The looting and stealing was, to a great extent, people simply trying to stay alive in the aftermath of a true disaster.

The night before in Baton Rouge, a young reporter asked a question at a news conference about who was going to protect the people of that city from the people who had been brought in from New Orleans. The implication was that the thugs and criminals were being evacuated and plopped down in their midst. There were some of those, especially in the group that went to Houston. But given the pressure we were under to evacuate as many people as quickly as we could, there was no way we could do background checks on each and every one of them. They

were not terrorists, I told the reporter. They were fellow Americans and
human beings in need of help.

Many Americans do not understand one significant issue about that
New Orleans have-not group we were evacuating. That have-not group
was created when the source of a large number of jobs, the city's port,
moved into the mechanized era and people found themselves out of
work. The people were still there. Their homes in the 7th and 9th wards
were still there. But the jobs were gone. The city did not change to meet
that need over the years and the only thing left for the poor were low-
paying tourism jobs or drugs. The drug culture came in with a vengeance
and generally took over the poor neighborhoods. Since the storm, it's
come back even stronger.

There is a natural racial tension along much of the Gulf Coast. It is
especially evident in New Orleans and has been there a long time. But
there is a certain dichotomy to it. People of all colors mingle on the
street socially and do business with one another all day long. That interaction between races goes on in the French Quarter unlike in any other
city in this country. The racial divide is most evident in politics and economics. It doesn't take long in any argument or heated discussion about
those two issues for race to become a key factor.

The business community in New Orleans convinced Ray Nagin to
run for mayor in 2002 because he was one of them and not part of the
longtime political families that had controlled New Orleans and Louisiana for many years. But Nagin, a Republican turned Democrat, created some tension with Blanco during the 2003 gubernatorial campaign
when he supported her opponent, U.S. representative Bobby Jindal, a
Republican of Indian descent.

There was never any indication that race was an issue between the
governor and the mayor. Neither wanted this to happen on their watch. I
think Blanco was basically a good person concerned about the welfare of
the people. But there were undertones of conflict and tension because of
the differences between them of politics, race, and gender and those were
played up or hinted at in the media more than they should have been.

While some white commentators blamed Nagin and the black community for the problems after Katrina, some black activists claimed that
"America let this happen because these people are poor and black." It
really hurt to hear that somebody would think the government allowed
this to happen. I had served my country for thirty-four years and it
was offensive to me to hear people say the federal government did not

move as fast as it could because most of the people trapped were poor and black. I was part of that government and by implication was being accused of criminal neglect. And then somebody said the government had bombed the levees to kill black people. The problem with stupidity is that it can't be cured, and there was a lot of stupidity from blacks and whites making the rounds after Katrina. Ignorance can be fixed; stupidity is for life.

Even prominent blacks in the entertainment industry and politics were chiming in without much knowledge of the situation. Jesse Jackson said after visiting New Orleans that he did not see any black people in charge. A few days later somebody apparently pointed out to him that the mayor is black and that I am black. What the hell more did he want? It was probably good that the people of New Orleans had limited access to this news. Had they heard that nonsense it could have started riots. The people waiting for evacuation might have burned that city down, their anger fueled by the nonsense spouted by those with virtually no real knowledge of the situation but with the most to gain politically or economically and the least to lose.

The media were all too willing to ensure that the American public got a healthy dose of the racial tensions and economic disparity in New Orleans after the storm. That in turn had a negative impact on law enforcement officials and National Guard soldiers huddled down at the end of Convention Center Boulevard waiting to assist in the delivery of the food and water. They were of the opinion that this was a city ready to explode, that snipers were on every rooftop, and that gunmen, most of them poor and black, were running loose in the convention center. In addition, many of those same people charged with maintaining security were expecting a third-world scenario in which thousands of hungry and starving people rush the relief trucks and create a dangerous situation for all involved. I was not sure what to expect.

In a telephone conversation shortly after five o'clock that morning, Bennie Landreneau and I discussed details of the delivery of the food and water. We planned to put it on the north end of the Riverwalk Marketplace parking lot just north of the convention center. Since the parking lot was virtually empty we could line people up single file starting at the south end. That would give us some space between the supplies and the bulk of the crowd. We still were not sure what the reaction would be but we wanted to make sure that if there was any trouble we would have some room to maneuver the trucks and soldiers out of harm's way.

We also discussed the rules of engagement, or ROE, for his Guard soldiers. They were armed with M16 rifles, M4 carbines, and 9mm pistols. They had live rounds but none in the chamber. They had the right to protect themselves if they were fired on. We decided from day one we would not have loaded weapons, including no magazines in the weapons. Bennie and I agreed that it was important for this operation to be planned and executed as a humanitarian mission, rather than a combat mission. We were delivering food and water and helping save the lives of American citizens so it was important that we convey that message to the people we were helping and to the American public, who would be seeing it live through the embedded CNN crew following me.

He said he would pass the word that the troops should go in with weapons down, not weapons up as if they were patrolling or expecting trouble. We would have several dozen vehicles filled with soldiers coming in to help control the crowd if things got out of hand but we needed to do it in a way that was not threatening. We didn't want another Kent State. They were not trained for crowd control.

Just a few minutes before noon the first of the cargo trucks carrying relief supplies came rolling down Poydras Street and turned right past Harrah's onto Convention Center Boulevard. As soon as that first truck came into view I realized that the word had not gotten down to the soldiers' level about how they should carry their weapons. A soldier leaning over the cab of the lead truck had his M16 up and ready to fire, as if he was on patrol in downtown Baghdad, not downtown New Orleans. At the same time about a half-dozen trucks filled with heavily armed New Orleans police and SWAT members from across the country pulled out into the street. Every officer in those vehicles had their weapons at the ready as if expecting an ambush.

"Get those damn weapons down!" I shouted to the soldier in the first truck. "Hey! Weapons down! Weapons down, damn it! Put the weapons down!"

I started moving down the line of trucks. "Put that weapon on your back! You're delivering food!" I yelled at the soldiers.

That incident was memorialized by CNN, which aired it and my rather indelicate remarks live. Nothing was bleeped out. Sometimes my mouth gets the better of me but in this instance I felt justified ordering those National Guard soldiers, even though I did not command them, to put down their weapons. I wanted the crowd to know we were there to help and did not consider them dangerous. The message we were trying to send was one of humanitarian assistance, but the soldiers were sending a message of fear.

I asked Command Sergeant Major Marvin Hill and a National Guard military police officer to walk down the line of trucks and instruct the rest of the soldiers to put their weapons down and not add to the tension. The soldiers quickly complied.

Just before dark that night, Bennie Landreneau called and asked if we could meet at the Superdome. He said he had something he wanted to discuss with me in private. By that time many of us were starting to get some sense of progress because the area around the Superdome was just about empty.

Bennie had heard about the issue with the weapons and confronted me when we finally met. "You can't tell my soldiers what to do," he said with an edge in his voice.

I told him I did what I thought was necessary at the time. He still did not like it and made it clear that I commanded the federal forces and he commanded the Louisiana National Guard forces.

"You're right," I told him. "I can't tell them what to do. I'm sorry."

We had a good working relationship and I wanted to make sure we kept it, but at that point, with all that had happened that day, I really did not care who was right. We had achieved the effect we wanted and needed at that particular moment.

Bennie also was upset about me personally supervising the unloading and placement of the food and water at the convention center. He thought that was something his soldiers should have done. My explanation was that because of all the unknowns we were dealing with that day, particularly the concerns over what might happen when we dropped off the relief supplies, I wanted to be there in case there were serious problems. I felt it was incumbent on me to be at the leading edge of that particular problem rather than sitting at a distance waiting for reports from my staff.

The food distribution turned out to be anticlimactic. When we finally told people they could get food and water there wasn't a lot of movement. A few people got up and casually strolled over to the supplies. Of the 15,000–18,000 people, only a few hundred showed up. Not a lot of those MREs were eaten. They ended up sitting in that parking lot for weeks. When there was no big rush for the food and water I knew we had it made and we were not going to have any trouble with these people as long as we kept our promise to get them out of there in a reasonable amount of time starting the next morning.

After we dropped off the food and water we drove back down Convention Center Boulevard and passed some people who were living large despite the circumstances. They had coolers full of ice and food and beer. One guy held out a Miller Lite and said, "Thanks for coming to get us, brah. You want a brew?"

It was already pushing ninety steamy degrees and that Miller Lite looked mighty good. That thing was sweating cold. I just smiled and shook my head.

Of the dozens of journalists who interviewed me during my stint as commander of JTF-Katrina, at least 90 percent would ask questions like "How do you feel today?" Or "How does it feel to be back in your state?" Or "How does it feel to be involved in an operation saving your own people?"

My feelings were never an issue on this particular mission. My focus was on the task at hand because thousands were suffering. If I let my emotions intrude they would interfere with rational decision making at a time when many of the city and state leaders were letting their emotions adversely affect their decisions. That was understandable, though. They were victims, as were many of their relatives, and could not help but be overwhelmed by the enormity of the situation.

That is not to say that I kept my composure the entire time. One incident that got to me came that Friday afternoon, shortly after we had completed the food and water drop and the people were lining up to get the supplies. My staff and I were walking north on Convention Center Boulevard with Barbara Starr of CNN when a young African-American woman wearing a purple football jersey with number 16 on it and a purple-and-white hat came walking toward us. She could not have been much more than twenty years old, if she was that. She had twin baby boys, one in each arm. As she got closer one of the babies started to slip out of her grasp. Blood was coming out of the child's nose, a sign of severe dehydration. I took that baby and gave it to my executive officer, Lieutenant Colonel Ron Rose. Then I took the other baby and handed it to my aide, Captain Scott Trahan.

We turned the woman around and had her walk with us two hundred yards or so to the river, where a Coast Guard barge was tied up. Another woman who had a baby that looked like it was having problems came out of the crowd and we motioned her to come with us, too. We took those two young mothers and their three babies to the barge. The Coasties got some milk and other fluids for the babies and the medics began treating them and the mothers for dehydration. Once we were sure they were in good hands we left and walked back to the corner of Poydras and Convention Center Boulevard, where our vehicles were parked. Seeing those babies made me think of my own grandson and the experience got to me a bit.

By the end of that Friday I was exhausted yet exhilarated by the good we had done not only for the people at the convention center, but especially for those two young mothers and their babies. It was a day in which a lot went right and we won some battles. But we all knew there was still much to do before we could call our mission a success.

CHAPTER 10
Lessons Learned for Building a Culture of Preparedness

1. The National Guard needs to review whether troops coming to a national disaster need rifles. It's harder to lift someone when you are in full combat gear. Not every National Guard soldier is qualified to do law enforcement and only law enforcement should have weapons in a disaster situation.

2. National Guard troops should not have to run food and water distribution outside the disaster area. Local communities need to organize volunteers or hire survivors for this task.

3. States need to ensure rules of engagement are given in writing to National Guard soldiers.

4. National Guard and federal troops work well together; they share the same oath, uniform, and equipment. While politicians argue, troops work it out on the ground.

5. Private contract security guards with assault rifles and shotguns should not be used to protect property. This is America, not Baghdad.

11

"A John Wayne Dude"

BY THAT FIRST SATURDAY AFTER HURRICANE KATRINA CAME ASHORE, it was apparent I had become the face and voice of the federal rescue and relief effort to much of the media and the American public. I never sought the role and did not particularly want it. Governor Kathleen Blanco and Mayor Ray Nagin should have been front and center for the media throughout the crisis. But they often were unavailable or sent mixed messages that were not helpful to the overall effort. That was understandable, though, because they, like tens of thousands of others along the Gulf Coast, were victims of Katrina and were having problems coming to grips with that victimization. Blanco and Nagin had been dealing with this for over a week and just because they were public figures did not mean they were immune to the kind of emotional damage the storm and its aftermath inflicted on so many people.

My unofficial and unintended role required me to stand in front of the media and try to keep the record straight about our progress. It was also my intention to present a face of calm and control in the midst of all the chaos. My straight, if occasionally profane, talk about our efforts to save lives and move people out of the city was meant to bring a sense of clarity and direction to the effort. Many people seemed to appreciate that. But whenever I spoke to the media, which was frequently, I always tried to follow the Zumwalt Rules so the public would get the message we wanted it to hear.

It was necessary at times to provide Military 101 lessons for members of the media who had not done their homework before being sent to New Orleans and apparently were getting little guidance from their editors and producers back home.

The media had two misconceptions about the military effort in New Orleans that seemed to linger like a bad cold. The first was that I was in charge of the entire operation. I had to dispel that notion almost daily. I was not in charge of anything more than the federal forces assigned to JTF-Katrina. I had no control over the National Guard forces or any of the civilian federal agencies. My job was to coordinate and collaborate with all of the above to try to get maximum efficiency out of our efforts. The other misconception the media had was that the Army Corps of Engineers was under my command and its work to plug the holes in the levees and dewater the city was my responsibility. At no time was the Corps of Engineers under my command but some members of the media had trouble understanding that.

Had they done their homework they would have known that the U.S. Army Corps of Engineers is an entity distinctly separate from the U.S. Army. It has its own chain of command and its own missions. The Corps of Engineers has far more civilians in it—nearly 35,000—than it has members of the military—fewer than 1,000. I gave the Corps the support it needed for work on the levees by providing heavy-lift helicopters that were not otherwise engaged in search-and-rescue missions.

Yet because the organization's name contains the word *Army* the assumption by many in the media was that the Corps fell under my jurisdiction. A brigadier general from the Corps was on the JTF-Katrina staff to advise me but whenever questions arose about what was being done to repair or replace the levees and who was at fault for them breaking in the first place, I deferred to the engineers. We were tracking their progress closely because the more quickly the levees were patched and the city was dewatered the sooner we could start ground searches of the more than 250,000 buildings my staff in Atlanta had estimated were in the our area of responsibility.

Ray Nagin was probably the person most responsible for me being placed in the somewhat awkward position of being the voice of the post-Katrina effort. On the night of Thursday, September 1, Nagin went on WWL radio in New Orleans and strongly criticized the federal response to the Katrina efforts. But for reasons I have never understood, he had high praise for me.

"Now, I will tell you this—and I give the president some credit on this—he sent one John Wayne dude down there that can get some stuff done, and his name is General Honoré," Nagin said in the interview. "And he came off the doggone chopper, and he started cussing and people started moving. And he's getting some stuff done."

Nagin's remarks did not reach me until several days later. I was both amused and embarrassed. In a way it was an honor to be compared to a man many people admire as a man's man and a rugged hero. But John Wayne was largely a creation of Hollywood, a man who read scripted dialogue and knew what the end to each of his movies would be before filming started. I was engaged in a real-life disaster. There was no script. There was no rehearsed dialogue. There were no do-overs. We were flying by the seats of our pants and trying to come to grips with a national tragedy. I wasn't John Wayne. I was Russ Honoré trying to do the best possible job under very trying circumstances without any idea what the ending would look like.

Some of my critics complained that I went to New Orleans looking for one last shot of glory before retirement. That is such nonsense it is not even worth discussing. But my critics were after me not only because I was not shy about getting up in front of the media on a daily basis, but because what JTF-Katrina did and how we did it did not fit protocol or preconceived notions about how the military should handle disasters.

"He was just making stuff up as he went along," I have heard people say. But that's what happens in a real disaster. That's the art of war fighting. Leaders take what they know and what they have trained on and deal with the situation at hand to the best of their ability in the midst of constant change. In any battle the enemy always has a vote about how things go. In this case the enemy was Katrina. *We* didn't have a plan because *no one* had a plan for the levees breaking and the city being flooded. If the city had not flooded it would have been the Defense Coordinating Officer from Fifth Army and ten or fifteen soldiers working with FEMA to assist the recovery of New Orleans. That was the plan. Katrina rendered that plan totally useless.

It's easy to plan and theorize in a clinical environment when no lives are at stake. When a leader in that situation starts being creative and innovative, people say he is "adaptive" and "thinks outside the box." That's something we have been talking about in the Army for years. But when I started doing that in a real-world situation the deep thinkers back at the Pentagon started complaining that I wasn't following protocol or sticking to the plan. My method of operation was to look at what the task at hand was, who could best do it, and how could we complement one another to get that task done. We did have the proverbial wiring diagram but it was built after we got to New Orleans and was adjusted to meet our needs as we went along.

After Nagin's remarks started making the rounds in the media I was constantly besieged for interviews and requests from the media to follow me for a few hours or a day. I tried to accommodate everyone because the media had a vital role in informing the American public of what was going on in New Orleans and what the military was doing to assist the civilian authorities in the relief efforts. If I could get that story out it would help efforts all the way around and the American public and the people of New Orleans would be the better for it.

General Peter Schoomaker, who was chief of staff of the Army at the time, would call occasionally and get a briefing on what we had done and what we had planned for the days ahead. One night after seeing me on a TV interview he called and said, "Damn it, Russ, don't become a celebrity."

And I said: "Okay, Chief. But you know I'm just trying to do my job."

"Russ," he warned again, "don't become a celebrity."

Schoomaker was a great coach and a good sounding board for me throughout the Katrina operation, as was General Dan McNeill at Forces Command in Atlanta. Whenever things were not moving as I thought they should or people tried to overstudy things I called Schoomaker or McNeill and they unclogged things in a hurry.

Some members of the media had the idea that I was selected for the JTF-Katrina job because I was from nearby Lakeland. That was about the furthest thing from the truth imaginable but it is probably the biggest myth that lives today. The real reason I was picked was because the majority of space affected, Mississippi, was in my area of responsibility, so it was easier for me to oversee operations there and in Louisiana than it was for someone from Fifth Army to take on the responsibility for Mississippi. Shortly after 9 A.M. Central Time on Saturday, September 3, Bush held a news conference in the Rose Garden to announce the deployment of additional federal troops. Over the next few days, he said, more than 7,000 soldiers and Marines from the 82nd Airborne Division, the 1st Cavalry Division, the 1st Marine Expeditionary Force, and the 2nd Expeditionary Force would be sent to New Orleans as part of JTF-Katrina. We already had more than 21,000 National Guard soldiers in the region, about 13,000 of them in Louisiana, plus 4,000 active-duty forces specifically tasked with doing search and rescue and providing logistical and medical support.

There's an old Louisiana saying: "Who's washing and who's drying?" The number of washers and dryers has to be kept in balance. If too much is washed too soon things get wrinkled because there are not enough dryers. It was the same way with the forces we were bringing in. We had to keep the washers and the dryers in balance or things would get out of whack. The resources we were providing and the mix of forces coming in had to be able to perform the tasks that were the priority of the governor and the mayor or else the efficiency we were seeking would suffer.

Maximum effectiveness for those forces and for me was my goal. I did not stay in Atlanta or move my headquarters into downtown New Orleans or put myself in Baton Rouge next to Mike Brown and the FEMA folks, because my effectiveness as a coordinator and a collaborator was best utilized at the point of attack. A number of military people criticized me for going to the scene instead of staying behind in Atlanta. That's what a commander is supposed to do in wartime and that's how they would handle disaster relief and recovery. But unlike a war zone, where people are shooting, this was a permissive environment. The difference between combat and a humanitarian mission is that combat is nonpermissive. After being involved in all those tabletop exercises in years past it was my belief that I needed to be on the ground at the focal point of the disaster. There's a big difference between going to Baghdad on a combat mission and going to New Orleans for a humanitarian mission.

If we could bring in the federal troops to save lives and be enablers to the local population, whether it was for medical supplies or food or whatever, then we would be doing our jobs. The National Guard was doing full-spectrum operations including law enforcement and security. Those of us on the active side were going to do everything we were asked to do minus law enforcement. It was clear in my mind what my role was, even though a lot of people in uniform and in the media were confused by the fact that there was no single person in charge, and the operations worked because of collaboration and coordination between the active forces and the National Guard.

Some active officers have this concern about the ability of the National Guard to perform in a complex environment such as Katrina. I had no such reservations because First Army trained many of these National Guard soldiers and my son is one of them. I was confident they could do whatever was asked of them. As I told President Bush the day before, it was not necessary to have a single overall commander. The active and National Guard forces would work together to get the job done for the nation.

The National Guard brings a particular asset to disaster operations. Since 1996 all states have signed onto a congressionally sanctioned plan known as the Emergency Management Assistance Compact, or EMAC. Through the EMAC, governors who declare a state of emergency can request assistance from the governors of other states. Often those states are contiguous or nearby. This has worked well among many of the southern states during hurricane season, when National Guard soldiers and law enforcement from one state are sent to another to assist in cleanup and recovery.

But what we were dealing with after Katrina was something much, much larger. The National Guard Bureau was pushing this beyond normal EMACs and much to its credit was able to quickly mobilize troops from around the country and get them into the region. Some general officers in the Pentagon expressed concern about how this would work, although soldiers on the ground had no real problems working together. Any problems JTF-Katrina encountered were dealt with immediately or headed off before they became major stumbling blocks. Much of that was a result of the relationships I had built over the years with the National Guard units that First Army trained.

Two National Guard division headquarters were sent into the region to assist. The 35th Infantry Division out of Kansas, under command of Major General James Mason, went to Louisiana. The 38th Infantry Division out of Indiana, under command of Major General Greg Vadnais, went to Mississippi. I had experience working with both and was their senior rater on job performance. They did not work directly for me in New Orleans but I was able to go to them outside the normal chain of command and tell them, "Let's talk through this."

Soldiers from the 82nd Airborne Division and 1st Cavalry Division started arriving late Saturday afternoon. They were exactly the right units for the mission we needed them to do. They were to go door-to-door in their assigned areas and look for the living and the dead. These were combat units with strong noncommissioned officer (NCO) leadership. Many of the NCOs were veterans of Iraq or Afghanistan and knew how to operate and communicate quickly and effectively in difficult situations.

We put the 82nd Airborne soldiers in their distinctive maroon berets in the French Quarter and teamed them with the 35th Division. We had National Guard soldiers with law enforcement authority in all the active units down to platoon level. There were not many people in the French Quarter at the time, although it was bone dry, and as long as we had a presence in there people were not likely to go wandering in if they did not belong. That carried us for several days before we reset the National Guard troops because of a big push to put soldiers in some of the smaller cities around the state where help was needed with food distribution.

The 35th was stretched from the French Quarter to the Garden District, which contains some of the most expensive real estate in America. The area from St. Charles Avenue, which has a streetcar line running down the middle of it, to the river, had not been flooded but we needed to get soldiers into the area to check on those houses and the people who stayed behind. With that part of the city being patrolled around the clock and the rest of the city flooded, the police could control access to much of New Orleans by blocking the interstate off-ramps.

The 1st Cavalry Division soldiers were assigned the West Bank. It's actually south of the city but for whatever reason they call it the West Bank. I asked Nagin at one point, "Why do they call it the West Bank? It's south of the city." And he said, "General, don't try to understand it. That's just the way it is. It's the West Bank."

That area is residential and was difficult for the media to get to because of the floodwaters, so the 1st Cavalry Division was largely ignored despite the great job its soldiers did patrolling and looking for people who had inexplicably stayed in their homes and were in need of food, water, or rescue. Once we got those troops in position we started searching houses, apartments, and businesses to see if anyone was alive and needed help.

We had a bit of a dilemma at one point when the mayor told me that if we ran into people who were still in their homes we should bring them out because he had issued a mandatory evacuation order. "I cannot force people to leave," I told him. "My priority is to keep them alive."

The active forces had no authority to remove anyone from their home. All we could do was offer assistance if they wanted to leave and food and water and medical treatment if they wanted to stay. Only law enforcement officials could make those people leave and we were not in the law enforcement business.

That ended up being another source of friction between Blanco and

Nagin. Who has the authority to force people to evacuate their homes in a disaster such as Katrina? We were told that the mayor can direct it, but that it has to be approved by the governor. The concept of people being forced out of their homes by the government plows ground that had not been plowed before, at least in Louisiana. Mandatory evacuation and forced evacuation are two different things. Mandatory evacuation means people are supposed to leave but are not forced to. If they stay behind they just won't get any public services. Forced evacuation means people will be removed from their homes by force.

There was also the question of which people were going to be forced to leave. Should those whose homes are dry, who haven't been flooded out, and who have food and water and generators for electricity be forced to leave? If so, why should they be forced to leave? That would mean more stuff for police to watch and more people to feed at the other end. Or should only the poor people whose homes were flooded be forced to leave? Do they have fewer rights than those who didn't get wet?

These questions were never answered but are likely to come up again in other states when a disaster of Katrina proportions hits. Florida residents in particular have a habit of ignoring storm warnings and either refusing to leave or waiting until the last minute to get out of town. If another Andrew is bearing down on Florida, will the governor order mandatory or forced evacuations? And if they are forced, who's going to do the forcing? The police and National Guard? Any governor who tries to do that and then has the storm veer off or not be as strong as predicted would likely suffer the political consequences. Forced evacuations are a tricky legal issue that disaster-prone states are going to have to come to grips with if the nation hopes to develop a fully functional culture of preparedness.

We decided to call patrols by the active-duty soldiers "presence patrols" rather than "security patrols." We were there to assist, not do law enforcement. In that way we were able to mitigate having combat troops on the ground in New Orleans. If those patrolling soldiers saw looting and did not have a National Guard soldier with them capable of doing law enforcement, the orders were to call the police and let them handle it. To most looters, though, there is not a lot of difference between a police officer and a young soldier with an M16 or M4. The looters probably figured they were in a world of hurt either way. But by Sunday we had law enforcement from all over the country coming in to help out, so the manpower shortages among the New Orleans police as a result of illness, overwork, or desertions were minimized.

For many people in New Orleans those soldiers, whether active or National Guard, were a comforting presence. For others they were life savers. We gave soldiers orders that if they found someone alive in a house they should first ask if they needed medical attention, food, or water. We would supply whatever they needed. Then the soldiers were to ask if they wanted to be evacuated. If they said no, we left them alone. If they wanted out, we helped them get out.

One day early in the searches, Command Sergeant Major Wolf Amacker of the 82nd Airborne told me about one of his staff sergeants, a two-tour combat veteran, who walked up to one house and knocked on the door. An older lady wearing an apron answered. She looked at the young soldier and said, "I have had enough." She pulled a pistol out of her apron pocket and walked into the kitchen. The sergeant followed her and started talking to her. About thirty minutes later he had the pistol in his hand and was helping the woman leave the house. He had saved her life.

I have said many times since first hearing the story, "Thank God it was a soldier who found her and not one of the hair-trigger, private security guys we had running around down there." That sergeant realized her gun was not a threat to him and talked the woman out of killing herself. But that shows how deeply affected emotionally many people in New Orleans were after they had been trapped in their homes or had decided for whatever reason not to evacuate. It also shows the character and professionalism of those soldiers who came to New Orleans.

On another occasion we had some soldiers from the 82nd go into one of the public housing projects. The first floor of the apartments was flooded and people had moved up to the second floor. This housing project was closer to downtown than it was to the 9th Ward and many who had stayed there were living off food and water they were taking out of a nearby Wal-Mart. When the 82nd soldiers went into the project they told the residents that they could get trucks and boats to take them to the convention center for evacuation.

The people said they didn't want to leave. They said they were hearing that anyone who went to the convention center was being locked up. So the noncommissioned officer in charge of that patrol offered to take two members of the group to the convention center and leave two of his own men behind as a show of good faith. They did that but when they returned the people said they didn't want to leave that day. The next day, when the 82nd soldiers went back, everyone was gone.

My guess is those people did not want anyone to know who they were and what they were doing. The two who had gone to the convention center learned that anyone who came to heliport Superman DZ across the street from the convention center and wanted to get on the bus for Houston first had to give their name and then were searched for weapons and drugs. They also had a doctor look them over. Bags and purses were examined for contraband. Gang members did not want to be documented like that so they ran off and hid somewhere else in the city. The New Orleans housing projects have been a systemic problem for the city as a breeding ground for crime where gangs, drugs, and guns flourish. But the 82nd Airborne Division soldiers handled the situation as well, if not better, than anyone could have.

That image of New Orleans as a crime-ridden city is one reason we started seeing so many private security guards after the first week. People kept complaining that the active military and National Guard did not have any clear-cut command structure but the private security element was even worse. These guys had no command and absolutely no control. It is understandable why a homeowner not used to handling firearms might want to hire a private security guard or two for their home in situations such as this. But these guys were riding around in pickup trucks armed to the teeth and almost looking for trouble. What made even less sense was that FEMA hired several hundred private security guards when it had thousands of National Guard and active-duty soldiers available to protect its offices and staff members.

Not long after Admiral Thad Allen took over FEMA from Mike Brown, I went to Baton Rouge to meet with him. A private security guard with an M4 carbine was guarding the door to his office. I was in my standard Army combat uniform with my name tag over the breast pocket clearly visible along with the three black stars on my shirt and three silver stars on my beret.

"Where are you going?" the guard asked.

"I'm going to see Admiral Allen," I told him.

"Okay," he said, "let me see your ID."

"You've got to be shitting me," I shot back.

"That's the rule," he said. "I have to see everyone's ID card."

I did not pull the "Do you know who I am?" routine but rather than show him my military ID card I pulled out my Louisiana driver's license. He examined the license then nodded and allowed me to pass. It was just ridiculous. This was a humanitarian mission, and here these wannabe Rambos were running around with loaded weapons. A year later, when I returned for the one-year anniversary of Katrina, the private security guards were still there. Somebody made a lot of money off that deal.

The complete opposite of those private security guards were our uniformed soldiers. The soldiers, whether active duty or National Guard, quickly understood and accepted the spirit in which this humanitarian mission was being carried out. They constantly impressed me and made me proud to be a soldier with the manner in which they handled themselves and how much goodwill they spread wherever they went in New Orleans.

I have written in earlier chapters that I tried to keep my emotions out of this entire operation. Getting those babies some help on Friday got to me a bit. So did another incident during the first week of the house-to-house patrols.

I was sitting in a folding chair smoking a cigar out in front of Superman DZ one afternoon when a woman who looked to be a child of the sixties pedaled up on a Schwinn bicycle. The bike had a basket in front with an MRE in it and another basket behind the seat. She had long, stringy gray hair and was wearing a psychedelic flowered blouse and sandals that made her look like an aging hippie. She reminded me of Janis Joplin.

She stopped in front of me and said, "The troops said you're in charge."

"Well, I guess I am," I replied.

"I just wanted to tell you," she went on, "that those young men have come around every day for the past few days to check on me and make sure I was all right. I really want to thank you and your soldiers for doing that."

I just kind of nodded my head in thanks and smiled at her.

Then she said something that stunned me.

"I want to tell you something. I spent many years hating the Army because my brother got killed in Vietnam. And from the time he got killed until now I hated the Army. I never really understood what you do except kill people. But when I saw these boys coming through trying to help people and offering them food and water, my whole idea about the Army has gone from hate to respect."

That was a pretty powerful moment. That made me juice up a little. It was a good thing there wasn't a camera on me just then. We talked briefly and she mentioned she was a painter and had decided not to evacuate because her house had not flooded. She was worried that if she left it unattended it would get looted. I sympathized with her and tried to assure her that the police were doing everything they could under the circumstances to curtail the looting.

That conversation later brought up an interesting point in my mind about what happens after a hurricane or some other major disaster. Where do these scavengers come from who try to take advantage of other people? Is there something in the American gene pool that causes that? When we see the effects of that sort of behavior on the American people's psyche, it's devastating.

The average American is shocked by the fact that people are trying to break into stores and homes in the immediate aftermath of a disaster. That first night after the storm went through Mississippi, people were back in their homes, or what was left of them, with guns to protect their property because the scavengers were coming in from the water to see what they could steal.

When we look at the culture of preparedness, what sort of lessons do we learn from that? We will never change the criminal mind. Law-abiding people are well aware of the lengths criminals will go to in order to take advantage of any lack of civil authority. That's why a lot of people don't want anyone else to know they've left their home after a disaster. It makes their home a target for the scavengers. But our soldiers, who were under orders to break into homes to look for survivors and bodies during the latter rounds of searches, did tens of thousands of dollars of damage to front doors, back doors, and windows looking for people. That could have been avoided had there been some criminal-proof system to let searchers know no one was at home, and where the owners or residents could be reached. In a mass evacuation you want to know which houses are empty so you don't waste time searching them.

In a high-crime area many people don't want anyone to know they have left their house even if it's for a quick trip to the grocery store. They leave the lights or the TV on. That idea of leaving some sort of universal signal is counterintuitive to a mass evacuation. The crooks would pick up on that pretty easily unless there is actually a mandatory evacuation. Then everything could be secure. But a lot of people refused to leave their homes, their pets, and their property in New Orleans because they would be vulnerable to looters. Some even brought in their own private security guards.

This is an issue in which technology could make a major contribution to the culture of preparedness. What we need is a system that would give homeowners who evacuate in times of disaster some peace of mind about the safety and sanctity of their property while letting authorized search-and-rescue parties know if the house is vacant or occupied. The standard alarm system will not work because most rely primarily on land-based or cell phone lines. When those lines go out, as they did after Katrina, the systems are worthless. The answer is something more innovative that is storm, earthquake, tornado, and looter proof.

By the Sunday after the storm we were starting to see some light at the end of the tunnel and knew it was not a train bearing down on us. The breach in the 17th Street Canal had been closed by the Corps of Engineers and pumps were at work gradually dewatering the city. The Superdome and convention center had been evacuated. The two downtown hospitals were finally empty. People were still walking downtown to the convention center and the Superdome looking for help or evacuation after a full week of gutting it out in flooded homes. We got them what they needed, which usually was evacuation. But often they needed medical attention before we could move them because they were ill, injured, or simply dehydrated as a result of not having enough to drink in the oppressive heat.

It was about that time that we had a portable military field hospital make its way to the convention center. Doctor Jullette Saussy, the director of emergency medical services for New Orleans, was to be in charge of the hospital and insisted on putting it at the north end of the building. I thought it would be a better fit at the south end. She had not seen the inside of the facility but I had. Only the front part of the building had been used by people waiting to be evacuated. Most of the rest of the facility, which runs for ten and a half blocks, was untouched and was pristine clean. The doors to the exhibit center had been locked and the crowds had not gotten into that area.

Doctor Saussy wanted to triage and treat on the scene and I wanted to move people out as quickly as possible. We got into a heated argument and she reminded me she was the senior medical officer in New Orleans. I reminded her I was the senior military commander and that this was a military hospital. I was going to put it where I damned well thought it would best serve the people who needed treatment.

We eventually put the hospital at the south end of the building where

Emergency Preparedness Kit

Figure 1: Batteries, Moist Towelettes, Antibiotic Ointment, Whistle, and Emergency Preparedness Booklet

Figure 2: Battery-Operated Radio

Figure 3: Battery-Powered Flashlight

Figure 4: Light Stick

Figure 5: N95 Breathing Mask

Figure 6: Working Gloves

Figure 7: Rain Poncho, Survival Blanket, and Plastic Sheeting

Figure 8: Personal First Aid Kit

Figure 9: Toiletries

Figure 10: Duct Tape and Batteries

Figure 11: Complete Emergency Preparedness Kit

(Photos by Richard Yoo)

1

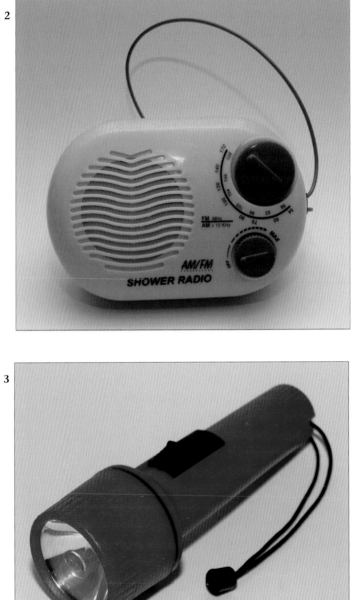

2

3

4

5

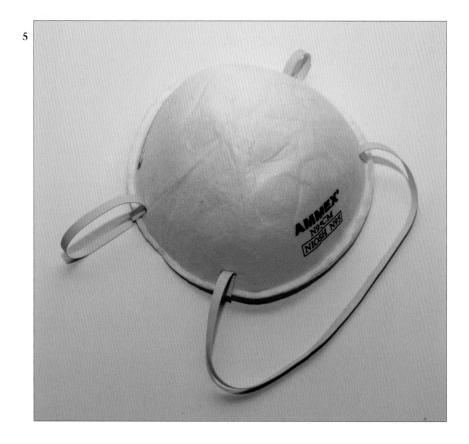

6

7

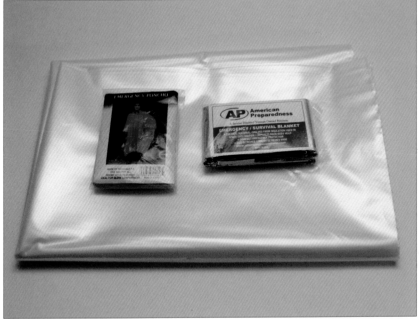

8

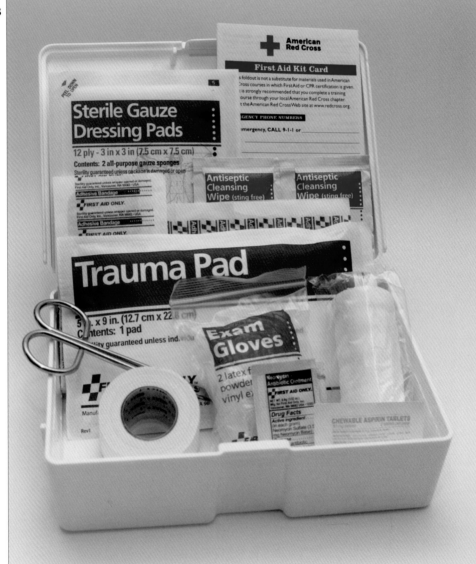

Sterile Gauze
Dressing Pads

12 ply - 3 in x 3 in (7.5 cm x 7.5 cm)

Contents: 2 all-purpose gauze sponges
Sterility guaranteed unless package is damaged or open
First Aid Only, Inc., Vancouver, WA 98661 · USA

Adhesive Bandage

■ **FIRST AID ONLY.**
Sterility guaranteed unless wrapper opened or damaged.
First Aid Only, Inc., Vancouver, WA 98661 · USA

Adhesive Bandage

■ **FIRST AID ONLY.**

**American
Red Cross**

First Aid Kit Card

This foldout is not a substitute for materials used in American
Red Cross courses in which First Aid or CPR certification is given.
It is strongly recommended that you complete a training
course through your local American Red Cross chapter.
Visit the American Red Cross Web site at www.redcross.org.

EMERGENCY PHONE NUMBERS

For emergency, CALL 9-1-1 or _____

Antiseptic
Cleansing
Wipe (sting free)

Antiseptic
Cleansing
Wipe (sting free)

Trauma Pad

5 in. x 9 in. (12.7 cm x 22.8 cm)
Contents: 1 pad
Sterility guaranteed unless ind...

**Exam
Gloves**

2 latex f...
powder...
vinyl e...

Neosporin
Antibiotic Ointment

■ **FIRST AID ONLY.**

Drug Facts
Active ingredient
(in each gram)
Neomycin Sulfate (3.5
mg Neomycin Base)...

CHEWABLE ASPIRIN TABLETS

Manufa...

Rev1

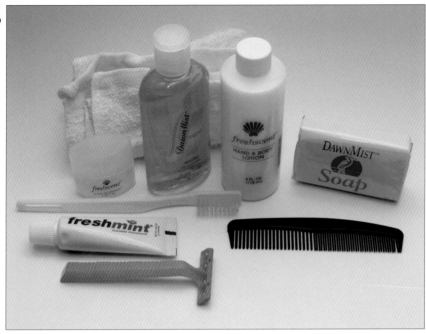

we had more room and fewer distractions. After a few days she ended up agreeing with my assessment. But over the course of the next few weeks she more than once gave me her opinion as a medical officer about the way she thought things should be done. She was not bashful about it, either, and I acquired a great deal of respect for her. She is one strong and opinionated woman. She stood up to me and the police and the fire department and did a great job of running that hospital even though she was a victim of the storm. She had lost her home, and her children had been evacuated, so she was dealing with all that at the same time she was dealing with medical issues of those who stayed behind. New Orleans and JTF-Katrina were lucky to have her at such a critical moment.

Also that Sunday we started seeing the first of what would become a steady procession of dignitaries, politicians, and celebrities with which my staff and I had to deal. The first group included Secretary of Defense Donald Rumsfeld; General Richard Myers, chairman of the Joint Chiefs of Staff; and Admiral Tim Keating, the commander of Northern Command. I met the group at the airport in Baton Rouge and we flew to the Louis Armstrong New Orleans International Airport by helicopter.

This was only my second meeting with Rumsfeld, although we had conversed several times over video teleconferences. Our first meeting was on my fifty-sixth birthday in September 2003. When I walked into his office at the Pentagon that day he looked at me and said, "You look kind of old."

I mentioned that I thought General Douglas MacArthur was seventy-two when he commanded the invasion at Inchon during the Korean War, although I later learned he was actually two years younger. Rumsfeld seemed to brighten at that, looked at me, and said: "I'm seventy-two. That's a great age."

We talked about his wife's love of gardening, which is an interest of mine, and he kidded me about my Louisiana accent. When I saw him again that Sunday in Baton Rouge he laughed and told people, "He can just keep talking. I can't understand what he's saying anyway."

Rumsfeld surprised me with his knowledge of New Orleans and its traditions. He had been a naval aviator in the 1950s and had frequently flown into the airfield at Belle Chasse, just south of the city. He told a wonderful story about going into the French Quarter during his visits and having a good time. He knew there was something special about New Orleans and he fully realized what a major disaster could do to the culture of the city. But he also knew it was a city challenged by crime, poverty, and health issues.

The New Orleans airport was foot-dry, and the ill and elderly were being taken there in stretchers for evacuation by air, so we pushed a military police company out there for security. Senator Bill Frist of Tennessee, who also is a doctor, flew into the airport unannounced on Saturday to lend his assistance. He was one of the selfless volunteers who kept politics in check and simply did what he could to ease the suffering of some of those folks. And he did it without any fanfare or expectations of publicity.

By that Saturday night the weight of the world was off our shoulders. We had evacuated the convention center. But no matter how well we thought we were doing, little things we did not anticipate were likely to jump up and bite us in the butt when we least expected it. Over the next few days that happened innumerable times as we gradually made the transition from search and rescue and evacuation to recovery. We were still plucking people off rooftops but the numbers were diminishing rapidly and we could start to think about embarking on the task of finding the bodies of those who had not survived.

That issue of remains recovery eventually put me at odds with Mike Brown of FEMA and officials from the state of Louisiana because of the way they wanted to handle the situation, which essentially was to hand it off to DOD and the young soldiers under my command. It was not a job for which they were trained and was not something I wanted them to do. That was an issue that for their sake I could not back down on.

CHAPTER 11
Lessons Learned for Building a Culture of Preparedness

1. Use life experiences to "adapt and overcome." In the Army, it's a way of life. The poor learn to make do with what they have.

2. Some things take time, but keep the team focused on doing things with speed. When saving lives, minutes and hours, not days, are crucial. "You are looking at a calendar and I am looking at my watch."

3. Leaders must learn to adapt to the situation. Work with what is available. Praise people who take initiative to solve problems. The

culture of most first responders is one of being able to adapt to most situations and save lives. Too many elected leaders and the media focus on who screwed up.

4. Be wary of symbolic response. A lot of organizations will want to post their flags in the disaster area without really helping solve the problems.

12

Mike Brown's Exit

DURING MY TENURE AS COMMANDER OF STANDING JOINT FORCE Headquarters–Homeland Security in Norfolk, Virginia, from 2002 to 2004, one of the studies my office worked on dealt with mortuary affairs in the aftermath of a national disaster. That study became part of the Department of Homeland Security's 2004 National Response Plan (NRP), which was a product of the post-9/11 world. The U.S. Department of Health and Human Services (DHHS) was given overall responsibility for handling mass casualties as a result of a pandemic, terrorist attack, or natural disaster such as a hurricane. DHHS further developed its plan to have mortuary operators pool resources to handle remains that under normal circumstances are the responsibility of first responders such as local police and fire departments or emergency medical services.

In those normal situations the handling of remains is a relatively simple and clear-cut task since bodies generally are not lying around in large numbers. But Katrina did not give us anything simple or clear-cut. It broke every system and undid all the plans. There was no way of telling where the bodies were and neither the state nor FEMA had the resources to do searches of the magnitude required. Every one of the 250,000 or more structures and pieces of property in the greater New Orleans area would have to be searched inch by inch for the dead and missing. Who was to do that? And who was responsible for identifying those bodies and removing them to a storage facility? Again, neither FEMA nor the state nor DHHS had that sort of capacity.

In the middle of the second week of Katrina operations, FEMA started pressuring me as the military commander to take responsibility for that mission. They thought that since the Department of Defense could tap into more resources, we could handle all aspects of remains recovery. They wanted us to find the bodies, identify them, tag them, bag them, and haul them off to a mortuary. The NRP says DHHS can request assistance from the Department of Defense for this but we were now being asked to do far more than assist. We were being asked to bear the full responsibility for something that could have a long-lasting impact on many families because of the distinct possibility of getting identifications incorrect. There are technical and legal issues related to the identification of remains for which the infantry soldiers at my disposal were not qualified or trained. It appeared that the thinking of FEMA was that because we had a large number of soldiers who had been in combat and saw people killed or seriously wounded, they would have no problems handling this job.

I immediately started pushing back hard on that idea. I knew we were going to have serious issues not only dealing with the numbers of remains, but also in getting access to many of the bodies. The water was still too deep in much of the city, especially in St. Bernard Parish just across the river. In addition, those bodies had been out there for a week by then. Our troops recover bodies on the battlefield but often it's their buddies who have just been killed. They put them in a body bag and it's done. What FEMA was asking us to do was find bodies that had undergone some degree of deterioration in the stifling heat and brackish water. Many of the bodies were bloated and decomposing. These soldiers were not trained for that sort of duty. The National Response Plan envisions the bodies being laid out in nice neat rows so they are easily identifiable and easily transportable. The soldiers would be finding bodies trapped behind or underneath furniture, stuffed into attics or crawl spaces, or simply floating out in the open.

We had only about fifty-five active-duty soldiers with a Disaster Mortuary Operational Response Team (DMORT), which specializes in this type of mission, left in the United States. They were at Fort Lee, Virginia, and were scheduled to deploy overseas in a few months. The majority of soldiers with those special skills were already in Iraq or Afghanistan so we were looking at dipping into a pool that was already extremely shallow.

It takes a special person to develop the skills and have the composure necessary to deal with decomposing remains. It is not something I would be able to do. I have always believed that a commander should not ask a soldier to do something he would not do and I certainly did not want to do this. My primary concern was that a lot of these young privates had not been to combat before, although many of the senior noncommissioned officers had. It was impossible to tell what the long-term effects this type of operation would have on these soldiers.

The state of Louisiana had hired James Lee Witt, the former FEMA director under President Bill Clinton, and his emergency preparedness and management consulting firm shortly after Katrina hit. It is my understanding that Witt, a Texan, advised state officials about a Texas company called Kenyon International Emergency Services to assist in the identification and recovery of bodies. This particular firm sent people to Thailand and Indonesia after the 2004 tsunami and was made up of retired medical officials, coroners, and military officers who had done this work in the past.

On Sunday night, September 4, I was in a meeting with Michael Chertoff, secretary of the Department of Homeland Security; Mike Brown of FEMA; a representative of Kenyon; and Major General Bill Caldwell of the 82nd Airborne. Brown said since I opposed using active-duty soldiers for this work I had to sign a contract with Kenyon on behalf of the Department of Defense for that firm to do the work. I responded that my troops would help find the bodies and transport them to save some manpower. Many of Kenyon's people were getting up in years and were not in the best of shape to be working in this heat. But identifying bodies and getting them into bags are technical issues that needed to be handled by professionals. These soldiers were not trained for that.

Brown kept insisting I had to sign the contract. Finally, I blew up at him: "I really don't give a flying shit what you do. We'll be there to support you but we're not going to sign a contract. And if you don't have this shit worked out in the morning, I am going to tell the American people about it."

I slammed my hand on the desk and stomped out of the room. I flew back to Camp Shelby and said nothing more about it but by ten o'clock the next morning Louisiana officials had signed the contract and gotten my soldiers off the hook for what everyone knew was going to be a particularly gruesome mission.

It must have been some contract. A year after the storm, a public interest group out of Oakland called CorpWatch published a report called "Big, Easy Money: Disaster Profiteering on the American Gulf

Coast," which claimed that Kenyon recovered 535 bodies, about one-third of the casualties in Louisiana, and charged the state more than $6 million, which came out to roughly $12,500 per body. After reading that report I breathed a sigh of relief that I had not allowed myself to be pressured into inflicting that mess on the Department of Defense.

Once the contract was signed we put the troops into position to assist the recovery teams. The soldiers joined with various state and federal agencies in the house-to-house searches, which were done in two stages. The primary stage involved simply knocking on a door and seeing if anyone answered. If they did we asked them if they wanted or needed assistance in any way. If no one answered, we moved on. In the second phase we actually went in and searched the premises. Once that search was completed the building was marked with a special symbol to indicate to others the date on which it was searched, who searched it, and what, if anything, was found.

Those symbols, which were still on many houses in the 7th and 9th wards for years after the storm, became one of the enduring symbols of the post-Katrina operation. Searchers made a large X in luminescent paint somewhere near the front entrance. In the northern quadrant of the mark was the date the structure was searched. The western quadrant contained the numerical designation of the military unit that did the search, or the letters, such as DEA for Drug Enforcement Administration, of the agency that did the search. The eastern quadrant contained information about any hazards in the building while the southern quadrant was reserved for the total number of people found inside and whether they were alive or dead. On occasion, some buildings were searched more than once and it was not unusual to see two sets of markings on some houses in the area that suffered the heaviest flood damage.

When we held a news conference to get the word out about how the operation would be conducted, the media were told in no uncertain terms they were not welcome to ride along with the recovery teams.

"There will be zero access to that operation," I told them. "It would not be good to have pictures of people, the deceased, shown on any media."

"Does that mean you are denying us from reporting on this?" one reporter asked.

"No, what I am denying you is a ride. There is nothing that says I have to give you a ride while we are searching for remains. Everybody knows it's a horrific event."

My reasoning was simple. I did not want CNN or Fox carrying live feeds of us recovering bodies and showing the addresses of buildings. It was entirely possible that a relative would be watching that and see Granny or their Aunt Nelly carried out of the house in a body bag and learn about the death that way. That was no way for people to find out that a loved one had died in the flood. I understood the media's concerns and appreciated what they were doing to get the story out to the American public but I was not going to back down on this.

Many news organizations saw this as an effort on my part to prohibit them from covering the story of remains recovery. Within hours of the news conference, CNN and its lawyers were in federal court in Houston seeking a temporary restraining order against FEMA, claiming the media's First Amendment rights were being violated because we were imposing prior restraint on their newsgathering operations. Two days later our lawyers decided we had to back down a bit and clarify our position. They drafted a statement for my signature that said, "All personnel assigned, attached or under the operational or tactical control of the JTF-Katrina Commander, are prohibited from barring, impeding, or preventing civilian news media from their newsgathering and reporting activities."

In fact, the media were not being denied or impeded in any way, shape, or form. They were simply being denied access to government transportation because of operational necessities, which was within my right as the JTF-Katrina commander to do. No one was stopping them from going anywhere. I was just not going to help them get there.

As we moved into the second week of operations we were starting to get a number of volunteers flowing into the city. They were ready to do what was necessary to save people, help out with distribution of food and water, clear away the mountains of debris that the storm had left, or rescue and care for the thousands of dogs and cats stranded or abandoned by their owners who left town. The pets issue was one of those stray bullets that came zinging at me out of nowhere and will be dealt with at greater length in the next chapter.

Katrina created a large volunteer force of Americans who dropped everything they were doing to come to New Orleans. That's something that is wonderfully unique about this country. I can't say enough good things about the people who came to help their fellow Americans. Even though some of them initially were hesitant because of the media reports of widespread rapes and shooting, thousands showed up and helped us save many lives and ease the hardships of a number of storm victims.

One of the more memorable of those volunteers was a sod grower and debris removal contractor from Elberta, Alabama, by the name of Edward "Eddie Boy" Woerner. Eddie Boy, as everyone called him, had loaded up a truck with ice and tents and was getting ready to head for Mississippi two days after the storm hit to bid on a debris removal contract. Then a friend called and told him he had seen a news report that the New Orleans police were on duty around the clock but no one was feeding them.

Eddie Boy loved to grill and had used those skills to keep his employees fed after Hurricane Ivan tore through Alabama in 2004. He decided that rather than bid on a contract to remove debris in Mississippi, he would go to New Orleans and feed the more than eight hundred police and other law enforcement officers on duty.

He arrived at the police command center at the corner of Poydras Street and Convention Center Boulevard shortly after noon on Sunday, September 4. He quickly got two more volunteers to assist him and before long had his barbecue grills going full-blast under the Harrah's Casino awning, cooking hamburgers and hot dogs first for the police and then for more than 1,200 soldiers in the area. With the support of Brigadier General Mike Terry, the logistician for JTF-Katrina, who ensured that Woerner had refrigeration trucks and other supplies that he needed, those grills were kept going day and night and at times were feeding 6,000–8,000 people a day.

When the story started getting out, people from all over the country contributed food and money. The Elberta Little League, which had an annual grilled sausage sale to buy uniforms for the players, offered three thousand pounds of meat. When I learned no transportation was available to get the meat to New Orleans, I authorized a helicopter to fly over there to pick it up. That drove the lawyers up the wall when they found out about it but eventually more than $500,000 worth of food and supplies found their way to Eddie Boy's grills.

Eddie Boy and his crew stayed around for three weeks, working virtually nonstop to keep law enforcement, soldiers, sailors, and Marines fed. We had MREs available but when fresh-grilled hamburgers and sausages are available, who wants to eat something out of a plastic pouch? Those Alabama boys cooked so much that it took months to get rid of the grease spot on the driveway under the awning at Harrah's.

One of the perks of being the JTF-Katrina commander was complete access to civilian leaders across the federal, state, and local spectrum.

There was not one time when I needed to see someone that they did not stop what they were doing and either come out and see me or have their staff come out and bring me in to see them. And when I called they were always available, with the exception of one—Mike Brown, the FEMA director. He was always difficult to get on the phone in the week and a half he was there.

Other than that, Brown and I got along well. He was extremely pleasant and affable in all our meetings. It was obvious early on, though, that he was somewhat overwhelmed by the circumstances he found himself in. It was not within my jurisdiction nor was it my responsibility to criticize him or point out the shortcomings in the way he did his business. He was a political appointee and JTF-Katrina was working for him as much as it was working for the governor and the mayor.

In the media, Brown was the face of all that went wrong in the run-up to Katrina, and the cleanup after. In their eyes Brown was the very model of inefficiency and ineptitude in federal disaster relief. As events unfolded, it became clear to me that here was a man whose confidence far exceeded the capabilities of FEMA to quickly execute in the wake of a large-scale disaster. FEMA had weathered several hurricanes in Florida the year before and felt it had a handle on the template for disaster relief and recovery. Katrina created her own template and neither Brown nor FEMA was prepared to deal with it. The old template had to be thrown away and the new one built from scratch. That was something to which Brown and the FEMA staff had difficulty adjusting.

On September 2, the same day President Bush came to New Orleans and met with Kathleen Blanco and Ray Nagin, the president stopped earlier in Mobile, Alabama, where he met with Brown. In remarks after that meeting Bush uttered the words that were seized on by the media as emblematic of the federal government's inability to understand the full scope of the disaster.

"Brownie," Bush said, "you're doing a heck of a job."

It was almost like a kiss of death. The media jumped on that and began a full-scale investigation into everything Brown had ever said or done. From that moment on he was a marked man.

Exactly one week to the day from that pronouncement by the president, I was summoned to Baton Rouge for a news conference. I thought it would be another update on events and the progress we were making. I met Chertoff and Vice Admiral Thad Allen in Brown's office and exchanged pleasantries with Brown, telling him it appeared that things were going well and we were headed in the right direction. He looked at me and said, "You don't know why you're here, do you?"

"No, sir," I replied.

"They're sending me back to Washington," Brown said.

I was stunned. I knew things had been rough for him but had no idea they were this bad. Congress and the media were looking for accountability and immediate response and they did not see it in Brown. Chertoff did most of the talking at the news conference. I tried to blend into the background and disappear. I said nothing. I didn't want to say anything. This was a political issue and it would not help us or the effort to get New Orleans back to normal if I stuck my opinions into the middle of it. I felt uncomfortable just being there.

Before we walked out to meet the media, Chertoff turned to his press aide and asked, "Can I be no-holds-barred on this?" He was told he could. But Chertoff and the White House obviously wanted it to appear that Brown was being called back to Washington to capture lessons learned. Reporters immediately pounced on the fact that he was being replaced at a critical time in the operations and naturally assumed he had been fired. It put Brown in a pretty awkward position.

Later that night Brown sent a message to me on my BlackBerry. The subject line simply said: "Thank you."

"General," Brown wrote, "thanks for your kind words prior to the press conference this afternoon. Getting to know and watch you was a privilege, sir. Godspeed in your work."

He signed off: "Best regards, MB."

I thought it was a classy thing to do under extremely difficult and embarrassing circumstances. Three days later, after Brown returned to Washington, he turned in his resignation.

Brown's problems in Louisiana were to a great extent of his own making. He became an expert marksman there: every time he shot he hit the target—his own foot. The rather intemperate e-mails he sent throughout the crisis were an embarrassment to the administration once they were released to the public. He seemed more concerned about what shirt to wear for a news conference and whether he should roll up his sleeves as the president did than he was about the welfare of those suffering. He also spent all his time in Baton Rouge instead of jumping into the middle of the fray in downtown New Orleans. It was almost as if he wanted to avoid the unpleasantness he would see there. In times of crisis the American public wants to see its leaders out in front and in a

humanitarian crisis they want to see them on the scene. That's one reason Bush received so much undeserved criticism—he did not get there
early enough. That's also one reason I received more praise than was
deserved.

Comparatively speaking, there was a significant difference between
Brown and me in how we were able to do things. If a request came to
me and the capability was available to do it, it would get done. But if
a request came in to Brown, unless it was a life-or-death matter that
request went first to the staff and then a mission request had to be made.
Brown was a coordinator, not a commander, and had few resources at
his immediate disposal. He was a cowboy hat with no cattle. He had no
more than 2,200 people in FEMA when Katrina hit. They had connectivity to resources that were called forward at the time they were needed
but he could not just snap his fingers and make five hundred buses or
much of anything else magically appear.

On the other hand, as commander of JTF-Katrina I was able to get
the assets available to me moving much more quickly. The task force
had 20,000 people on the ground, nearly three hundred helicopters,
more than twenty ships, and hundreds of trucks. We had *stuff* readily
available and did not have to contract for it. Mike Brown had no assets
at his immediate disposal and had to rely on a bureaucracy that is not
designed to be a first responder or a fast responder. FEMA relies on contracts.

Brown came into Katrina with a lot of confidence because of how
FEMA had handled the storms in Florida the year before. But none of
those storms challenged the organization under his leadership as Katrina
did. He was one of those unintended consequences whose confidence
exceeded his competence and he could not hide it. He became a victim
of the storm. People simply lost confidence in his ability to handle the
job and he was hauled back to Washington to account for it. A disaster like Katrina has a way of killing people and destroying reputations.
Poor Mike Brown thought he was doing a great job and ended up getting fired.

It bothers me to this day to hear people say that what happened after
Hurricane Katrina was the president's fault or FEMA's fault. Many people
had unrealistic expectations about what could have and what should
have been done. Were we late? Yes, we were late. I wish we could have
been there the day the storm hit. But we weren't. The storm had a vote
on how fast we got there. Federal officials agonized over that as much as

anyone. They felt very strongly about what happened and wished they could have done more and done it more quickly.

FEMA, by the very nature of the laws that created it and restrict what it does, is not only a slow responder, it is also an inefficient responder because of the way the bureaucracy works. There is a story about one FEMA contract that may or may not be urban legend but it is indicative of problems in the agency as it tried to work through the post-Katrina chaos.

This story concerns a truckload of ice contracted out of Indiana to be sent to New Orleans. FEMA supposedly sent the driver by way of Atlanta. Once he got there he was told he needed to go to Norfolk, Virginia, because Hurricane Ophelia was starting to threaten the coasts of Virginia and North Carolina. So the driver headed to Norfolk. But not long after his arrival he was told it was too dangerous to stay and he needed to go back to Atlanta. In Atlanta he was told he should head on down to Camp Beauregard, Louisiana. The poor guy was bounced all over the Southeast before he was able to deliver that load of much-needed ice. There was just too much bureaucracy for FEMA to have any effective control close to the ground.

My sense toward the end of the second week of JTF-Katrina was that we could start looking at redeploying some of the troops. Our main missions had been accomplished, civil authority was being restored, and our role was coming to an end. That's about the time we started getting word about Ophelia and the potential threat it posed. Just as we were getting our legs under us from Katrina, Ophelia was making a move toward the North Carolina coast. Now our eastern flank was being threatened even as we were trying to recover from the damage to our southern flank.

We started making arrangements to get people in place if we got any sense that Ophelia would become a major event but I started thinking to myself, Oh, shit. What's next? Fortunately, Ophelia was mostly a wind and rain event as a high-pressure system kept most of the damaging winds out to sea. We dodged that particular bullet.

Meanwhile, other stray bullets were coming my way from all directions, none of which were anticipated. Some were coming from Washington. Some were coming from Northern Command. And some were coming from the most unexpected sources I could ever have imagined, such as pet lovers. Everybody seemed to have an agenda and to hear it from the people with those agendas, we were not doing anything right.

CHAPTER 12

Lessons Learned for Building a Culture of Preparedness

1. The Department of Health and Human Services needs to develop a more effective plan to deal with human remains. Using contractors is expensive and not effective. Another option is for each state's National Guard to have a DMORT platoon as backup to DHHS.

2. Metal caskets should have a stamp that identifies the remains. When caskets float out of graves as a result of flooding, it requires a DNA test to verify remains.

3. We need a national standard for marking homes that have been evacuated. If searchers don't know if anyone is in the home, they have to break in to make sure no humans or animals remain in the home.

4. Be careful of e-mails. The "e" in e-mail means "evidence." If you don't want to see it again, do not put it in an e-mail.

13

Avoiding the 1,200-Mile Screwdrivers

IN ANY MILITARY OPERATION, WHETHER IT IS WAR OR HUMANITARIAN assistance, a certain amount of second-guessing and Monday morning quarterbacking takes place even as events are developing. Higher headquarters sends out senior mentors, off whom commanders can bounce ideas and receive suggestions that are well rooted in experience. My senior mentors were retired Marine Corps General Charles Wilhelm and retired Coast Guard Vice Admiral Jim Hull. Historians and staff officers also are dispatched to take notes for after-action reports and lessons learned. Brigadier General Tony Cuculo III was in charge of a team of officers capturing lessons learned from JTF-Katrina.

Those are the obvious. The not-so-obvious are the attempts to influence ongoing operations in e-mails, offline telephone conversations, or the occasional personal visit from senior officers or members of Congress. On top of that, staff officers in the Pentagon have a habit of watching events unfold from the safety of their offices and try to influence them with extra-long screwdrivers. These are what I referred to during JTF-Katrina as 1,200-mile screwdrivers.

Some of the more insistent of these screwdrivers were urging me to take a lower profile and push the National Guard side of the story harder. The first of those came Thursday afternoon, September 1, even as we were struggling to find enough resources to get people out of the

Superdome. It was sent from higher command through Major General Rich Rowe, the operations chief at Northern Command and one of the people with whom I was in almost constant contact. In an e-mail message he wrote, "Guidance is 'guard' in NO and 'guard' to fullest extent possible for tasks in LA and MS. NGB supports. EMAC working. OSD and CJCS agree with this."

The translation was that the people at the Pentagon wanted me to make it clear that the National Guard, not the active force, was doing the bulk of the heavy lifting for the Katrina operation. After the evacuation, the National Guard Bureau, the Office of the Secretary of Defense, and the chairman of the Joint Chiefs of Staff thought I should fade into the background and be a less visible presence and a less insistent voice, according to Rowe's message. This operation, in the minds of some senior officers, was supposed to reflect well on the Guard, not on the active Army, and especially not on me personally.

My response was a simple, loud, and clear "GOT IT."

The problem with complying with that suggestion—it wasn't really a directive, more of a strong suggestion from officers above Rowe—was that the National Guard did not have an overall commander on the ground to provide a clear assessment of what was happening in Louisiana and Mississippi. The National Guard Bureau chiefs were back in Washington, D.C., with their 1,200-mile screwdrivers trying to fine-tune things from there, although much credit goes to Lieutenant General Steven Blum and Lieutenant General Clyde Vaughn, director of the Army National Guard, for doing a remarkable job deploying the National Guard to Louisiana and Mississippi.

My proximity to the problems gave me a much better feel for the problems we were dealing with at any particular moment. By the time the people in Washington heard about a problem, studied it, and then sent out a fix through their staffs we had solved dozens of complex issues. We were in a constant problem-solving environment in which decisions had to be made quickly in order to save lives and keep things moving forward.

That friction between the National Guard and the active component of the armed forces remained constant throughout the operation. When we had our first JTF-Katrina commanders' conference on board the USS *Iwo Jima* on September 14, as a courtesy we invited Major General Bennie Landreneau and the National Guard division commanders from Kansas and Indiana. Bennie and one of the division commanders showed up. As the mission progressed it got harder and harder to get the National Guard generals to our meetings, except for Landreneau. The word we were getting was that they were being coached from back home not to go to any meetings with me.

That was fine with me, though, because I was able to speak through Landreneau. Bennie and his forces were coordinating efforts through the commander of the 82nd, who had 7,000 troops in the area, plus ground troops from the 1st Cavalry Division. Brigadier General Doug O'Dell was in charge of the Marine forces deployed in St. Bernard Parish and they were also working with National Guard units in the area.

The people with the 1,200-mile screwdrivers always seemed more concerned about planning to get things done instead of actually getting them done. I was into execution rather than planning. I had to constantly be on guard for people outside the JTF-Katrina chain of command who wanted to put their 1,200-mile screwdrivers into my back. Higher headquarters thought its responsibility was to micromanage and overcontrol me. I did not want to be controlled by Northern Command because I would have ended up being told what to do and where to do it rather than doing the things that needed to be done at any particular moment.

We were so far ahead of the people at Northern Command and the Pentagon that at times they found out what we were doing only because they were watching TV or reading our daily reports. Even some members of the JTF-Katrina staff later criticized me for that, complaining in congressional testimony that "we track General Honoré's location by watching CNN." If this had been a combat operation I could have understood why people wanted to stick to strict structure and follow a plan. But this was a permissive environment. We were trying to help people, not kill them. We were on American soil and were not being shot at. It was necessary for the leadership to be out front at the point of attack because it facilitated getting the most things done in the least amount of time. It also meant changing plans on the fly if a particular situation dictated.

When the 82nd Airborne took over from the Oklahoma National Guard's 45th Brigade we did it with a couple of guys standing out on the street looking over a map of New Orleans. If we had given this to officers at Fort Leavenworth it would have taken three days for them to figure out how to do it. When the 82nd took over we saw soldiers in maroon berets moving in and soldiers in Kevlar moving out. It wasn't rocket science. This was America. This was not Baghdad.

Once the *Iwo Jima* got upriver on September 5, the Navy, Air Force, Marine, and Coast Guard bosses put together a digital mapping system that divided the city into grids to make it easier to search for people stranded on their roofs. A street address to a helicopter pilot has no relevance to what he is trying to do. Somebody has to translate that address into a grid coordinate or latitude and longitude. An aerial grid allows everyone to be on a common sheet and pilots can deconflict their flight plans so they are not running into each other.

Some of my critics complained we should have done that before we went to New Orleans. Their idea was to stop first and make a plan. But we never figured we needed an aerial grid for the city of New Orleans when we worked for First Army. That was not our area of responsibility. If anybody had an aerial grid it should have been the Louisiana National Guard or the people doing the evacuation planning. This was yet another example of not being properly prepared for the worst-case scenario. Someone may have thought at one time about an aerial grid but no one ever took the initiative to actually do one. As a result, we had to develop one from scratch. Until we were able to do that we just had helicopters flying around the city looking for people stranded on their roofs. When it's a matter of saving lives, the idea is to just get out there and get after it. Having a plan is certainly not more important than saving a life. To stop and develop a plan to save lives at the expense of lives would have been unconscionable, if not criminal.

After taking command of First Army in the summer of 2004, I read a book about how General Omar Bradley commanded First Army during World War II. Bradley and his staff would sit down at night and talk about the next day's tasks. There were no briefings and no decision folders passed from officer to officer. Today the Army has these big, elaborate, long-ass briefings with hundreds of PowerPoint slides that basically talk about what happened yesterday. By the time the briefers start talking about what is going to happen tomorrow, nobody has any energy left and people are nodding off all over the place. In a situation like Katrina the civilian officials tell FEMA, the National Guard, or the active forces what they need and those agencies respond to the requests. It is not necessary to overstudy the problem and come up with some elaborate plan that delays results by days. The mayors know what they need. I let my staff and the Northern Command staff know that was the way

JTF-Katrina would operate. Needless to say, I was not always the most popular guy on the block.

By the third week after the storm we were getting hit hard and fast by congressional delegations and stray bullets from other groups and agencies. In addition, President Bush came to New Orleans three more times after his brief visit of September 2. He was there on Labor Day, September 5, and was back exactly a week later, spending the night on the *Iwo Jima*. Three days later he gave a nationally televised speech from Jackson Square in the French Quarter assuring the people of New Orleans and the rest of the country that those suffering would get all the federal assistance they needed.

During that September 12 visit Bush also went down to St. Bernard Parish to meet one of the great characters of Louisiana politics, Henry "Junior" Rodriguez, the parish president. Junior, as everyone in Louisiana knows him, is one of those larger-than-life characters. He has a full head of white hair and is almost as wide as he is tall. He walks with the aid of an elaborately carved walking stick that he takes everywhere. Junior was not nationally known until he started showing up on CNN on a regular basis to complain about the slow pace of the federal response. He is well-known in Louisiana so it was not surprising that Bush's aides convinced the president to go to St. Bernard Parish.

Junior had sent President Bush a letter on August 29 after the storm surge caused the levees to fail, flooding not only the 7th and 9th wards but also St. Bernard Parish, which is adjacent to the 9th Ward. In the letter Junior pleaded for help, saying the parish was largely under water and the people had no food, water, sanitation, power, or communication, and that parish officials had no means of helping them.

"Absolutely no attempt has been made to communicate with me regarding the catastrophe that has occurred to the citizens that I represent," Junior wrote.

"I cannot believe that in a country as sophisticated as the United States of America that the leadership in the White House cannot somehow communicate NOW with me and the local government that I represent."

Junior went on to charge that the disaster "is a direct outgrowth of the neglect of the Federal Government to address the costal [sic] erosion problem of southern Louisiana."

After the president met with Junior, the deputy White House chief of staff, Joe Hagin, called me and said there were some issues in St. Bernard

Parish that were of concern to the president and that I needed to get over there to find out what was going on. When I got to Chalmette, the parish seat, I found Junior and we went into this small office that had no air-conditioning but had about twelve people in it already. Everybody was sweating like crazy in the stifling late-summer heat. Junior started carrying on and raising all kinds of hell about how New Orleans was getting all the attention and St. Bernard Parish wasn't getting any.

He said he wanted to know what he was supposed to do because his parish was contaminated from the oil and chemicals that came with the floodwaters. I told him the Marines had been there for several days and none of them had gotten sick. They were wearing rubber gloves and always washed their hands before they ate. And when they came out of the muck they were getting sprayed down to reduce the risk in the event there was contamination. Junior kept insisting the place was contaminated. I told him we had been taking water samples and they were being tested by the Environmental Protection Agency and we'd have an answer back to him the next day.

After leaving the meeting I put in a call to E. Renae Conley, president and CEO of Entergy, the power company that supplies that part of Louisiana, to ask if she could get line crews into St. Bernard Parish to pick up the big power lines so people could start moving on the roads.

"General," she responded, "I would do that but Junior Rodriguez has told everyone the place is contaminated. I'm not going to send my men in there if the place is contaminated."

I said we would have a better reading on that the next day when the EPA came out with its analysis. And sure enough their findings were the same as ours. The EPA recommendations were to avoid getting the stuff on exposed skin, wash hands before eating, and get sprayed down after walking in the muck and everything would be fine.

Junior's initial emotional reaction to the disaster was much the same as Ray Nagin's. It was a function of the art of exaggeration that is part of the Louisiana culture. It's the art of exaggeration to get an empathetic response from people. Junior was looking at the long-term rebuilding of his parish and not at the short-term effects of what he was saying. It was much like the police chief of New Orleans saying "snipers" at a time we were asking grandmother bus drivers to go into the city and pick people up. The statements may have had some sliver of truth in that people may have been shooting and this mud was not something anyone would want to pick up and make mud pies out of but there were no snipers and the whole parish was not contaminated.

Those small, quantifiable words—*sniper* and *contaminated*—had second- and third-order effects on the people we were trying to help and the volunteers on whom we were depending for assistance. The volunteers wanted to be able to work in a permissive environment in which they were not going to get shot and not get sick from contaminated mud and water.

That was a real lesson in communicating and dealing with the media. Empathy can be sought to a point. But there is also the possibility that too much overexaggeration can result in people disregarding what is being said because whoever is saying it appears to be out of control. That's what happened to Kathleen Blanco, Ray Nagin, Junior Rodriguez, and Police Superintendent Eddie Compass III at one time or another during the crisis.

Another part of our effort that third week was to get a good assessment of what happened in Plaquemines Parish, where the storm first made landfall on the Gulf Coast. Benny Rousselle, president of the parish, and I drove down to Buras, the little fishing community that took the hardest hit.

This part of the Mississippi River delta is the heart of the fishing industry on the Gulf Coast. As we drove down Highway 23 with the Mississippi on our right and the Gulf of Mexico on our left we saw fishing boats all over the place. They were in the road, on top of the levees, and on top of one another. This parish had been hit as hard as Biloxi and Gulfport.

We drove until the road ended and then we got out and walked up to the levee. The storm surge had cut a swath through the levee like a giant backhoe. That water was so powerful it ate the ground away from the levee and bent the steel sheets that were driven in by a pile driver. When we topped the levee a scraggly dog came running up to greet us. Following him was a Cajun guy without a shirt or shoes. He was carrying an empty gas can.

"Who are you? What are you doing?" the parish sheriff, who was with us, asked.

"My name's Muskrat," the man replied in his lilting Cajun accent. "I survived the damn storm out here."

We looked at each other in surprise and asked him if he was okay and if he wanted an MRE. He took the MRE and said he needed some gas for his boat. He said he needed to get out of there. He said he was going to go on some of the smashed boats and get some gas but the sheriff told him it wasn't a good idea to go on private property and take the gas. Muskrat was talking loud, as if he had been drinking seawater instead of fresh water and his system was a bit out of kilter. When the sheriff finished talking Muskrat turned around and walked off without his gas but with an MRE in his hand and his dog right next to him.

Muskrat was the only sign of life we saw down there. Everybody else was gone. It was like going into an area where a nuclear bomb had hit. There was virtually nothing left standing for the last hour of driving into Buras. Most people had evacuated, except for Muskrat, because the eye was coming right at them. I don't know how he survived, except that God seems to smile at times on drunks and fools.

The people in that part of the state are storm-savvy. They don't build large, substantial houses because they know they are likely to get knocked down or flooded by the storms coming out of the Gulf of Mexico every so often. Most have good evacuation plans and leave the area as soon as it appears that the eye of a hurricane is heading at them. They had been through this before and likely will go through it again, but because they had developed their own culture of preparedness they survived Katrina.

Plaquemines Parish had been devastated, but since it wasn't a humanitarian issue as was the case in St. Bernard and Orleans parishes, it was not as pressing for us to get in there and get to work immediately. My role down there and in other parishes was as an enabler. I would talk to a parish president, take a look at the damage, and then come back and call Admiral Thad Allen, who had taken over for Mike Brown, to give him a list of priorities and suggest what FEMA might want to take a look at.

Once I became a visible presence on television my BlackBerry and telephone went into overdrive with messages from people who either wanted to get contracts or had a complaint about some of the contracts that were being let in New Orleans. I had nothing to do with any of the contracts but was hearing all sorts of stories, such as the one about a company from Jacksonville, Florida, that supposedly was supplying peanut butter and jelly sandwiches at thirteen dollars apiece. That's a bit much, although I was never able to confirm that it actually happened. Stray reports like that were usually handed off to Thad Allen and FEMA to handle.

People defaulted to me on all sorts of issues: everything from rescuing pets to the contracts to parish presidents whining about not getting enough attention from the federal government. They all seemed to think I had this magic telephone number to the White House and could get them anything they needed. I had that number, but only used it a couple of times because I had to be careful about how frequently I called in favors from the White House staff and the president. I needed to keep some goodwill in reserve in the event my mouth got me in trouble once too often.

So many odd things happened after we completed the evacuations and the search and rescue that it is difficult to remember all of them. A few stick out in my mind, though, as being symbolic of the occasional strangeness of the operation.

On one of my visits to the governor in Baton Rouge I was stopped by an FBI agent who asked if my helicopter was returning to New Orleans. "We've got some shooters we need to put on a building we have to protect," he said. As we boarded the helicopter for the flight back, seven heavily armed, grim-faced FBI agents with night-vision goggles climbed inside. They never said a word from the time we picked them up until we dropped them off atop a building downtown. To this day I don't know what building they were on, why they were there, or how long they stayed.

On Saturday, September 3, the State Department called the Joint Chiefs of Staff at the Pentagon about an issue it had. The message was relayed to my headquarters at Fort Gillem and was then passed on to the Louisiana National Guard with me and a number of other people in the "carbon copy" line. The "high priority message" said that "Dept. of State national security documents of highest level located on 12th and 13th floors of building" at 333 Canal Street. "Soldiers must secure building. No one will enter the building once secured, until authorized personnel arrive to retrieve documents."

I thought those must be some of the most important documents in the Western world for that much emphasis to be placed on their protection. Only later did I learn that the building in question was where passports are processed. There must have been a great deal of concern about terrorists wading through the floodwaters to steal that personal information.

And then on Tuesday, September 6, we received a message that a colonel deployed in Iraq had sent to Fort Hood, Texas. Fort Hood sent the message to Forces Command in Atlanta, which in turn sent it to my headquarters at Camp Shelby, where my staff sent it on to me. Seems this particular colonel's grandmother was in New Orleans and he was worried about her welfare. He provided her name and address and we sent soldiers from the 82nd Airborne and the 45th Brigade to check it out.

After the soldiers found her I received the following message: "Their assessment is that she is 'a tough old bird.' They found her house partially under water. She is living in the home and refused to leave the premises. They provided her food and water and will periodically check in on her since she is in their [area of operations]."

JTF-Katrina's role after the evacuations and rescues was partially to increase the number of enabling tasks we were doing, whether it was ferrying shooters to the top of a building in downtown New Orleans or finding somebody's tough old grandmother in the middle of the floodwaters. Perhaps one of our more gratifying enabling tasks, and the one that probably got the most news coverage, was bringing in the dogs and cats.

On Monday, September 12, Gloria Starr, my secretary at Fort Gillem, sent me a message: "Most all callers are very appreciative of what you and the military are doing, but most also want more to be done for saving the pets . . . I wanted to make sure you were aware that the stranded pets are more of an issue today than they were last Friday when we started receiving phone calls."

Her note was especially timely because as the soldiers were going from house to house on their patrols they were bumping into a lot of pets that had either been abandoned or were just wandering the streets. We received one report that some soldiers were shooting strays. I immediately called the brigade commander and told him we were going to take a big-time ass-whipping if this was true. I was never able to confirm that report but knew if even a hint of it hit the print or TV media we would have People for the Ethical Treatment of Animals and all sorts of animal lovers coming down on us.

I was also getting e-mails from my wife, Beverly, and daughter Kimberly asking me to go to Kim's apartment to see if the cat and a hamster she left there when she went to Florida just before the storm could be rescued. I could not in good conscience use up assets or take the time to run a personal mission like that until long after we had things under control, so Gumbo the cat and Hammie the hamster would just have to wait to be rescued. I could only hope they were not dead by the time I managed to carve out some time to rescue them.

I called back to my chief of staff, Jim Hickey, in Atlanta, and Colonel Chris DeGraff at Camp Shelby and told them we were going to make a statement that from then on the troops would rescue dogs and cats they found abandoned, whether in homes or on the street. We ordered a bunch of cages and dog-catching sticks and they arrived at the New Orleans airport the next morning. The collection point for the animals was Zephyr Field, a minor league baseball stadium in Metairie. After that announcement about saving the pets was made at a news conference, Mrs. Starr said she had seventy or eighty e-mails from people congratulating us on our decision. Animal lovers are networked and will be a friend forever if you look like you are one of them. But they will hang your ass out to dry if they think for one minute that you are not responsive to what they want.

We did not have to make a special effort to rescue dogs and cats. But I know the importance of pets to many people. They become members of the family. Some people risked death in the wake of Katrina by not evacuating simply because they did not want to abandon their pets. Americans put so much emotion into their pets that even before we left New Orleans and disbanded JTF-Katrina we had people saying that in the future we cannot have an evacuation plan, whether federal, state, or local, that does not include pets. Don't fool around with dogs and cats.

And don't make jokes at their expense. At one point we had so many reporters around New Orleans I started telling people that "I can't swing a dead cat without hitting a reporter." When one of my public affairs staff advised that cat lovers might get upset with me for saying that, I changed it to "I can't swing a stick around here without hitting a reporter."

Once I started to get some breathing room I decided it was time to go look for Kimberly's pets. Rick Leventhal of Fox News wanted to go along even though he had no idea where I was going. I didn't want to tell him because if a story about me rescuing animals showed up on television the chief of staff of the Army would have jumped all over me for trying to become a celebrity. But Leventhal persisted and finally I said, "If I take you with me you cannot film any of this." He agreed and we headed out to Kimberly's apartment.

When we finally got there I was relieved to see it had not been flooded. But the complex was absolutely trashed with tree limbs. An oak tree about four feet thick had crashed down on Kimberly's yellow Volkswagen Beetle. The place was really a mess. I was starting to feel sorry for her as we worked our way through the debris when a Honda Accord pulled into the parking lot. In the front was a couple from Indiana. An older woman, possibly the mother of one of them, was in the back crying.

The couple's voices were quivering as they told us they had just driven down from Indiana to look for their daughter. She lived in this complex but they had not seen her or heard from her since the storm and they were worried. It put things into perspective for me. At least I knew where my daughter was and knew she was safe. We gave that family some words of encouragement and moved on. There wasn't much we could do except pray they found their daughter safe in another part of the country.

Kim had locked the door to her second-floor apartment and I did not have a key. The manager of the complex was gone so we had a choice of either breaking down the door or trying to find some other way in. Lieutenant Colonel Rich Steele, my Public Affairs Officer, and my aide, Captain Scott Trahan, finally climbed up to her balcony and discovered she had left the sliding glass door unlocked. They got in that way and unlocked the door for the rest of us.

As soon as we stepped inside we were hit with this overpowering smell of rotting food from the refrigerator. But Gumbo was sitting on the bed patiently waiting and although Hammie was dehydrated and not in good shape we took him along as well. After we locked the door we called Kim to tell her that the animals were safe. Sergeant Major Hill and Rick Leventhal chided her about the messy condition of her apartment, which embarrassed her to no end. Some time later on a trip to Baton Rouge for a meeting, I turned the cat and hamster over to one of my sisters. The cat is still alive but the hamster didn't last too long.

The deeper we got into the operation, the more insistent was the message coming out of Washington that everything we did needed to be documented and watched closely so it did not get lost in the corruption of Louisiana politics. That's a hell of a thing for victims of the storm to hear but that was the prevailing attitude of many people who thought Louisiana was a cesspool of political corruption. That attitude can be understood to some extent, especially when it comes to the 9th Ward. How did that happen? How did these people become so disenfranchised? Was it that donor culture, where people came to be dependent on government assistance and expected it every month? Was it the corruption for which New Orleans and Louisiana politics have long been known? Was it the dysfunctional local governments at the city and parish level?

That aura of, and potential for, corruption made me particularly careful of everything JTF-Katrina did and everyone with whom we dealt. I was representing not only myself but also the U.S. Army and by extension the federal government. It would have been very easy to get caught up in that culture of corruption and there were some things I had the good sense, or the blind, dumb luck, to back away from before they became problems for me or my staff.

The official congressional delegations that started coming to New Orleans were not a major issue, because once we had the Superdome and convention center evacuated and the bulk of the search-and-rescue operations completed we had plenty of people to handle them. It was clear to me that the missions of these delegations were to assess performances across the board and to begin looking for who was at fault for the slow federal response. The primary concern of most members of Congress who came to New Orleans was not the people who had been evacuated, not the people who had lost their homes and most of their worldly possessions. No, instead the focus was on who had screwed up. The Democrats were looking to pin something on President Bush and his administration. Even the Republicans were upset with the pace of the effort and wanted to find someone to blame, especially if it was a Democrat like Governor Blanco or Mayor Nagin. Finding blame was the name of the game.

I was questioned quite extensively by Senator John Warner, of Virginia, a Republican. He was on the Senate Armed Services Committee, the Select Committee on Intelligence, and the Senate Committee on Homeland Security and Governmental Affairs, and he probably knew as much as anybody in government about how the military could and should operate in disasters such as this. He was very interested in my views on federalization and whether in an event such as Katrina it should be done more quickly. He wondered if Congress should consider streamlining the federalization process.

I told him we had gone through that conversation the previous week and that I was aware of scenarios where we should federalize. Those were events involving terrorism, a nuclear or biological weapon, or some incident involving multiple states. I said I understood the law that spelled out when troops should be federalized but that it was worth reviewing. It was even more important to review the policy in the aftermath of Katrina because governors in other states facing catastrophes may look at what happened in Louisiana and be reluctant to ask for federal troops until it's too late.

The following year Warner included wording in the Defense Authorization Act for 2007 that was designed to make it easier for the president to federalize military and law enforcement forces in times of emergency. The new law gave the president the authority to declare martial law if in his opinion a state was unable to properly carry out its law enforcement functions or if a situation was such that it "deprives people of a right, privilege, immunity, or protection named in the Constitution and secured by law or opposes or obstructs the execution of the laws of the United States or impedes the course of justice under those laws." Even to a nonlawyer such as me that wording opened a lot of troublesome doors for the president, the states, and civil libertarians. Governors and local law enforcement agencies pushed back hard on it and in 2008 that language was changed back to the original.

By the end of the third week of post-Katrina operations, FEMA, with Thad Allen at the helm, was functioning more smoothly and with much more discipline. It was working closely with Nagin and the presidents of St. Bernard and Plaquemines parishes to establish their priorities. With Allen coordinating non-DOD activities, including FEMA, my role changed from being a coordinator to more of a collaborator. I was getting clear messages from Northern Command through my public affairs staff: it wanted me to back off and let Allen become the face of the Katrina operation. That was fine with me because the active forces could not do much more with the special skills they brought to the fight. It seemed a good time for JTF-Katrina to pull out of New Orleans and head for home. But before we could do that another major storm started heading our way. Her name was Rita and she appeared to be as big and as nasty as Katrina had been.

CHAPTER 13

Lessons Learned for Building a Culture of Preparedness

1. Don't overstudy the problem. When FEMA, a mayor, or the governor asks for something to be done, just do it. When you are trying to evacuate folks, there is no time to ask lawyers what they think of your plan.

2. Every high-risk large city needs to have a joint search-and-rescue map made. This is vital to synchronize helicopter operations and deconflict air routes.

3. FAA needs to establish restricted airspace over the disaster area. News helicopters and private helicopters bringing in business assessment teams can be a danger to search-and-rescue air efforts.

4. Leaders need to be careful about what they say on television. If you say your city is contaminated, or that there are snipers in your city, this could have second- and third-order effects.

5. Be prepared to take time for congressional visits. If you have a Katrina event, they need to see it so that they can go and budget for the response.

14

Dancing with Rita

ON SEPTEMBER 14, 2005, LESS THAN THREE WEEKS AFTER KATRINA ravaged the Gulf Coast and flooded New Orleans, I was invited to Baton Rouge to listen to a speech by Governor Kathleen Blanco to a joint session of the Louisiana legislature. I felt good about the progress we were making even though parts of the New Orleans were still underwater and the water, sewer, electrical, and communications infrastructure in the southern part of the state was still being stitched together.

Vice Admiral Thad Allen of FEMA and Lieutenant General Steven Blum, head of the National Guard Bureau, had seats with their names on them right up front in the audience. No seat was reserved for me. I stood around until somebody offered me his seat. When Blanco started speaking she thanked FEMA and the National Guard and led the assembly in a standing ovation for Allen and Blum. She never mentioned me or the efforts of the more than twenty thousand federal troops in the state.

It wasn't that she didn't know I was there. I was sitting right in front of her. I talked to her before the speech. I shook hands with her and met her family. But that speech was her way of telling me who the hell I was and what my place was in Louisiana. That was the perception I got from her speech. She wanted to put me in my place.

I thought my relationship with Blanco was good. I don't know to this day if the snub was political or racial. I know she saw me as Bush's guy in New Orleans. But to recognize Blum, who had not even been on the ground and had watched the situation from Washington, was an obvious slap in my face. In my heart I want to believe she ignored me and the federal troops because of the old federal-state friction and not because of my race. But I spent twenty-three years in that state being snubbed because of my race and could not help but think that this was more of the same old crap my family had been hearing for years.

After the speech, several dozen members of the legislature lined up to shake my hand and thank me. I never said anything directly to Blanco about that speech. But I was insulted then and remain upset that she seemed to go out of her way to ignore me and the work done by the active military forces. I met with her several times after that, including as we were moving into position to deal with Hurricane Rita. She even had me to dinner at the governor's mansion and presented me with the Louisiana Legion of Merit. But I thought it best to ignore her speech and push forward because there was still work to do and did not want to let the sense of humiliation I felt interfere with that.

In a late 2007 telephone conversation I had with Blanco informing her of my pending retirement, she told me she appreciated what I had done for the state and for New Orleans but complained even then, more than two years after Katrina, that I did not initially come with enough troops. She did not understand then and still does not understand that bringing in large numbers of troops in those first few days after the storm would have created a logistical nightmare. We were trying to get people out of the city, not in, and we had to build the capacity to do that. She wanted a sizable contingent of federal forces but did not want to federalize the forces that were there. She was conflicted and was having difficulty making decisions, a problem that affected many of the state and local leaders. They were all victims of the storm.

On my fifty-eighth birthday, September 15, 2005, First Army storm watchers back at Fort Gillem began tracking an area of disturbed weather north of Puerto Rico and the Virgin Islands. It was beginning to drift westward, but had no real definition and gave no indications it would become a hurricane. Still, any weather disturbance at that time of the year heading into the warm waters of the Gulf of Mexico has to be watched with concern and suspicion.

By September 18 a tropical depression had formed with seventy-mile-per-hour winds. It was given the name Rita, the seventeenth tropical storm of that busy season. A mandatory evacuation of the Florida Keys was ordered. Two days later, on the morning of September 20, Rita became a full-fledged hurricane and its winds increased to one hundred miles per hour as it pushed through the Florida Straits south of Key West and into the bathtub-warm waters of the Gulf.

As we continued to track the storm and it began to grow—by September 20 the winds were in excess of 140 miles per hour and increasing—our worst fears began to be realized. Rita had the potential of following much the same track as Katrina. It also had the potential to be an even larger and more destructive storm than her older sister. In fact, by September 21, Rita was a full-blown Category 5 hurricane with sustained winds of over 180 miles per hour. It was one of the four most powerful hurricanes ever recorded.

The fear in New Orleans was almost tangible. People who had begun to drift back to their homes were frightened, and rightly so. Those who had weathered Katrina now began to doubt the wisdom of trying to ride out Rita. The governor, the mayor, and the New Orleans city council began verbally sparring over whether to order a mandatory evacuation. That was when the mayor came to me and said he wanted my help in forcing people to leave their homes.

I just shook my head and told him, "I don't have the authority to do that."

All of us knew that a direct hit could undo much of what had been done to dewater the city and start restoring the infrastructure. Even if the eye of the storm missed New Orleans, the rain it dumped would create problems on top of problems. Only this time we had the assets we needed for evacuation; buses were on standby in downtown New Orleans. We were prepared for Rita.

Yet during a news conference on September 20 to talk about preparations for Rita, many of the reporters asked three-week-old questions. They were stuck on Katrina and, to my way of thinking, stuck on stupid. I've been shaped by the military writings of the German strategist Clausewitz, and generals George Patton and Douglas MacArthur. But I've also been shaped by the blues and country music. Thoughts from songs that I've listened to for years creep into my head on occasion and sometimes come flying out of my mouth when I least expect it. That's what happened during that news conference about our preparations for Rita. I kept trying to tell reporters about what we were doing to evacuate people in the event the storm made landfall in southern Louisiana but some of them kept asking why we had not done this for Katrina.

"You're asking last-storm questions for people who are concerned about the future storm. Don't get stuck on stupid, reporters. We're moving forward," I admonished them.

But one reporter persisted. "General," he began, "a little bit more about why that's happening this time, though it did not happen last time . . ."

At that point I wanted to make my point perfectly clear. I turned to look at him, pointed my finger, and said sharply, "You are stuck on stupid. I'm not going to answer that question . . . Let's talk about the future. Rita is happening."

I had heard the song "(I'd Have to Be) Stuck on Stupid," by Blues singer Shirley Brown, when I was puttering around in my garden back in Atlanta before the storm and the words stuck with me. The context I used the phrase in, though, was not about the relationship between a man and a woman. My concern was getting the media to focus on what was happening at that moment, not what happened three weeks earlier. We could examine the past at a later date. At that moment it was time to look at today and the future and what we had to do to be proactive on the next storm. That was one of my key leadership teaching points—keeping people focused on the future and moving forward, and not looking back until the appropriate time to do so.

As Rita continued to plow through the Gulf it appeared more and more that it would move northwest and hit either southwest Louisiana or southeast Texas. Northern Command put out an order establishing a Joint Operations Area that set an imaginary north-south line just west of Baton Rouge. JTF-Katrina was to control everything east of the line. Fifth Army had everything west of the line. Northern Command said it would control Navy assets and send them where it thought they might be most needed.

In the meantime, the Navy forces that were part of JTF-Katrina and the Coast Guard collaborated and came up with their own plan. The Navy, which had its ships already floating back out to sea, was to handle everything east of the Sabine River, which forms part of the boundary between Texas and Louisiana. The Coast Guard had everything west of the river. It thought the big fight after the storm would be in the Galveston-Houston area and the Coasties wanted to be the first on the scene there.

On September 22, I met with Blanco again and provided her the details of the instructions I had received from Northern Command. She was not at all pleased with that news. She said she wanted me to be in charge of the federal response for all of Louisiana. She did not want to deal with another JTF that had its primary focus in Texas. I saluted and marched on and let her work out the jurisdictional issues with FEMA, DOD, and Northern Command.

Northern Command had gone into a deliberative mode at this point and wanted me to wait and see what the storm did before moving any assets. But I did not want to wait for the approval from a staff officer in Colorado Springs before moving some of the task force to where it could provide the most assistance. The Northern Command staffers pulled out their 1,200-mile screwdrivers and went to work on me. But I said that as long as we were in the state we were going to be on the scene when the storm hit.

On the morning of the 23rd my staff and I headed for Lafayette, Louisiana, about fifty-five miles west of Baton Rouge on Interstate 10. While en route I called Bill Caldwell, the commander of the 82nd Airborne, and told him to move his soldiers to Lafayette to prepare for Rita. The 82nd was getting ready to redeploy to Fort Bragg but before dark on the 23rd, Caldwell had a brigade and all its equipment positioned in Lafayette. Those 82nd Airborne troopers were incredibly nimble.

In Lafayette we took up residence in the 256th Brigade's headquarters across the road from the airport and hunkered down for the night. Before we secured our satellite communications inside the armory I received a call from Lieutenant Governor Mitch Landrieu asking for an aircraft to move the critically ill from Lake Charles Memorial Hospital. I worked with my staff in Atlanta and Northern Command and got the mission accomplished just before the winds got too strong to fly in.

I spent that evening with the men of consequence from Lafayette and Lake Charles talking about the level of their preparations. We were treated to a great seafood and Cajun feast at Prejean's restaurant before the storm came ashore, and we returned to the armory at about 10 P.M. By that time it was raining in sheets and the wind was blowing about fifty miles per hour. Everyone carved out a little spot for themselves to get a few hours' sleep. I lay on a cot but never slept. It reminded me too much of my youth and those nights we spent listening to the hurricanes pass over and around us, pelting our old wooden house with rain that often seeped through the cracks in the walls while the winds shook the tin roof in the darkness.

The rain we received from Rita was the first that fell on New Orleans and southern Louisiana in nearly a month. It was as if Katrina had sucked all the moisture out of the atmosphere. The good weather let us work uninterrupted through the search and rescue and the evacuations. It was almost as if Mother Nature gave us a little break. That was a good thing, though, because people were miserable enough. More rain would have added insult to injury.

Shortly after 2 A.M. on the 24th, Rita came ashore between Sabine Pass, Texas, and Johnson Bayou, Louisiana. Its intensity had dropped significantly as it approached the coast and by landfall was down to a Category 3 storm with winds of 115 miles per hour. It was not nearly the storm it had once been, or that we feared it would be, but it was still a nasty lady.

By midmorning the next day we were up and moving south by road through Lake Charles and Calcasieu Parish into Cameron Parish, which is in the southwestern most corner of Louisiana and had taken a pretty good beating from the wind and rain. Officials there did excellent work evacuating most of the residents. But Cameron Parish is sparsely populated and it is easier for people to leave there than it is for people to evacuate New Orleans.

On the way down I called Rear Admiral Joe "Killer" Kilkenny, who was in charge of all the Navy assets in JTF-Katrina. Kilkenny said the Navy was already at work rescuing people. They had plucked more than a hundred from Pelican Island, one of the barrier islands off the Louisiana coast.

"We came in like surfers on a surfboard following the storm in and it was a hell of a ride," he said. "We also have seven hundred or eight hundred sick Marines on this ship."

This once again was a clear demonstration that the active forces, whether Navy, Army, Marine or Air Force, could do a great deal more good if they were in position before a storm hit. The Navy put out to sea and weathered Rita in deep water but was prepared to head in and do what it could as soon as the wind and waves died down. A brigade of the 82nd Airborne and my staff were on the ground within easy driving distance of where the storm hit nearly a day before it made landfall. We did not have to wait for the governor to make a request to DOD. We were already there.

In addition to the active forces available for duty after Rita, the 256th Combat Brigade from the Louisiana Army National Guard redeployed home after nearly a year in Iraq and was ready to help. Among them was my son, Sergeant Michael Honoré. He flew directly from Iraq to Alexandria, Louisiana, and the following day picked up my second command-and-control vehicle and drove it to Lafayette. The satellite telephone communications in the first vehicle had gone out as a result of the rain. He and other members of the 256th made an immediate transition from combat operations in Iraq to preparations and response for Hurricane Rita in their home state.

On the way to Cameron Parish we decided to stop in Lake Charles and see the mayor, Randy Roach. We heard there had been some flooding in the city so we went to the courthouse, which also served as the parish EOC. No lights were on in the building. Outside the courthouse was a small generator on a platform about eight feet off the ground. It was too small to do much of a job but at least it was off the ground, which was good. Not even the New Orleans Police Department had put its emergency generator somewhere other than the ground floor. During Katrina it got flooded and was useless. Nearly three years later it was still at ground level.

At least in Lake Charles there was some sense of a culture of preparedness. But as I looked around it became apparent the generator was far too small for a city that is right in hurricane alley. Lake Charles has a large oil refinery, a casino, and a major basketball arena. It is an economic engine in that part of the state and sits right off the interstate, but officials had done little to make adequate preparations other than the evacuation for the storm.

I went into the courthouse and saw the mayor and the homeland security chief. They were happy to see me because I represented a quick infusion of federal money and assets.

"Okay, general," the homeland security chief said, "here's what I need. I need gas for police cars."

I could not believe what I was hearing and went off on him. "What the hell are you talking about?" I said. "You make gas for the world."

He said the man they usually purchased their gas from had evacuated. I asked if it had not occurred to him to think ahead and have a truck full of gas parked where they could get to it after the storm. By this time I had just about had it with the donor culture of people standing there with their hands out waiting for the government to do everything for them.

"Why didn't you tell me this yesterday when we were in Lafayette?" I said.

"The disaster hadn't hit yet. I couldn't spend any FEMA money then," he replied.

I called back to Lafayette and asked that a gas truck be sent to Lake Charles. This was amateur hour. At one point the chief of the parish council wanted to close the interstate highway through the city because he was concerned about people coming in to loot or people coming back early when there was no electricity. I told him I did not have the authority to do that and did not think he had the authority to disrupt travel on a federal highway. He asked the sheriff to block the state roads going into Lake Charles. I finally called Colonel Henry Whitehorn, commander of the Louisiana State Police, and he convinced Lake Charles officials they could not close the highway.

We finally left Lake Charles and pushed our way down to Cameron Parish with state police leading the way. At the parish line we saw police officers blocking the road with an old M114 armored reconnaissance vehicle. Seeing something like that sitting in the middle of the road is a sure sign that beyond there, things must really be bad.

As we drove west on state Highway 14 and then south on Highway 27 all we could see was the top of the road. Everything else was underwater. Dead alligators and dead cattle were lying in the shallows on both sides of the road. And scattered everywhere, on the road, in the water, hanging from power lines, fence lines, and trees were these large, black balls of fur. As we got closer we could see they were nutria rats, which live in the swamps and bayous. Some were the size of small dogs.

After driving about thirty or forty minutes we came to the Cameron Prairie National Wildlife Refuge. We got out of the vehicle and walked across a wooden plank walkway to the visitor's center. Smaller Louisiana parishes have as their governing bodies what are referred to as parish police juries. They function much like county commissions but are a remnant of French influence from centuries earlier. The president of the Cameron Police Jury was a man by the name of Scott Trahan, the same as my aide, Captain Scott Trahan. They chatted briefly but quickly discovered they were not related.

Freddie Richard, Jr., the director of the Cameron Parish Office of Emergency Preparedness, also was there. The parish, the two officials told us, was cut in half by the floodwaters from the hurricane.

We asked if they needed anything, and they just looked out over the landscape and thought for a moment. Virtually everything was underwater. They said they could use some food and water to sustain them for a while. By that time Brigadier General Doug Pritt of the 41st Infantry Brigade from the Oregon National Guard, which had been assigned to work Lake Charles and points south, had found me, as had my helicopter. We coordinated for Pritt to push some food and water to Cameron Parish and I asked Lieutenant Colonel Rose, my operations officer, to go back to the Lake Charles airport to pick up a short-term supply of food and water.

Pritt went back to the airport separately to pick up a larger supply and told me later that when he got there he saw a bunch of trucks and a bunch of trailers separated from one another. Drivers were sitting in the trucks as if they were waiting for something. When Pritt started looking in one of the trailers for MREs and water, someone came out of a travel trailer and asked what he was doing. Pritt said he was looking for supplies to take down to Cameron Parish.

"Okay, we'll send it down there," the guy told him, "but I'm going to have to find the trucks first."

The trucks were just sitting there waiting for the trailers to be hooked up to them. So Pritt went over to one of the drivers and said, "What are you doing here?"

And the driver replied, "We're waiting to haul stuff for FEMA." Talk about a dysfunctional organization. But this was typical of the bureaucratic blunders I saw throughout Katrina and Rita.

When Rose returned with a helicopter load of food and water I turned to Trahan and Richard and told them, "Boys, the Lord is going to descend on you. You're going to have some stuff coming in here because we want to make sure you have everything you need."

Within an hour another helicopter landed with a FEMA assessment team. I was talking to Thad Allen on the phone at the time and he asked, "Russ, how the hell did you get there so quick?"

"I was here ahead of the storm and the Navy has already been in here doing rescues," I replied.

"Do you see any of my people there yet?"

"Even as we speak, they are landing."

I hung up the phone and waited as the FEMA rep got off the helicopter. She never made eye contact with me but asked, "Who's in charge?"

Scott Trahan turned to her and said, "I'm Scott Trahan and I'm the parish president and this is Freddie Richard, our emergency management director."

"I'm from FEMA," the woman said, "and I'm here to do an assessment of what your needs are."

Trahan looked at her for a second and then got a big smile on his face. "You're too damn late," he told her. "General Honoré is here and he has given us everything we need."

I told her I would send Thad Allen a full report and that she was needed more in Lake Charles, where there was a larger population. So she got back on the helicopter and headed for Lake Charles.

Later that day I received word that President Bush planned to come to southwestern Louisiana on Tuesday, September 27, to assess the damage Rita had done. I headed back to Lafayette to set up shop there. Marc Mouton, a disaster relief official and city councilman who was working with us in Lafayette, found one of the few vacant motel rooms available in Lafayette for me. But after only a few days the motel manager came to me and said I had to leave. He told me the University of Louisiana at Lafayette Ragin' Cajuns football team had a home game that weekend and the room was reserved for fans coming in.

Here we were in the wake of two major hurricanes with people still living in school gymnasiums and basketball arenas and those not affected by the storms were focusing on football. The whole Gulf Coast was worried about football games. The amount of energy that sport consumes is just crazy. It's out of control. And that goes on four months out of the year. The number of senior leaders in any given state, especially in the South, who are out of position on football weekends frightens me. Government provides a completely different response if something happens during the week than if it happens over a weekend. On weekends the C students are in charge. I was in my headquarters every day. Where were these guys?

Every time I go to church I pray, "God, please don't let a hurricane strike on a Saturday during football season." We'll all be screwed if it does.

The president got an aerial tour of Cameron Parish on the 27th because it was still too rough to drive in. From the air, the mostly rural parish looked even worse than it did from the ground. The parish was a veritable war zone. What little had been there was washed away or blown to bits. The physical destruction was unbelievable. The one building that survived was the courthouse in Cameron, built in the 1930s by the Works Progress Administration to the one-hundred-year floodplain; it sat ten feet off the ground.

After the brief tour Bush met with some of the local mayors. It was obvious from their conversations with him that they were expecting miracles from the federal government. He wasn't responsible for officials not having enough gasoline or generators or high-water vehicles. He wasn't responsible for their lack of planning. He wasn't responsible for the media not flocking to southwestern Louisiana as they had done to New Orleans. But the mayors were complaining to him about all those issues and more. Finally, he said to them, "General Honoré is here. Tell him what you need and he'll get it to you." And with that JTF-Katrina got the mission to help the Rita victims.

At one point during the Rita operations I got roped into saving some livestock. I was out somewhere in Cameron Parish the week after the storm and these five farmers said to me, "General, you want to go out and ride with us? We are finding cattle and dropping hay for them. But the problem is that all the water around them is now salt water. And when cattle drink salt water they get mean. So all these cows now have an attitude."

They were not talking about your normal dairy cows, though. They were talking about huge Brahma bulls. Those Louisiana cowboys were going after them with airboats, four-wheel drive vehicles, and horses because those cattle are their livelihood. Being a farmboy at heart I decided to join them and they gave me a little mare named Strawberry Wine to ride. I thought I was doing pretty well until one of the cowboys said, "Okay, General, go down there and rope that calf and bring it back."

I had told them all about growing up on a Louisiana farm but it had been thirty-seven years since I put a rope on anything. I said to myself: "This may be a little above my skills level."

I called to these guys in an airboat and said, "That looks a little deep for me over there. You guys better go get that calf." I didn't put a rope on anything the whole day but I successfully negotiated my way around there on that little mare. I had the best time riding around with those Cajun cowboys because they were not looking for handouts; they were helping themselves.

I knew it was time to leave Louisiana when a lawyer told me we could not use a helicopter to save some cattle. If people lost cattle they could request compensation for those losses from FEMA. In some cases it appeared that people took excessive risks with their cattle and other property knowing there was this big government reimbursement umbrella that protected them.

I heard one rancher talking about how he had three hundred head of cattle before the storm but could only round up about one hundred after it. But another rancher whispered in my ear that this guy never owned more than one hundred cattle in his life. Did he file for compensation for those two hundred head of phantom cattle? I don't know, but a lot of people found a lot of ways to get money from the government.

One of the more unusual issues the task force dealt with after Rita was the floating caskets that popped out of their burial vaults. They were all over the place in southern Louisiana. Some of them had hoofprints on top and when I asked what those were all about I was informed that during floods cows will try to get on top of the burial vaults to get out of the water and will end up popping the lids. When the water rises, the caskets float out.

We had to call in the DMORT because we wanted to make sure that Aunt Nellie was reburied in Aunt Nellie's grave. That task was anything but simple. The DMORT soldiers had to take the caskets to Lake Charles to do DNA testing so they and state officials could figure out which body should be returned to which grave. That was one of the most complex pieces we had to deal with.

I kept saying to myself the whole time I was in Cameron Parish, "We can do better than this. Why do we wait until the day after the storm to figure out we need gas? Why do we not have a generator big enough to power the whole courthouse? We live in a hurricane-prone area. Why aren't we better prepared?"

The houses in Cameron Parish that survived Rita were built just slightly higher than the surrounding ground. The folks who lived in those houses were back in no time. The people who built slab on grade, like so many in New Orleans, came home to water and muck up to their ankles and higher. All it would have taken to avoid many of these problems was a little planning, a little foresight, and a little dedication to the culture of preparedness within each family and community.

Whose responsibility is it to ensure that a house is built a few feet above the floodplain? The individual homeowner? The local government? The federal government? It is first and foremost the individual homeowner who bears that responsibility. But if he does not do it, should the government be obligated to pay damages if the home is flooded? Why punish all the taxpayers for the lack of planning and preparation of a few?

Or should the federal government mandate that homes and businesses in flood- and hurricane-prone areas be built to certain standards that will give them a fighting chance even in the worst of disasters? At what point do federal government mandates become draconian? And is that a proper role for the federal government?

These are all questions that have to be dealt with and answered to the satisfaction of federal, state, and local officials, as well as every American at risk of being a victim of a disaster, which essentially is all of us. Until we start confronting these issues, we will never be able to create a true culture of preparedness in this country.

The federal response to Rita showed me how it could serve as a template for future disasters. There was no reason we could not do elsewhere what we did in southern Louisiana. We brought in assets early and put them near the edge of the storm, and were ready to go to work within hours, rather than days, after the storm blew through. It seemed a reasonable approach to the disaster relief. What I did not anticipate when we tried to implement that approach just a few weeks later, as Hurricane Wilma approached Florida, was the pushback from National Guard commanders and from the politicians who were listening to their Guard commanders. Unfortunately, by taking that position they put their citizens at risk.

CHAPTER 14
Lessons Learned for Building a Culture of Preparedness

1. You must understand state and local government. In small towns, counties, or parishes, the mayor and homeland security are part-time positions and the sheriff may be the principal decision maker. At the state level some principals—for example, the attorney general or the secretary of agriculture—do not work for the governor and may be from a different political party.

2. The governor is in charge. Everyone coming to help must understand that. All agencies coming to help are subordinate to the governor of the state. What members of Congress say is important but on this team the governor is the owner, general manager, head coach, and quarterback. Everybody else is on the team.

15

Wilma: Twisted Sister Number Three

ON LABOR DAY IN 1935, ONE OF THE MOST POWERFUL HURRICANES ever to hit the United States mainland came ashore in the Florida Keys. It packed sustained winds in excess of 185 miles per hour and pushed ahead of it a storm surge estimated at twenty feet. It was stronger than 1992's Hurricane Andrew, a Category 5 storm that killed sixty-five people and did more than $26 billion in damage in South Florida.

Living and working in temporary camps in the Florida Keys that summer of 1935 were hundreds of World War I veterans who had been run out of Washington by federal troops after seeking bonus money they had been promised years earlier. The veterans were lured to Florida by the promise of jobs building a highway and a railway line from Miami to Key West.

As Labor Day approached, warnings went out that a powerful storm was headed for the Keys but officials in charge of the camps delayed shipping the vets out of the danger zone. The trucks that could have carried them to safety were locked up for the weekend. A train sent from Miami arrived too late to make the return trip north and became a victim of the storm.

More than four hundred people died in that hurricane, among them at least 259 World War I veterans. The federal government absolved itself of any blame, as did the state of Florida. Both decided the warnings issued had been sufficient and called the deaths "an act of God" even though both governments were responsible for the welfare of these veterans, most of whom knew nothing about the power of hurricanes. It was one of the early examples of Florida officials believing they knew best how to deal with the annual storms but it is an attitude that persists in that state to this day.

In mid-October 2005, Hurricane Wilma embarked on a meandering path across the Caribbean. It moved slowly westward and blossomed into a Category 5 storm before raking the Yucatan Peninsula and turning northeast into the superheated waters of the Gulf of Mexico. It picked up speed as it rumbled across the open waters in search of the Florida coast. I had been back in my headquarters in Atlanta for little more than two weeks before Wilma, which was more powerful than either Katrina or Rita, began to bear down on Florida.

My staff and I immediately went to work to implement the Rita model of disaster preparedness. We looked at federal facilities in the state where we could send troops ahead of the storm while we asked for Navy ships to be off the coast to provide post-strike support. If this storm was as dangerous as it appeared, Florida would need a lot of help and the more federal assets we could put on the left side of the disaster the better off the state would be on the right side. My boss, General Dan McNeill, decided that if the storm hit he wanted Fifth Army, under the command of Lieutenant General Robert Clark, to deal with Wilma and that First Army would support him.

I called Fifth Army headquarters and asked that Brigadier General Mark Graham, who had been my deputy on JTF-Katrina, be sent to St. Petersburg, where I had picked out a building suitable for a headquarters. I sent some members from my staff down there and then got in touch with Northern Command to check on its plans. It had twelve helicopters ready to preposition in Florida and had given a warning order to a Navy battle group to be prepared to assist after Wilma hit.

I also called The Adjutant General of the Florida National Guard, Major General Douglas Burnett, to check on his preparations. What he told me was a stunning revelation of how jealously Florida was guarding its turf.

"The governor's position," Burnett said, "is that any of this stuff that comes to Florida would be under my command."

That may have been what the governor wanted but that was not the way things worked in the real world.

"Doug," I told him, "the current rule is that DOD is not going to put an Army active-duty division or Navy task force under your command. It's just not going to happen. What we will do now is create [an active-duty] commander based on the size and scope of the storm and he will come in and work in support of you and FEMA."

We continued moving in that direction until we received word from the Pentagon to stand down. We were not to put any additional active troops into the state. We were not to have ships standing by to assist. The word from Florida was "We can handle it on our own."

Florida officials apparently had pulled some strings in Washington. They felt the Florida National Guard, with its Emergency Management Assistance Compacts (EMACs) with other states, could handle the situation. No federal help was needed or wanted. That was the message that came back to me. It was typical of what I had been hearing for years. The state had been through so many hurricanes that officials there believed they knew better than anyone else how to handle them. They could do it themselves. So we stood down and waited and watched and prayed that the storm would not be as severe as it was threatening to be.

Wilma's strength dissipated as it approached land and it hit the west coast of Florida near Naples on October 24 as a Category 3 instead of the Category 5 it had been. It churned its way across the southern end of the peninsula, cut Interstate 95, and left more than six million people without electricity. Some had to go without power for more than two weeks.

Two days after the storm, Burnett called and said he was trying to get some C-5 aircraft to fly in food. We had gone through so many MREs during Katrina and Rita that we had none immediately available for victims of Wilma. But Burnett said he had found some prepackaged meals in Texas. So we sent those C-5s to Texas to pick up the meals at a cost to taxpayers of tens of thousands of dollars. If we had been allowed to prepare on the left side of the disaster as we tried, additional food and water would already have been in the state.

That raised a big question in my mind. If Florida is so well prepared for hurricanes and did not need any federal help, where were their stocks of prepositioned food? Why had no one thought to store food ahead of the storm so it could be retrieved in a hurry after it hit? Florida officials were not thinking of preparation and the left side of the disaster; they were still attuned to response and to the right side.

Florida scares the hell out of me for two reasons. First, my daughter, her husband, and my grandchild live there, as well as my youngest daughter, Kimberly. State officials have not done enough to develop a culture of preparedness and that easily could affect my immediate family. Second, the people in that state are very obstinate about evacuating. They are reluctant to leave their homes or condominiums for any reason, even a major hurricane. That's an attitude that goes back decades. The people in the Florida Keys often refuse to evacuate ahead of a storm. There was an extremely low evacuation rate for all the storms that hit Florida in 2004. New Orleans and the Mississippi coast had an evacuation rate of about 80 percent for Katrina but Florida cities have never come close to that.

That is why there is such a great potential for a storm with the power of Katrina to have a significant impact in Florida. The state generally does the right things. The government has the capabilities and is well organized. The National Guard is superb and led by a very competent commander in Doug Burnett. The problem is that the culture of the people is to not evacuate. Many residents are just too complacent about hurricanes. The Labor Day storm of 1935 is ancient history. Even Andrew was a long time ago.

Wilma was not a major storm. The only federal assets we used during Wilma were those cargo aircraft that brought in the food. The water, sewer, electricity, and telephone communications came back slowly but were minor inconveniences compared to what the people in New Orleans had to deal with after Katrina.

But what the pre-Wilma drama between federal and state officials once again demonstrated was the long-standing friction between them. Those turf battles are constant. They exist even among different federal agencies. Everybody wants to be in charge and nobody wants to take the blame when things go wrong. If we are to create a true culture of preparedness in this country, those turf battles have to end. Clear lines of responsibility have to be drawn outside the political arena in order for such a plan to be implemented and for it to work.

I wanted to be able to emulate for every hurricane or other natural disaster our ability to get to the left side of the event as we did for Rita. I've always been reluctant to say how much better we did for Rita than for Katrina because the situations were totally different. For Rita, we were already in the state with federal troops and thousands of National Guard soldiers. I was in the area hardest hit by Rita four hours after the storm went through. It took me twenty-four hours to get into Mississippi after Katrina.

Still, the Rita model is where I see the future, especially with megacities. If we are looking at a storm that is likely to hit Miami in three or four days, we need to move federal resources to the edge of the city and hunker down so we can get to work as soon as the winds die down. That's in direct opposition to what happened in Louisiana when the governor said: "We got it. We got it. We . . . oh, shit."

When they say that, it becomes the president's problem and he takes the heat for state and local officials hesitating to bring in federal assets.

Before Rita hit Texas, state officials there said they did not need any federal troops. They ended up looking like heroes because the storm was not that bad. It worked there. If it had been Katrina-like and swamped Galveston or Houston or both, I have no doubts the governor of Texas would have been on the telephone to Washington demanding immediate assistance and complaining to the media that the federal government was too slow in responding.

If federal assets can be moved in early enough, problems on the right side of the disaster can get tamped down a lot quicker and they won't become national issues. I like being on the offensive. But that's leaning way to the left side of the disaster and doing something before it happens. The Stafford Act discourages that kind of thinking. For two years prior to Katrina I tried to get naval forces afloat into position to move in right after a storm. I was not successful until Rita. What many people do not realize is that rescue assets can move in by sea a lot more quickly than by land or by air.

The present disaster response system is based on the "pull" model of operations. An event happens, local authorities ask for help, and that help is pulled into the area. We have to base our response more on the "push" model. If we see an event about to occur we push resources into the area ahead of it. I do not know why it is so difficult for so many people in state and federal government to understand that. It's a basic concept of good planning and preparation.

The Atlantic and Gulf coasts have a number of vulnerable cities. Why wait to get resources in there? Why wait for a request from the governor through FEMA? Why wait until we start getting news reports about people needing food and water and people dying? Get on it early. Preposition assets. We cannot prevent hurricanes. However, we can limit the adverse effects they have on people and communities.

When we see a Category 5 storm heading for Florida we need to do a Rita plan and prepare for it. We need to assume the electricity is going to be out. We need to assume the cell towers are going to go down. We need to assume we're not going to be able to pump gas or make telephone calls. So why not bring in the satellite communications, put them in a well-protected structure, and then as soon as the storm passes bring out the system so communications can be reestablished within hours instead of days? Recovery moves in a positive direction much more quickly that way.

But being proactive can be an expensive proposition and state and local governments generally will not spend the money necessary to do it. There is a great reluctance to fund a "What if?" worst-case scenario. That's a risk they would rather not take because politicians are more concerned about this scenario happening: a Category 2 or Category 3 storm is heading for a highly populated area. Hundreds of thousands of dollars are spent evacuating people from retirement homes and assisted-living facilities. More money is spent bringing in federal assets. Then the storm doesn't hit and people start complaining about all the money that was wasted.

But what would people rather do? Move those people who can't move themselves and keep them safe? Or let them stay where they are and run the risk that after the storm many of them will be dead, like the elderly and infirm at St. Rita's Nursing Home in St. Bernard Parish, where more than thirty people died in Katrina's floodwaters?

For most financially strapped state and local governments there is no money to budget for three or four evacuations that could take place every year in hurricane-prone areas. This is the sort of thing that calls for a collaborative effort. This is where the insurance companies need to get involved because they can either pay to help move people or they can pay the life insurance when they die. Which is cheaper? We've got to reduce this from a gamble to a risk. There are going to be times when we evacuate people and the storm is not going to mature. That's a risk. But I would rather take that risk than the gamble of leaving people in place to die.

The other question is, should we have retirement homes and assisted-living centers near the coast, where they are particularly vulnerable to hurricanes? Should we have those homes and hospitals just a few miles from the water? That is something communities need to consider, although it is intuitively obvious to me that those homes should not be placed near the water. Granny doesn't need to be watching the beach. She's had her shot at that. She needs to be in a safe and secure environment. She can be taken to the beach once a week or once a month. Putting those homes near the water is gambling with lives.

Local governments have to be involved in disaster preparedness and so do private businesses and the insurance companies. All it takes are some minor preparations and some foresight. Any number of little things can be done to mitigate the damage and help people recover more quickly. That was something I learned from Rita. I learned as many lessons from that storm as from Katrina because I was more of an actor in Rita. I got a better feel for the art of what can be done to reduce or eliminate many of the post-storm problems.

What I saw in New Orleans was the flood. What I saw in Mississippi was the storm damage on the coast and a lot of structures that got chewed up. What I saw in Rita, especially in Cameron Parish, was that small things can be done to reduce the impact of the storm on people and property.

That's the same for those who live in the 7th and 9th wards of New Orleans. It's not that people should not be allowed to live there, as some commentators have suggested. People can live there, but there must be building codes that mandate houses be raised a certain height above ground level so that if the city floods the damage can be minimized. People can live there if they build to that standard and accept the risk that every once in a while they are going to have to live through a flood. They can accept the risk, but it does not have to be a gamble.

Extensive disaster preparations cost a little more and are a little more inconvenient. But it is one of the ways homeowners in disaster-prone areas can get to the left side of the disaster. They can prepare. When people do not prepare properly for disasters, is it because of ignorance or stupidity? Ignorance can be fixed; stupidity is for life.

CHAPTER 15

Lessons Learned for Building a Culture of Preparedness

1. "Leaning forward," the first effort of any army going to battle, is to first get there. Deploy ASAP. The president and the governor will make the decisions on employment after deployment.

2. We can and should do a better job in prepositioning assets prior to the storm's arrival.

3. The federal government can position equipment, people, and supplies prior to hurricanes and floods, and away from fire areas, before the event becomes a disaster.

4. FEMA should not be trying to run a supply chain distribution system. This should be done by people who do this every day. FEMA should be involved, but this is best handled by businesses that do it every day rather than a few times a year.

5. DOD, the National Guard, and Northern Command need to figure out procedures for federal forces to go to a state and work smoothly with and for the adjutant general without interference from the National Guard Bureau. We need a system for disasters where the federal forces can be under the operational control of the governor in order to save lives.

16

The "E" in *E-mail* Stands for Evidence

I HAD BEEN BACK IN MY OFFICE AT FIRST ARMY HEADQUARTERS IN Atlanta just a few days when word reached me that congressional investigators wanted to see all my e-mails from my tenure as commander of Joint Task Force–Katrina. The tone of the request gave me the impression that members of Congress were suspicious about what we did and how we did it. In Richard Nixon's day, secret tape recordings enabled investigators to track down who knew what and when they knew it. In this era, e-mails and cell phone text messages leave an electronic footprint that is easy to follow.

Some people in the Pentagon were upset with me because I had not always followed protocol and had been a little too high-profile for their liking. My relations with the congressional delegations that came to New Orleans were generally good, and they gave me no reason to believe I had done anything criminal or had violated my oath as an officer in the U.S. Army. In my heart I felt we had done the best possible job under the circumstances. I was proud of how the military personnel under my command had responded and believed the people we assisted appreciated our efforts because we were constantly getting thanks from them.

It was made clear that at some point I would be called before the House or Senate or both to testify under oath about our operations. There was always an undercurrent of concern about whether there may be a disconnect between testimony and what investigators could show I said or did through e-mail or text messages. My objective was to tell the truth but what I remember having said or written in a text message or e-mail may not have been what it actually was. If there was a general lack of consistency between the two, people were likely to get suspicious of me.

My staff went to work doing the after-action reports and lessons learned for higher headquarters as soon as we returned from New Orleans. I tried to refocus my energies on training National Guard and Reserve troops for Iraq and Afghanistan. At the same time my staff was involved in the rather complicated process of handing Fifth Army the nationwide responsibility for disaster assistance and preparedness. First Army would take on the job of training National Guard and Army Reserve soldiers from throughout the United States except for Alaska and Hawaii. Fifth Army would get the role of defense support to civilian agencies.

The decision to do this came a year earlier than expected. The chief of staff of the Army wanted a three-star headquarters dedicated to Northern Command for disaster response for the entire continental United States. I did not think this was a good idea and pushed back hard on it. In my way of thinking it was the wrong way to create a culture of preparedness among those National Guard leaders who would be called on to respond to disasters. Under the new system all the relationships that First Army leaders developed during the training cycles would be lost and the effectiveness of the response in times of disaster could be the worse for it. I lost that battle and eventually had to bring all the National Guard and Reserve units west of the Mississippi under the First Army training umbrella.

Within a month of my return from Katrina, a team of four Senate investigators, Republican as well as Democrat, came to interview me with a court reporter in tow. It can be a little intimidating any time investigators show up and make you swear under oath that you are telling the truth. I told them I would tell the truth as I saw it, although other people may have different versions of that truth. The truth can sometimes be relative depending where you are sitting. If you were in Baton Rouge or Washington, D.C., during Katrina you had a completely different view than if you were at the Superdome seeing the frustration in people's faces and smelling the unwashed bodies and human waste. Your perspective was different if you were spending eighteen-hour days in the air-conditioned Pentagon watching events unfold on television than if you were slogging through the 7th or 9th ward in suffocating heat smelling the dead bodies, rotten garbage, and stagnant water.

Those investigators had the luxury of being able to zero in on a particular day, hour, and minute from the perspectives of many different people and ask specific questions about that moment. They often asked leading questions about something someone else had said or done and wanted to know what I knew about it. Often they would preface their questions with "Someone from FEMA said . . ." or "It was reported in the media that . . ." and then ask me what I knew about it.

I was specifically asked about the charge by Philip Parr, FEMA's deputy Federal Coordinating Officer for Katrina, that I canceled the helicopter evacuation of people from the Superdome. I told the investigators I did not have the authority to cancel that. All I did was give my best military advice and that advice was that the Coast Guard helicopters would better serve the people of New Orleans by doing search-and-rescue missions, not evacuations from the Superdome. Buses, not helicopters, were the preferred method of evacuation because they could take more people out more quickly. We simply did not have enough helicopters to both save lives and do evacuations. The number-one priority was to save lives of those people most at risk. The people at the Superdome were miserable because of the heat and lack of hot food, cold water, and sanitary facilities. But they were foot-dry and not at risk of drowning.

They also asked a lot of questions about Mike Brown, specifically my interactions with him and my thoughts about him. I told them I personally had no problems with him but that Brown came into Katrina over-confident because he had successfully dealt with the storms in Florida the year before. Katrina simply overwhelmed that confidence and his ability to handle the storm. Brown and FEMA were not able to deal with the impact of the storm as quickly as people thought they should. Somebody was going to be blamed for that and as the leader Mike Brown bore the burden of responsibility that is part of being a leader.

How the investigators approached issues and often how they asked questions seemed to depend on what political party they came from. Republicans implied it was the governor and mayor who screwed things up. Democrats implied it was FEMA and the president who screwed it up.

I spent six hours being grilled by those Senate staffers. They were tough but thorough and there was a definite deliberateness to the manner in which they went about their business despite the political implications of some of the questions. That thoroughness was reflected in the final report issued by the Senate in May 2006, *Hurricane Katrina: A Nation*

Still Unprepared. It was balanced and addressed many of the issues that
needed to be addressed regarding federal response to disasters.

The only other federal agency to question me about the DOD
response to Katrina was the Government Accountability Office. The
House of Representatives, which did its own investigation, never questioned me once. Its report, *A Failure of Initiative,* issued in February 2006,
seemed to have been hastily assembled with little interest in interviewing the actual participants. Instead the House report seemed to rely to a
great extent on newspaper clippings, broadcast reports, and testimony
from angry National Guard colonels and lower-ranking FEMA staffers.
The House report took shots in all directions, including a number at
me even though its investigators never interviewed me. When there's
very little chance of getting shot it's easy to shoot in any direction. That
report never gave any of us who got shot at a chance to shoot back.

The House report makes me sound like a cowboy who always was
doing things outside this imaginary framework that FEMA thought was
in place. The FEMA people seemed more enamored of the process than
the results. And anybody who knows me knows I am not about process.
I am about results. The biggest job senior leaders have is being able to
overcome and adapt in difficult situations while looking for opportunities to get things done. We should never blindly follow process.

Much of the FEMA testimony to Congress was a reconstruction of the
truth. FEMA staffers tried to blame other people for screwing up their
plan. I was the one person singled out as having come in and screwed
it up. But in virtually every case those who did not like me for not following their plan admitted, "Well, Honoré was operating independently
but he got things done."

If they thought I had screwed up and intentionally delayed people
getting evacuated from the Superdome I ought to be court-martialed
because that would have been inflicting cruel and unusual punishment
on those people. Nobody in their right mind wanted to see anyone
spend any more time at the Superdome or convention center than they
had to. The priority of work from the governor and mayor was to save
lives, evacuate people from the Superdome and convention center, and
provide food and water, in that order.

What slowed the response and getting people evacuated was the enormity of the task, not DOD's difficulty coordinating and communicating
with FEMA and the state of Louisiana. Nobody could communicate or
coordinate in those early days. The storm saw to that. To have someone

come along months later and say our inability to coordinate and communicate with FEMA and the state of Louisiana resulted in delays in the evacuation was just plain bullshit.

One recurrent theme ran through both the Senate and House reports. It was what investigators called the absence of a "unified command." What that actually means is that investigators thought that because I was not sitting at the table with Mike Brown for the ten days he was there, and later with Thad Allen, there was no unified command structure.

I look at command from a military perspective. Command is getting the effects the commander is trying to achieve. Command is not a place; it's a function. A commander does not have to be at a particular place to command. The command is where he is located and I was located where I could do the most good. Baton Rouge was absolutely the wrong place for me to be. JTF-Katrina had two colonels with Brown, Colonel Al Jones and Colonel Bob Jordan, as well as Brigadier General Mark Graham and his team from Fifth Army, who were embedded at the Louisiana response headquarters. There was no reason for me to be there as well.

The emergence of the phrase "unified command" and the concept of who is in charge after a disaster was formalized by the National Response Plan. During my time in Washington prior to 9/11, the general thinking was that in the event of a disaster other than a nuclear attack, who was in charge would be determined after the event occurs, not before. After 9/11 people became enamored of this idea of a unified command system for every event. Under this system the key leaders would be sitting in one room at all times. That's not necessary with today's technology. Speaking with one voice is what is important to get the effects needed while providing a voice of confidence to the people who are suffering or in danger.

Some people seem to think that if we had had a unified command system in the hours after Katrina hit New Orleans, the buses magically would have been there Monday afternoon. While planning is going to help get assets into an area quicker, there is no way anyone can pull five hundred buses out of their butt in a couple of hours.

I don't stay up nights nor have I spent time feeling guilty that there was something we didn't get done. We, like everybody else down in New Orleans after Katrina, were doing the best we could under the circumstances. There is some criticism of the DOD response but generally speaking it was thought that the military did well and that's how we came out in the congressional reports. The only thing that bothers me about this is that some day my great-grandchildren will pull out the congressional reports and read them and say, "My great-grandpa was an asshole, wasn't he?"

The congressional committees taking testimony about Katrina started calling people in before Christmas of 2005. I was a little surprised my name was not on the early list, since I had been the task force commander. As the hearings went on they called my deputy, Mark Graham. They called the adjutants general from Louisiana and Mississippi. They called Rich Rowe from Northern Command. They called Steve Blum of the National Guard Bureau. I was not sure if they were giving me a pass or collecting evidence so that somewhere along the line I would be thrown under the bus.

My turn to testify came February 9, 2006, before the Senate Committee on Homeland Security and Government Affairs. I was not even one of the primary witnesses. It seemed almost as if I was an afterthought. The committee had already taken testimony from Philip Parr of FEMA, who said under oath that the agency had a plan to fly people out of the Superdome and that I came in and changed it. I wanted to respond to that. But that wasn't a point the committee wanted to pursue. The committee had already gone past that. In fact, the committee had gone past much of what I thought I would be asked about. I read my statement, answered a few softball questions, was thanked for my service, and was excused.

I later learned that because of the public image given me by the media as the voice of calm and reason after Katrina, no one on the committee wanted to be perceived as going after me. No one wanted to even hint that I had somehow screwed up. They were looking more at process and procedure and what needed to be done for future events. I wasn't criticized or overpraised. The committee allowed the American people to have their opinion of me.

I had no more input to Congress after finishing my testimony. I put most of that behind me and went back to work getting First Army ready to make the transition from its previous dual role to a single mission of training troops from all over the United States. One of the things we were working on at the time was intensifying the training for soldiers on identifying and defeating improvised explosive devices (IEDs), the roadside bombs that were the leading killer of American troops in Iraq.

A new type of IED called explosively formed penetrators (EFPs) was becoming more commonplace in Iraq. It was common knowledge in the military that these devices were coming from Iran and that information about them was readily available on the Internet. I did an interview with CNN about it and gave other interviews to national publications because of the seriousness of the threat we were facing. I made it clear that EFPs could kill every known ground system we had in our inventory, including the massive seventy-ton M1A1 Abrams main battle tank, which many thought virtually indestructible. It was a problem we needed to address but no one in the Pentagon wanted to talk about it. The fact is, I did send some of those desk jockeys over the edge and what is known as a 15-6 investigation was initiated to determine if I had done anything wrong and whether I should somehow be punished for it.

I thought they were going to take me down on that one. I don't know if the investigation was instigated by that cadre of retired generals who did not think much of Honoréspeak or by someone else but investigators came after me as if they had been standing in line for months just waiting for me to screw up.

The 15-6 eventually concluded that the information I had been giving to the media was readily available on the Internet. Still, I was not exactly cleared. I was given an ass chewing by the director of the Army staff, also a three-star general, and told not to say anything more about IEDs or EFPs. I also was given a letter of counseling. That's not quite as bad as a letter of reprimand but for somebody in my position it was a sure career ender. Not that I had any hopes of being promoted anyway. I was told before taking command at First Army that I was not going to be part of the four-star club.

My sense is that this investigation was done simply because there was a certain amount of pressure out of Washington to do something about me but to keep it in the Army family. I had my wrist slapped but it was not made public. It was all rather hush-hush because whoever initiated it did not want to look like bad guys after I had been crowned by the American people as a good guy.

I guess it was my own mistake for thinking that the way we pushed the envelope during Katrina would be accepted after the disaster. My policy had always been that if somebody asked me a question, I was going to tell them what I knew as long as it wasn't about a pending operation or violated national security. And I wasn't going to lie.

The whole investigation turned out to be a lot of nonsense, though, because within a month after it was completed I was back doing interviews about IEDs and no one ever said another word about it.

In the aftermath of JTF-Katrina there were certain people in the military and in politics who tried to minimize the work done by federal troops in Louisiana and Mississippi. Governor Haley Barbour of Mississippi said during congressional testimony that I had no role in his state and that federal troops had no impact there. According to him, the good folks of Mississippi did it all themselves. Louisiana Governor Kathleen Blanco never really recognized the contributions of DOD or my role in them, saying repeatedly that I did not show up with enough troops.

But their people know the true story. Whenever I go to Mississippi I can't go into a restaurant without someone coming up and wanting to shake my hand or buy me a drink. It's much the same in Louisiana, especially in New Orleans. People stop me on the street, shake my hand, thank me for the soldiers' efforts there, and want to know when I'm coming home to run for office.

Much of that recognition and the reputation I gained were a result of the great job the soldiers did in New Orleans and Mississippi. But a part of it is because of the media spotlight that focused on Katrina, New Orleans, and me for so long and with such intensity.

CHAPTER 16
Lessons Learned for Building a Culture of Preparedness

1. We are accountable to the American people for what we say and what we do or fail to do. Expect to hear it again.

2. Leaders take responsibility for the good, the bad, and the ugly. You can try and pass the blame, but you cannot pass responsibility.

3. It takes teams of leaders and workers to get things done. You may not like everybody on the team, but you must work together to accomplish the team's mission, particularly in postdisaster lifesaving efforts.

4. If you don't worry about who gets the credit, you can get a lot done.

5. The true art of leadership is to avoid a crisis. If a crisis occurs, the leader has to do more than get people to do what they want to do. The challenge is to get people to do what they do not want to do, for the common good.

17

The Role of the Media in a National Disaster

THE MEDIA WERE BOTH AN OCCASIONAL ANNOYING HINDRANCE and a frequent great help in the early days of the Katrina operation. They were a hindrance because of the intrusiveness of the 24/7 news cycle and the insatiable appetite of the Internet, which demanded they come up with something new every few minutes whether or not that something new had been fully vetted. They were a great help because of that same 24/7 news cycle and Internet, which enabled them to get the story out to the world of what was happening in New Orleans, prompting tens of thousands of people to donate money or volunteer their time.

The media don't like to be used and usually will not admit they are being used. But in a disaster like Katrina we were using each other. They were using me and my military assets to get good stories. We, in return, were using them to tell our story to the public. There were, however, three serious shortcomings in the media coverage of Katrina, the particulars of which are offered here as constructive criticism of the news organizations that sent reporters to New Orleans.

The first was that few members of the media did their homework before they came to New Orleans. Hardly any had the vaguest concept of the roles that federal, state, and local government agencies have in disaster response. Most had no knowledge of the laws governing what active-duty troops were and were not permitted to do. Many had no idea the National Guard is a completely separate entity from the active forces. Only those very few who had served in the military or who had covered the military knew of the distinctions between the two. This was something we had to explain repeatedly and at times that basic lack of understanding prevented the media from telling the whole story. Katrina was on-the-job training for military affairs as well as disaster preparedness and relief for many in the media.

The second major shortcoming was that too many in the media were willing to report stories using suspect sources without getting that information corroborated. They did their profession, the people of New Orleans, and the American public a tremendous disservice by reporting sensational and sometimes incorrect information they could not or would not verify. They often went with the first version of a story without attempting to verify it. On numerous occasions in the first few days of the disaster that first account was incorrect, especially when it had to do with sensational reports of rapes and murders at the Superdome and Morial Convention Center. Those reports later turned out to be totally without substance.

The third major shortcoming was that too many reporters let their emotions get in the way of balanced reporting. They were shocked by what they saw, and rightly so. But when they allowed their emotions to override their professionalism they once again did their profession and the American public a disservice. There is a time for emotional reporting but Katrina was not it. Too many reporters who covered Katrina got on the emotions bus. When they stepped onto that bus they became part of the story and it detracted from what was actually happening. The media's job is to tell people where the bus is and what kind of shape it's in. Their job is not to get on the bus and become part of the story.

There is a point in time in any major event when some in the media become emotionally attached to a story and start to identify with the victims. They see the suffering and are frustrated they can't do anything to alleviate it. As a result, they make the decision, perhaps subconsciously, to get on the bus. When they do that they don't ask the right questions. When they do that they lose the ability to report honestly and fairly. At that point they have stepped into the story and have become part of it. Once the media are on the bus, the public starts to hear their voices rather than the voices of the victims.

It is not my intent here to be overly critical of the media and their performance during Katrina, because they provided a valuable service for the American public and for those of us who responded to the crisis. My staff and the Northern Command staff used live television shots on Monday and Tuesday after the storm to assess the situation. The media gave us the first view of what was going on at the Superdome. No one from FEMA or the state of Louisiana had the capability of passing back live footage from there.

The media did great work with their on-ground and aerial coverage from Mississippi as well. My staff looked at those reports and followed up on them if there was anything we needed to do to get resources into a particular area or address a specific concern. The media as much as any other institution or agency involved in Katrina understood the First Army concept of See First, Understand First, and Act First. They saw something that was about to happen, understood the importance of being there when it happened, and acted first to be in position to report on what was happening. The media were like first responders with communications. They filled a serious communications gap created by Katrina's devastation and allowed Mayor Ray Nagin to give the world the initial assessment of the horrific damage to New Orleans.

Those who watched the televised reports from New Orleans unfortunately got confused with the media's ability to get in there and report and the federal government's ability to get people out. It is understandable how the public got frustrated with the government after seeing Oprah Winfrey and nationally syndicated journalists on the ground because they left the impression there was freedom of movement into and out of the city. But this must be put into context: Oprah and those journalists were working for multimillion-dollar corporations and had all sorts of resources, including satellite phones and sport utility vehicles. They were working with relatively small crews. They were not trying to get tens of thousands of people out of the city.

One thing that concerned me about the early media coverage was that the local newspaper, the *Times-Picayune,* and the local television stations had to a great extent also become victims of the storm and appeared to have evacuated the city. No news products from any local sources were getting into New Orleans. I was not being asked many questions from local media and thought that a bit odd. I learned later that more than a dozen *Times-Picayune* reporters and editors remained in the city and continued to put out the paper, although it was online only and virtually no one who really needed that information could get access to it.

The third week of Katrina operations I went to Baton Rouge to meet with editors and reporters from the *Times-Picayune* working out of temporary offices in a former shopping mall. I told them that the majority of New Orleans residents were out of the city but that those people desperately needed information about what was happening. It was impossible to cover that story from Baton Rouge. The paper was shooting behind the target, writing the story of what happened last week rather than trying to reconnect the evacuees with what was going to happen.

"You're the mirror of what's going on here," I told them. "I grew up in this state. This state has a reputation. But God knows what this state would be if there weren't two strong newspapers in it that do public reporting. Y'all need to get back to New Orleans."

I urged them to tell the story that only they could tell. They knew city government. They knew the police department. They knew the levee boards and the hospital officials. The out-of-town reporters could not tell that story. Only *Times-Picayune* reporters who lived there could do it and to my way of thinking it was incumbent on them to get back in there as quickly as they could with as many reporters as they could muster and get that story out to the people who needed it most—the citizens of New Orleans.

All the top reporters in the country seemed to want a crack at the Katrina story. Many who came to New Orleans fancied themselves investigative reporters. They wanted to find that single cause or that single person who was to blame for what happened. They all wanted to be the case solver. But the story was so big and the failures so widespread there was no single answer to the question of who or what was at fault.

An old saying comes to mind whenever the media coverage of Katrina is brought up: Are you a thermostat or are you a thermometer? A thermometer tells the temperature; it is an unbiased observer. The thermostat controls the temperature. The role of the media is to be the thermometer. But sometimes they got confused. Sometimes they started trying to be the thermostat. That was especially true of some of the hotshots doing analysis from behind their desks in New York and Washington.

I was on a nationally syndicated television show one night when the host started talking about how the entire city of New Orleans was contaminated. Yet his network had just had a live feed from the French Quarter in which a female reporter was wearing what appeared to be high heels and a black party dress. So I asked him, "If the whole city is contaminated, why is your reporter wearing a party dress on the edge of the French Quarter? Certainly you wouldn't do that if the place was contaminated."

He stammered around for a bit and then went on to another subject. It was obvious he was trying to be the thermostat, not the thermometer.

He was not the only one who wanted to control the temperature in the room. It was obvious some reporters came in with a bias against President Bush because of the Iraq War. If they came wanting to make a point about the president they could make that point through the federal response to Katrina. Mike Brown was a Bush appointee and was the target of a lot of venom because of his association with the president.

Reporters have a great deal of discretionary power, much as the police do. The police don't have the right to impose punishment. But the police can make anyone's life miserable and can easily ruin reputations. A reporter can do much the same thing. A reporter can even serve as judge and jury. A reporter can conduct a thirty-minute interview and then do stories that can make anyone look like the biggest jackass in the world. There are few other disciplines that have that discretionary power.

Although I fully understood that power, I was not about to shy away from my duties to engage the media as often as possible and get our story out there. Every day I made time for the media. Often I started as early as 5:30 A.M. because of the importance of being on the morning shows to address any issues that may have popped up overnight. Still, I had the feeling that most of my interviews were like a ball hit into the sun; I had no idea where they went.

Starting the Thursday after the storm and then nearly every day until I returned to Fort Gillem in early October, half the people in my helicopter were media. I didn't go anywhere without them. It was the best way to get the story out. They stayed where I stayed, saw what I saw, and got their stories.

That's what made this operation different from Iraq. In Iraq a general will spend much of his time talking about plans. Reporters cannot listen to that and then report on it. But having the media hear me talking about things that were going to happen the next day in the New Orleans area only reinforced in minds of reporters and the public that we were moving forward and making progress. Plans can be discussed in a permissive environment but not in a nonpermissive environment.

We took virtually all filters off the media, except when it came to the issue of recovery of remains. Otherwise, the media go could wherever they wanted and talk to whomever they wanted. One reporter told me she did not think there would ever be another event where the media would have the unfettered access they had during Katrina.

Most of the public's perception about Katrina came through the media. That perception is why we came so close to having all the forces in the city federalized. The early reports about the rapes and murders at the Superdome and the convention center and video of looting made it appear the city was out of control and in need of martial law. Sure, things were bad. But they were not as bad as the media led us to believe.

Even after many of those reports proved to be false, the media usually did not go back and correct them. They failed to close the loop on that very significant piece of the story and there are many Americans out there today who still believe those initial reports. They heard only the bad and that stuck with them. If the media are wrong about something and it is not corrected the story takes on a life of its own. The media are in the business of capturing people's attention, not necessarily in closing the loop on stories. In any story there are going to be ups and downs. But if that reporter is always focusing on the downs and never shows any ups, he or she is on the bus.

For the first four or five days of the Katrina operation I was not able to watch that much television. The job of the public affairs teams from Northern Command, First Army, and JTF-Katrina was to put together media books for me. I read one in the morning as soon as I woke up. The other I read around midnight after returning to Camp Shelby. That gave me a platform to execute Zumwalt Rules when I met with the media so that regardless of the first question asked at the next news conference the answer provided often tried to correct a misperception that had been reported as fact.

As mentioned in an earlier chapter, if something happens in my formation I am going to be the one to speak and I am not going to read a statement. I never read a single statement written for me during Katrina. It was more important for me to say what I knew, not what someone else had written for me or what I felt or thought.

My public affairs team put together talking points on issues it thought I needed to address or correct. I did not want the media referring to information they received as coming from "a spokesman." The word *spokesman* implies that the information is secondhand. The reason the commander rather than a public affairs officer ought to be the voice after a disaster is that the role of the leader is to help shape what's going to happen tomorrow and give a true picture of what happened today. He should not be focused on what happened yesterday.

I developed an eighteen-point "react to media contact battle drill" that I put on cards to hand out to soldiers so they would have some sense of what to do if someone from the media wanted to talk to them. Because this was a permissive environment our soldiers were encouraged to talk about the jobs they were doing. Those eighteen points are included in Appendix 4, but the top two on the list were "Don't lie. Tell the truth" and "If you don't want to hear it or read it, don't say it or do it."

I spent a great deal of time invoking that second rule because I received an incredible number of questions about how things could have been done better. Instead of saying "no comment" or answering directly, I would say to reporters: "Look, you have just seen a no-shit disaster. People have been killed, property has been destroyed, a large number of people can't care for themselves, and the government is a victim here as well. The parishes, the city, the state are all victims of this storm. You know you're in a disaster when you lose the first quarter. If you don't lose the first quarter, if you don't lose communications, if you don't lose any lives, if you can account for everyone, you haven't had a disaster."

That concept of a football game as a metaphor for the Katrina disaster may have seemed a bit flippant at times but it resonated in that part of the country where football is a year-round obsession. My explanation to the media went something like this: If a good team is losing in the first quarter by four touchdowns, what does a good coach do? He is going to focus on the problem, not berate his players. He is going to look for ways to deal with the situation in the next three quarters. The reason we are here is that we have a disaster. We can sit around and talk about who's inept and who's inadequate and who's ineffective. Or we can focus on the next quarter. We can focus on keeping people alive and getting people evacuated. We can sit down later and talk about what went wrong in that first quarter but right now we have to focus on making things better.

If a hurricane comes to New Orleans, some people are going to lose. But how badly they lose is in direct proportion to where they are before the storm hits. The poor are going to lose harder. The sick and elderly are going to lose harder. Those who have not properly prepared are going to lose harder.

How to keep the disaster in context and focus on the task at hand was something I tried to stress repeatedly. In a crisis people get stuck on "what went wrong." I received very few questions about what was going to happen next or what sort of progress we were making. The media wanted to know what happened yesterday, why it happened, and who was to blame. A lot of time and effort was wasted transmitting negative energy and criticizing leaders after that first quarter was lost in New Orleans. That was effort that could have been more wisely spent improving things in the second quarter.

I came out of the JTF-Katrina experience with three recommendations for the media, the technology industry, and educational institutions that would enable all of them to be better prepared to deal with a major national disaster.

The first and simplest is that the media have to get a seat at the table in all disaster preparedness exercises. They have to play in those exercises. The problem with many media organizations is that they wait until after a disaster hits to figure out what they are going to do. Then they either send their top guy, who has been too busy to play in any of the exercises, or the first reporter who walks into the newsroom but who likely has little experience reporting on disasters. Disaster reporting is a learning process and the media have to be willing to spend the time and money to prepare their reporters to do it well.

The second recommendation is for journalism courses to include as part of their curriculum, and news organization to include in workshops, classes on the National Response Framework, as it is now known, as well as how to deal with all the ambiguities that reporters face when dealing with a disaster. Ambiguities sometimes lead reporters to think they are being told a lie. But there are some things a leader just does not know and the smart ones admit that. Reporters need to know how to deal with that.

Many reporters seem to think that the person in charge of something ought to know everything about what they are in charge of. I can get comfortable being in command and not knowing everything. But I will never be comfortable not knowing what I need to know. There are some levels of detail that I don't need to know because of my confidence in subordinates who know what they are doing.

The third recommendation is that media and the technology industry should partner to develop a system to provide a source of news to those who are stranded and at the mercy of the elements and the government. The media are using these people to get their stories. Why can't they find a way to give information back to those people?

In those first few days after the levees broke there was no information coming into New Orleans. We needed something to distract those people at the Superdome and convention center. We could have done that if we had been able to get some wide-screen television sets in there, powered by generators, to give the people some sense of what was going on and why it was so difficult to get them evacuated. I talked to the mayor about that the first day. We looked into it but it proved to be too difficult to do in a short period of time with everything else that was going on.

We even talked about getting some loudspeakers and a sound system to pipe in news reports or music through satellite-based radio networks such as Sirius and XM. Again, we were not able to do it because there was not enough time and our priority was to get people out of there.

In an event such as Katrina the media not only are reporting on an event, they are providing information to hundreds of thousands of interested viewers and readers. The people in Oregon were interested in what was going on in New Orleans but the people who cared most were the victims, yet they were completely left out of the information loop. We are not talking about spending a lot of money here but the big question is, Whose responsibility is it to do this? Is it the responsibility of local government or of the individual media companies? There is no reason it can't be a collaborative effort. Information needs to be pumped back to the people who need it most.

After Katrina some of the networks made a humanitarian gesture to help people reconnect with their families. They used their satellite communications and their Internet connections to do that. That was a glimpse of the possibilities the media can bring to the table in future disasters. The media can be part of the solution by using their technology to help people get through a crisis.

There is something in our culture or our value system that enables us to deal with those things that we can see. However, we are held in suspense by that which we can't see. God made the earth round for a reason. When people can see that horizon they can deal with it. But that horizon keeps moving and it is that unseen problem just beyond the horizon that gives people problems. We are worried about the economy, global warming, pollution, terrorism, the rift between the haves and the have-nots, and any manner of problems because we can see them. But we have become a culture that knows there will be unseen and unplanned events along the road of life yet believes that the government should deal with them. The true art of leadership is to see beyond the horizon and figure out what's next and how to optimize some of the technology to deal with those problems so not everything is left in the hands of the government.

My experiences with the media have been largely positive. Many Americans know me because of the media. There were times when the media could have damaged my reputation for my outspokenness. Some of the media bosses could have called my hand about using the word *bullshit* on live television. I personally got a bye from them. But it's also because of the media that I cannot go into the drugstore and buy my Preparation H without hiding it for fear that someone will recognize me and see me with it.

Because of the media attention I received during Katrina, people now listen to me talk about the lessons learned and why we must move forward in creating a culture of preparedness. The media will be a part of educating and bringing awareness to the nation of the need for that culture of preparedness. Despite their occasional shortcomings the media are a vital part of our democracy. Our democracy cannot survive without a relevant, open, and balanced media, and we cannot create a true culture of preparedness without their cooperation and collaboration.

CHAPTER 17

Lessons Learned for Building a Culture of Preparedness

1. Look at the media as a friend, like someone who will tell you that you have spinach in your teeth. Also expect the press to be like a mirror. It will and can give you a broad perspective of the situation: bad, ugly, and sometimes good.

2. Expect the press to sensationalize bad news, and that even if you have kept people alive, that good news will be trumped by the fact that you have not moved as quickly as the media think you should have.

3. A real disaster will cause you to lose the first quarter. That's what happens in a disaster. In the first quarter of a disaster people die, get injured, and property is destroyed.

4. The second quarter is the search and rescue. In a disaster, your requirements will exceed your capacity. If you can handle everything without outside help, it may not be a disaster that requires much federal help. But count on the press being there, as they should be.

5. You must make time to talk to the press. If you don't speak to them, others will. Be proactive and choose the three most important things you want the American people to know about. At the press event do not be afraid to say that you need help and where the help is needed.

6. Be aware of when the reporter has gotten on the emotional bus. Is the reporter telling the story, or has the reporter put himself or herself in the story?

7. Network and reporter bias does happen in a democracy.

8. Print journalists will want and need more time than most TV reporters. It's hard to meet the needs of print journalists who are not just looking for a thirty-second sound bite. But you can do several print journalists at the same time.

9. If you want a pet, buy a dog. This is a contested event! A news conference is verbal combat and don't forget it. If it is a love-in and you are not challenged by the press, then it's not a disaster, just news. Or, if they feel empathy for you, then it is the American democracy that loses.

10. Great reporters will already have an answer before they ask you the question. They will allow you to answer, then afterward show the American people the rest of the story. Most reporters are very smart people; it is the stupid ones that you need to avoid or be careful of. Ignorance can be fixed, but stupidity is for life.

11. With twenty-four-hour news cycles, there is still a premium on morning news that people see before they go to work and evening news that they see after work. That is where the big stories will get the details to them.

12. As much as possible, avoid any television shows that are on from 8 P.M. to 10 P.M. that are normally loaded with "you say, they say." They have much more time and it becomes entertainment, not news. True news programs are limited by time; they must get the headline and move on.

18

How America Can Create a Culture of Preparedness

I HAVE OFTEN HEARD THAT THE TWO MOST IMPORTANT DAYS IN ANY person's life are the day they are born and the day they discover the reason for their existence. For years I thought my primary mission in life was to provide for my family and serve my country. But during my six weeks as commander of Joint Task Force–Katrina I discovered that my entire Army career, if not my life, had been a training ground to help me understand the importance of creating a culture of preparedness. The Katrina experience put me in a position to take those lessons and encourage the American public through speeches and writings to embrace that culture because of its importance to the survival of the country.

During the last eighteen months of my command at First Army, I received and accepted numerous requests to speak about my experiences in New Orleans. People who listened to those speeches often told me they thought a lot about disaster preparedness but did little to actually put those thoughts into action. They had good intentions but seldom followed through on them and almost never committed the time or money to prepare themselves, their families, or their homes for a disaster.

Some of that failure to act is a function of a too-busy society overwhelmed by other problems and unwilling to take the time necessary to attend to the details of preparedness. But some of it is a function of believing that the government will step in and make things right when they go wrong. As we saw in Katrina, the government is not always in a position to do that as quickly or as efficiently as we think it will.

Often when I talk with state and local officials about their disaster preparedness plans they start the conversation with "What happened in New Orleans won't happen here because we're better organized." But that "better organization" is often a myth based on good intentions and false premises. Governors tell me that if they see a hurricane heading for a major city in their state they would order a mandatory evacuation. When I ask how they will get their key people back into the city after the storm passes they say they have a phone tree and people will call one another.

"Governor," I tell them, "if the phone tree works you have an inconvenience, you don't have a disaster. In a disaster the phones don't work."

So I ask why they don't have those workers and their families go to one central location, such as a military post or a major university, so they can be quickly recalled to get back into the city. If key city and county workers are allowed to scatter to the winds and a true disaster hits, it is going to be impossible to find them and get them back on the job.

That's exactly what happened in New Orleans after Katrina. Many of the essential city workers could not be found. The phones weren't working. There was no electricity and no Internet service. So how were they going to get those key workers back into the city? If the purpose of government is to take care of the people, why does the government think its responsibility stops when it orders a mandatory evacuation?

When states do their disaster readiness exercises, they seldom if ever worst-case any of the scenarios. That is, they assume the telephones are going to work and the computers are going to work and that all other communications systems will be functioning. That's because most politicians won't buy into planned failure in a training exercise.

Yet that is the direct opposite of what needs to be done and what we try to do in the military. The Army's National Training Center at Fort Irwin, California, has been so successful in preparing forces for combat because every plan devised by friendly forces is taken to the point of failure and beyond. Soldiers are expected to learn to work through failure. But to most people in the civilian world, especially those in politics, the idea of failure during an exercise is unacceptable.

It is counterintuitive to the political mind to take a plan that a state's experts train to and make that plan fail during an exercise. No politician wants to stand in front of the media and say that the disaster preparedness plan failed. But if those players are not forced to fail no one knows what the worst case will be. State and local governments will sell worst-case scenarios to the feds and the public so they can get the money through grants and taxes but will almost always resource the best-case scenario and hope it works. Many states and cities do disaster response exercises to give the impression they are preparing but the preparation often is purely symbolic.

As a nation we have become better prepared since 9/11 for national disasters but we are not nearly as good as we could be or need to be. One reason for that is that much of the focus has been on the National Response Framework, which deals with what happens after the event. What we need is a National Preparedness Plan that focuses on creating a culture that lives preparedness.

More than 40 percent of the population of the United States lives within twenty miles of the more than ninety-five thousand miles of coastline, which includes ocean beaches, lakes, and navigable waterways. This is a population at risk from hurricanes, floods, or tsunamis. What happened in New Orleans can happen even in those cities seemingly immune from major weather disasters.

In 1938 a hurricane that became known as the Long Island Express hit New York and several New England states with winds of 121 miles per hour and a storm surge in excess of seventeen feet. It overtopped Long Island, killed more than 700 people, and left 63,000 homeless. Some storm models indicate a similar storm would put up to ten feet of water on Wall Street and leave Long Island in ruins. The very same thing could happen in Charleston, South Carolina; Washington, D.C.; and Miami or Jacksonville, Florida.

A storm of that magnitude causing that much damage would create severe economic hardships throughout the country, just as Katrina did when it damaged oil rigs in the Gulf of Mexico and processing plants on the mainland. Gasoline prices went up and stayed there for several years. A tsunami on the West Coast hitting either Los Angeles or San Francisco also would create economic devastation throughout the country because of the amount of damage it could cause to the ports in those cities.

In addition to the natural disasters, we also are faced with the specter of pandemics for which the nation as a whole and most individuals are totally unprepared. Pandemics once were primarily local events and could be contained in a relatively small area. Now they can spread much more quickly because of interstate highways and commercial air travel. We are living in a new normal and have not prepared for it.

In the 1960s this country had a culture of preparedness. We were worried about the survival of the nation. We were facing off with the Soviet Union. We had missiles pointed at them and they had missiles pointed at us. We were talking about the doctrine of mutually assured destruction. The country engaged the education system and the business community to come up with a plan for mutually assured survivability. The country had three years of food stored in the event of a nuclear attack. We taught children how to survive a nuclear blast. The government had its own communications system. We had more than twenty Army divisions. When the president spoke he talked about the survival of the United States.

Things changed over the years. We are now down to ten Army divisions. We cut the size of the force and closed bases. Those base closures were based on economics and not what was best for the security of the country. We stopped thinking about the survival of the United States. Now we're thinking about making the economy work.

In recent years the government started outsourcing key national capabilities. Before my retirement, if I wanted to do a video teleconference with someone in Iraq I had to go through a commercial contractor. Cheaper, better, quicker now drives how we do business in America but cheaper, better, quicker also drives our ability to respond to disasters and that is not necessarily for the better.

The military went from analog to digital communications, so we no longer have the same ability to communicate long-range. Technology went away from that long-range capability to a system based on cell towers and cable communications. We are more vulnerable now because our communications are more fragile. The only phone working at Camp Shelby, Mississippi, after Hurricane Katrina hit was a Defense Switched Network, or DSN line, a relic of the Cold War. But it worked. The newer, cheaper, faster phone lines were knocked out. Technology changed and it reduced our redundancy and reliability.

Local governments are outsourcing their emergency medical services to private contractors because of the cost. It's a culture of competition for dollars rather than a culture of collaboration and cooperation for preparedness. In a disaster it is important to share information across the spectrum of government agencies and private contractors. Information that is contained within one agency or held by one contractor during a disaster is of no use to anyone, especially those who would benefit most from it.

My point in urging the creation of a culture of preparedness is that we know there are going to be disasters. Let's not wait until after the disaster hits and then respond. That's dealing with problems on the right side of the disaster. Let's start dealing with the left side of the disaster, before it happens. Let's start dealing more with preparation and mitigation than response. We will always need a robust response capability. But we can reduce what we need to do on the right side of the disaster by being better prepared on the left side of it.

What will it take to get this done? It must be driven by government policy. If we look at the big-muscle movements in this country, such as school desegregation, the response to polio and AIDS, and the cleanup of the environment, all were driven by policy at the federal level. Those issues never would have been dealt with as successfully as they have been had not the federal government established policy and then partnered with education and business to get the message out about how to deal with them.

Concern about AIDS becoming a national health problem is a perfect example of how government, education, and business worked together to deal with a potentially deadly issue. Education began teaching about it in the schools. Business saw a way to make money and save lives. Government did a full-court press on the public through the media. Hollywood got involved and started making movies about AIDS. It was a combined effort. We saw the goodness of cooperation between the public and private sectors supported by policy. We got to the left side of the AIDS issue and educated people about how to avoid contracting it.

We need to do the same thing with preparedness. At the present time preparedness is embedded with and competes with response resources. Most of the preparedness money is being spent on "stuff." It is not being used to coach, train, and teach to produce this cultural shift where people are thinking more about preparedness than response.

The role of government is to protect the people. Yet government has become more enamored of looking at the right side of the disaster, the response side, instead of the left side, the preparation side, where it can actually do more and do it more efficiently. By moving more assets to the left side of a disaster government can better shape the outcome on the right side and be in a more advantageous position to protect people. We need the equivalent of a Stafford Act on the left side of the disaster that funds preparedness or gives tax breaks for it. We can either pay on the right side of the disaster or the left side.

Responding to a disaster is a logistics issue. It's about moving people and food and water. We spend too much money doing that and not enough looking for solutions that can move us to the left side of the event. We need to stretch technology to ensure our survival on the left side. We can no longer do business as we did it in the past. It's a matter of survival. We cannot wait to respond. We cannot leave this to chance. The cost to respond to disasters makes the risk too high.

Based on what we saw during Katrina, state and local politicians can have a significant influence on creating that culture of preparedness. Why can't governments pass local ordinances that require drugstores and gas stations to be equipped with emergency generators? We need that redundancy so people can get gasoline or medicine after a disaster.

State politicians can write legislation to mandate that schools get back to teaching first aid. And they can mandate that college students take an elective in first aid or disaster preparedness and get credit for it regardless of what discipline they are studying.

We need substantive training in practical science at the college level and in grade school. That might include such topics as how to purify water in a disaster situation. We can invest in policies that force things to happen before a disaster so that when we do have one, not everything becomes a calamity.

Katrina hit two of the states with the worst health problems in the country. Obesity, diabetes, and heart disease are major issues in Louisiana and Mississippi. What do we do about people with chronic health problems? Many of these problems can be prevented by teaching kids that what they eat as children can have a long-term impact on their health. We need to invest more in wellness so health problems have less impact during a disaster. Some health problems can be made to go away through education, better eating habits, and exercise. The disasters are not going away.

Economics often plays a key role in what is done and what is not done on the left side of a disaster. Why was the generator for Charity Hospital in New Orleans at ground level? Why was the generator for the Veterans Affairs Medical Center at ground level? Why was the generator for the New Orleans Police Department at ground level? This is a city where a few inches of rain can produce major flooding. Yet the backup generators for these buildings were in the floodplain. Were those economic decisions or a matter of convenience? Whichever it was, when those generators were flooded they became a national problem. There have to be economic incentives for people who live in these high-risk flood areas to raise the utilities and backup power sources for a building above the flood line. That would be the power of the National Preparedness Plan. Goals would be set and incentives created.

Solutions will come but they may not all be from the government. A great many will come when business sees an opportunity to make money. That has happened in Florida, where Home Depot and Lowe's have ready-made hurricane preparedness kits for sale. All anyone has to do is take it home and break it out. These types of opportunities are going to pop out from large and small businesses. It has started, but it is not happening at the pace it should.

As much as government and the business community are responsible for helping create this culture of preparedness, individuals must share a significant amount of the responsibility for getting themselves, their families, and their homes in a position to survive the next disaster. A weather radio that wakes the family in time to get to a safe place in the event of a tornado or flood should be as much a fixture in every home as a television and a computer.

Each family should have a disaster preparedness kit well stocked with food, water, hand-cranked flashlights and radios, and cash. The cash is important because after a disaster ATMs are not likely to be working. We have become so smart about new technology that we have outsmarted ourselves. The new type of thinking I'm calling for is the heart and soul of changing the country and making it look at preparedness as we looked at survival in the 1960s.

People need to see first, understand first, and act first. People need to take a good, hard look at where they are living, understand there are certain times of the year they may be in danger from floods, hurricanes, wildfires, or tornadoes and act to deal with those events before they occur. Anyone who lives in a danger zone needs to have situational awareness and plan ahead. They need to get on the left side of the disaster.

Without a culture of preparedness it is almost as if we are gambling and using hope as a method. But we figured out a long time ago that hope is not a method; hope is hope. It's not a matter of *if* we are going to have a hurricane, it's when. It's not *if* we are going to have a pandemic it's when. It's not *if* we are going to have a flood or tornado or tsunami,

it's when. We need a concerted effort to build this culture of preparedness by developing a National Preparedness Plan. The future leaders of
this country need to make this a priority, because it's not just about hurricanes. It's about the new normal in which we now live. It's about our
survival as a nation.

Epilogue

ONE OF MY FAVORITE PLACES TO VISIT WHENEVER I AM IN THE NEW Orleans area is the battlefield at Chalmette in St. Bernard Parish. On that low, swampy ground in January 1815, Major General Andrew Jackson took about 5,000 irregular forces recruited from local militias, the bars of the city, and the crew of the pirate Jean Lafitte and defeated about 5,400 well-trained British regulars, considered at that time the finest fighting force in the world.

Some of the old-timers in New Orleans say Hurricane Katrina was the second Battle of New Orleans. Only this time the battle was with nature and with the state and federal bureaucracies. And we were doing it all under the ever-watchful and unforgiving eye of the media.

Had Jackson been forced to deal two hundred years ago with similar impediments it is doubtful he would have succeeded in defeating the British. However, it also is doubtful Jackson ever would have become a general had he been held to the same standards as today's officers. He was barroom brawler on occasion and something of a ladies' man. That sort of behavior would have kept him from getting anywhere near the general officer ranks.

Some people say my role as commander of JTF-Katrina was destiny. Three Honorés fought with Andrew Jackson as free men of color. I do not believe it was destiny for me to be there, although my wife, Beverly, believes that. A number of other people have made a great deal more out of what was merely a coincidence than they should, because I was not the story.

The story was the people of New Orleans. The story was the response to the devastation of the city. I was just the commander of the federal forces. Jackson worked with the locals to solve the British problem. I worked with the locals to solve the Katrina problem. I had far more resources than Jackson did. I did not have to scour the bars of the French Quarter or make deals with the local pirates to solve the law enforcement problems in those first few days. Jackson's recruitment of Lafitte's men would have been like me recruiting gang members to assist us.

Yet Jackson's initiative in gaining cooperation from a variety of groups and collaborating with them to protect New Orleans is still instructive today. It demonstrates that despite differences people might have in how they think things should be done, a leader able to get people to cooperate and collaborate can do far more good than one who sticks strictly to the wiring diagram drawn up for him. It was not until some-time after Katrina that I realized I tried to do much the same thing as Andrew Jackson did at the first Battle of New Orleans. I tried to make sure individuals and agencies cooperated and collaborated to the benefit of the residents of New Orleans.

Some people say I was successful. Some say I too often overstepped my boundaries and played outside the lines. If they want to beat me up about what I did, that's an ass-whipping I can take, especially if I stand in the shoes of the poor people who were trapped at the Superdome. I was trying to do the best I could for them and if I broke a few rules and bruised a few feelings along the way, so be it. I would rather have the respect of those people we helped than of those who are critical of me and the federal response.

I had a teacher who once told me, "Russ, you're a C student and you're always going to be a C student. But I'm going to give you three rules to remember to help you out in life."

Rule number one was to do the routine things well. She told me that if I was going to be a C student then I should be a champion C student and I could do that by doing the routine things better than anyone else.

Rule number two was to never be afraid to take on the impossible. She said champions are challenged by impossible things and believe they can do the impossible. Evacuating all those people from the Super-dome and the Morial Convention Center in a reasonable amount of time seemed an impossible task to some but I looked at it as a challenge to overcome.

Rule number three was to not be afraid to act in spite of criticism. I had my share of criticism from those in uniform and those in the civilian world. But I pushed on through it and used the comments that were constructive and ignored those that were destructive to our mission.

As with any major historical event, no one will be able to get the full picture of what happened in New Orleans and why it happened as it did until historians have had a chance to ponder all the complexities of

Katrina and its aftermath over the next twenty years or so. That puzzle had an incredible number of moving pieces. To fully understand why it turned out as it did, historians will have to go back and look at how dysfunctional the state and city governments were long before the hurricane and how their relationships with the federal government were anything but smooth.

One of the most enduring images of New Orleans after Katrina was the one of thousands of people at the Superdome standing hip to hip in their own waste without food, water, or sanitary facilities. That scene was not just a result of Katrina, it was the result of years of neglect and poverty. It was the result of the state and city governments being unwilling or unable to adequately prepare for the storm.

When I first saw all those people standing around helplessly in all that garbage I could not understand why no one organized a cleanup detail. Why did the National Guard not organize that? They could have handed out a few trash bags and told people to help with the cleanup. It is basic sanitation. Everyone is responsible yet no one wanted to take responsibility beyond basic security. There was no organization at the Superdome. To this day I do not know why. My only guess is that everyone was waiting for somebody else to do it. Not only did the government let it happen, but the people let it happen.

There is an expectation in many states, especially in the South, that if something is broken the federal government will come in and fix it. Our culture is one that says when something tragic happens it ought to get fixed right away and it is the federal government that should do the fixing. Well, this isn't television. This isn't *24*. Jack Bauer is not going to show up in the first five minutes and then fifty-five minutes later have everything solved. In real life there is no way to have a disaster in the morning and have everything back to normal by the next morning.

The culture of New Orleans is unique, and people admire it and go there to have fun. But one of the exacerbating issues at the second Battle of New Orleans was the realization by many in the media, if not the federal government, that this was a city with a large concentration of poor people. It had an antiquated medical system that barely met the needs of the people, and a police department that frequently was under investigation by the federal Department of Justice. This was an area that was economically depressed before the storm and most of the city's visitors just tended to look past it.

Part of the reason for that is what I perceive as a natural fear of the poor. There seems to be an expectation that if a bunch of poor people are put together they are going to somehow mess up. In New Orleans they were not only poor, but black.

It is not just the poor and black who are held in suspicion, though. From what I have seen of other disasters, anyone who gets evacuated is suspect and it does not matter if they live in the 9th Ward of New Orleans in a run-down shotgun shack or in the hills of San Diego in a multimillion-dollar home. During the California wildfires in 2008 I watched on television as armed National Guard soldiers walked around San Diego's Qualcomm Stadium, where the evacuees were being housed. One female Guard soldier had two weapons: a 9mm pistol and an M4 carbine. She looked as if she were in downtown Baghdad, not in America. Just who was she protecting herself against? It looked absolutely ridiculous.

In the years since Katrina I have returned frequently to New Orleans for speeches and conferences in which I try to impress on the audience the need, especially there, for the creation of a culture of preparedness. It is a city that will be on the mend for many years to come, a city in which the temporary FEMA trailers brought in for residents still dot the landscape in the 7th and 9th wards. Those residents are desperately trying to hold on to a small patch of land while they rebuild and recover.

A number of businesses in St. Bernard Parish did not come back. The buildings that housed them are empty shells of what once was but will never again be. Some of the residents and businessmen in the parish decided not to return after Katrina and thereby gamble their investments, their livelihood, or their lives on the low-lying, flood-prone ground or the levees that protect it. They moved to higher ground in search of fewer risks and peace of mind.

Will there be another Katrina?

The next Katrina may be worse. Some scientists say we have entered the "Age of Extreme Weather." *The New York Times* has reported that "there have been more than four times as many weather-related disasters in the last 30 years than in the previous 75 years" and that the United States has borne the brunt of majority of them. Global warming is being blamed as the culprit for the larger and more frequent storms and some scientists want to declare war on climate change just as we have declared war on cancer, drugs, and terrorism.

Whether climate change is the culprit for more powerful storms, they will occur, and hurricanes are, after all, only one type of disaster. We also face floods, earthquakes, tornadoes, wildfires, tsunamis, and pandemics. As a nation we cannot declare war on all forms of natural disasters, because those are not winnable wars. Disasters will happen. How we prepare for them will determine how well, or if, we survive them. The better prepared we are before a disaster, the more we will be able to mitigate its adverse impact.

Our best defense against these disasters is to go on the offense. That means pushing resources to the left side of the disaster before it hits instead of waiting for the right side to come. That means governments, communities, and individuals must begin to create within their own spheres of influence a true and sustainable culture of preparedness.

Appendix 1
Joint Task Force–Katrina Command Group

Lieutenant General Russel L. Honoré—Commander, Joint Task Force–Katrina

Major General Henry Morrow—Commander, Joint Force Air Component

Major General Scott Mays—Commander, Joint Force Air Component

Major General Douglas V. O'Dell, Jr.—Commander, Marine Forces JTF-Katrina

Major General William Caldwell—Commander, Task Force All-American

Brigadier General Mark Graham—Deputy Commanding General, JTF-Katrina (Forward)

Brigadier General Michael Terry—Commander, Joint Logistics Command

Rear Admiral Joseph Kilkenny—Commander, Joint Force Maritime Component

Rear Admiral Stephen Turcotte—Commander, Joint Force Maritime Component

Rear Admiral Ronald Bayless—Commander, Joint Force Maritime Component

Appendix 2
Joint Task Force–Katrina Hurricane Assessment:
Ten Quick Wins

1. Command and control—Determine who is in charge early in the event.

2. Preposition response forces—Too many assets positioned outside the affected areas when a storm hits will slow response times.

3. Single Department of Defense contact with Federal Coordinating Officer—Eliminates confusion over who is making requests.

4. Government employee disaster clause—Employees on government payrolls not able to do their jobs after a disaster should be required to assist in operations or lose pay.

5. Communications continuity—Need redundant emergency communications, prestaging of a separate network, and compatibility of communications assets.

6. Provide external support, including federal funds, to affected areas before the event.

7. Ensure federal and other agencies have workspace in state emergency operations centers.

8. Continuity of government plan—Governments down to the local level should have a plan to maintain continuity to quickly reestablish control in the wake of a disaster.

9. Preexisting contracts—Establish critical needs and utilize contracts to ensure support after a disaster.

10. Integration of industry—Form an industrial civic coalition/ partnership that gets commitments from industry to provide support and services in the event of a disaster.

Appendix 3
Nineteen Rules for Leadership During a Disaster

1. Arriving on the scene in a disaster—you must be the calm in the storm.
2. Work through the chaos and confusion—don't add to it.
3. Can't do everything at once—establish priority of work.
4. Look for quick wins.
5. In a disaster, you are the priority—if you ask for it, you'll get it.
6. Need decision superiority—See First, Understand First, Act First.
7. Collaboration is key—unity of effort, not unity of command.
8. Who else needs to know?
9. Public information critical in a disaster situation—keep lines of communication open.
10. Must give media access—if you're not speaking, someone else will speak for you.
11. Stay connected with those responsible—mayor, governor, president, broader command authority.
12. Track what those key leaders are saying so there are no contradictions.
13. Learn to deal with misinformation put out by others.
14. Real art of leadership is getting people to follow you willingly.
15. Audio and video have to match.
16. Leader can't be an observer, must be a player.
17. Leader takes responsibility for what happens—good, bad, or ugly.
18. Don't play the blame game.
19. Don't allow the media to interrogate you.

Appendix 4
Battle Drill: React to Media Contact

1. Don't lie. Tell the truth.

2. If you don't want to hear it or read it, don't say it or do it.

3. Give media access 5 A.M. to midnight. Set aside at least twenty to thirty minutes a day for interviews. Be prepared for action on contact.

4. Purpose: to provide information to the public. The American people have a right to know.

5. Talk about what you know, not about what you think.

6. Don't answer "How do you feel about . . . ?" questions. Focus on mission. Think about answers.

7. Interject humor with caution. Watch timing based on situation.

8. It's about us, not me.

9. The Army is an outdoor sport. Do interviews outside in an operational environment.

10. Have your Public Affairs Officer keep you posted on your boss's and your boss's boss's quotes.

11. Figure out your daily top three priorities of work and talk about them.

12. Get satellite radio and listen to national news a few times a day.

13. Don't be part of a public investigation. Don't let reporters act like prosecutors.

14. Build business relationships with reporters. Drink coffee, eat with them, and let them get to know you.

15. Be yourself.

16. Don't read any damn prepared remarks.

17. Don't do politics—focus on your mission. Don't compliment or criticize political leaders.

18. Use your staff to see first, understand first, and act first.

Appendix 5
Emergency Kits

The Ideal Situation

Emergency supplies can be simple or complex. It is recommended that you begin with the simple and work you way up as you learn more about what you would need and how to reduce the effects of disasters on you and your family. Ideally, each household should prepare and keep updated the following emergency supplies and kits:

HOME

Emergency supplies that are stored in a safe, health-conscious place.
* for when the emergency or disaster requires you to stay inside (shelter in place).

One or several emergency "Go" bags.
* one for each member of your household; or
* several for each kind of need you may have; or
* one on each floor of the home and in the garage for easy access.

WORK

An emergency supplies bag or box, primarily for your personal use.
* useful for both evacuation and shelter in place situations.

Your employer should also maintain emergency supplies for the company and its employees.

CAR

Emergency supplies that deal with each of your cars.
- items that you may need to get your car going, to provide emergency lighting, or to communicate with people when you need help.

General emergency kits or "Go" bags.

Specialized disaster evacuation items.
- when a catastrophic disaster is about to occur and you have to evacuate the area for what might be a long period of time.

SCHOOL

An extra backpack stored in your locker or dormitory room, or items stored in your main backpack that you carry around. It is a good idea to carry some items with your always (i.e., flashlight, whistle, bottled water, granola bars or other healthy snack food, surgical face mask, cell phone or text messaging device).

Generally, all of the above types of emergency supplies will have the same or similar items in them and they will be useful to you during almost all emergencies and disasters you will encounter. Having them stashed in several places will allow you greater flexibility in how you respond (go or stay) and how you sustain yourself when disaster strikes.

Important Tips

Store your kits in a convenient place known to all family members.

Keep a smaller version of the supplies kit in the trunk of your car, at work, and at school.

Keep items in airtight plastic bags, if possible.

Change your stored water supply every six months so it stays fresh. Drink what you have saved and replace it with fresh water.

Replace your stored food every six months. Eat what you have saved and replace it.

Rethink your kit and family needs at least once a year. Replace batteries, update clothes, etc.

Ask your physician or pharmacist about storing prescription medications.

Items for Your Emergency Supplies and Kits

HOME (INCLUDING HOME EVACUATION OR "GO" KIT)

There are seven basics you should stock for your home in the case of an emergency: water, nonperishable or ready-to-eat food, first aid supplies, clothing and bedding, communications devices, tools and emergency supplies, special items for medical conditions, and important documents.

You will probably have many of these items already in your home, so build your supplies, starting at home. For items you do not already have, start with the Dollar Store. Work your way up to Walmart, Target, Kmart, Big Lots, or similar stores. Last, you may want to visit a camping gear store or department store. Many disaster supply items are on sale throughout the year, so keep your eyes open for bargains.

Keep the items that you would most likely need during an evacuation in an easy-to-carry container. You should also store the same supplies in a "safe" area of your home, where you would "shelter-in-place," should an incident occur.

WATER

Store one gallon of water per person per day. This is for all your water needs. A normally active person needs to drink at least two quarts of water each day. Hot environments and intense physical activity can double that amount. Children, nursing mothers, and ill people will need more.

Keep at least a three-day supply of water per person (two quarts for drinking, two quarts for each person in your household for food preparation/sanitation).

If you bottle your own water, be sure to store it in food-grade plastic containers, such as soft drink bottles. Avoid using containers that will decompose or break, such as milk cartons or glass bottles.

FOOD

Store at least a three-day supply of nonperishable food. Select foods that require no refrigeration, preparation, or cooking, and little or no water. If you must heat food, pack a can of Sterno. You may also purchase Meals Ready to Eat (MREs) online or in selected camping stores for this purpose. Select food items that are compact and lightweight.

Include a selection of the following foods:

Ready-to-eat canned or packaged meats, fruits, and vegetables
(can opener)

Canned, boxed, or plastic container juices

Staples (deli mayo, mustard, and ketchup packs, salt, sugar,
pepper, spices, etc.)

High-energy foods or granola bars

Vitamins

Food for infants

Comfort/stress foods

FIRST AID KIT

Assemble a first aid kit for your home and one for each car.
(20) adhesive bandages, various sizes

(1) 5" x 9" sterile dressing

(1) conforming roller gauze bandage

(2) triangular bandages

(2) 3 x 3 sterile gauze pads

(2) 4 x 4 sterile gauze pads

(1) roll 3" cohesive bandage

(2) germicidal hand wipes or waterless alcohol-base hand sanitizer

(6) antiseptic wipes

(2) pair large medical grade non-latex gloves

Adhesive tape, 2" width

Antibacterial ointment

Cold pack

Scissors (small, personal)

Tweezers

CPR breathing barrier, such as a face shield

First Aid Manual

NONPRESCRIPTION DRUGS

Aspirin or nonaspirin pain reliever

Antidiarrhea medication

Antacid (for stomach upset)

Syrup of Ipecac (use to induce vomiting if advised by the Poison
    Control Center)

Laxative

Activated charcoal (use if advised by the Poison Control Center)

TOOLS AND SUPPLIES

Any and all available communications devices (cell phone, land line
phone, text messaging devices, GPS device, wireless laptop, walkie-talkies,
signaling devices, weather radio or any radio, portable television, etc.)

Help Sign

Mess kits, or paper cups, plates, and plastic utensils

Emergency preparedness manual

Solar, hand-cranked, or battery-operated radio and extra batteries
    (try to find those that will also charge your cell phone and other
    needed devices)

Solar, hand cranked, or battery-operated light or flashlight and extra
    batteries

Cash, traveler's checks, change

Nonelectric can opener, utility knife

Fire extinguisher: small canister, ABC-type

Tube tent

Small grill top and Sterno, grill, or portable propane-gas stove top

Charcoal or wood chips for cooking

Pliers

Duct tape

Compass

Matches in a waterproof container

Aluminum foil

Plastic storage containers

Signal flare

Paper, pencil, waterproof markers

Needles, thread

Medicine dropper

Shutoff wrench, to turn off household gas and water

Whistle

Plastic sheeting

Rubber gloves (surgical, heavy duty, chemical proof)

Disposable or cell phone camera

Map of the area (for locating shelters)

SANITATION

Toilet paper, towelettes

Soap, liquid detergent

Feminine supplies

Personal hygiene items

Plastic garbage bags, ties (for personal sanitation uses)

Plastic bucket with tight lid

Disinfectant

Household chlorine bleach

CLOTHING AND BEDDING

Include at least one, generally two complete changes of clothing and
footwear per person.

Sturdy shoes, work or waterproof boots

Rain gear

Protective helmets

Blankets or sleeping bags

Hat and gloves

Thermal underwear

Sunglasses

SPECIAL ITEMS

Remember family members with special requirements, such as infants and elderly or disabled persons.

FOR BABY

Formula

Diapers

Bottles

Powdered milk

Medications

FOR ADULTS

Heart and high-blood-pressure medication

Insulin

Prescription drugs

Denture needs

Contact lenses and supplies

Extra eyeglasses

ENTERTAINMENT (BASED ON THE AGES OF FAMILY MEMBERS)

Games (cards) and books

Portable music or video device

CDs or DVDs

IMPORTANT FAMILY DOCUMENTS

Keep and make copies of these records. Place in a waterproof portable container. You should also deliver a set to a trusted relative, friend, or attorney—out of the disaster impact area:

Will, insurance policies, contracts deeds, stocks and bonds

Passports, social security cards, immunization records

Bank accounts numbers, most recent bank statements

Credit card account numbers and companies

School records (transcripts, report cards, test scores, copies of diplomas and degrees)

Inventory and pictures of valuable household goods

Important telephone numbers

Family records (birth, marriage, death certificates)

Mortgage or lease documents

WORK EMERGENCY KIT

WATER
Store one gallon of water per person per day. It is recommended that you store a 3-day supply.

FOOD
Keep a three-day supply of nonperishable food—items like vacuum-sealed pouches of tuna, crackers, granola bars, deli mayonnaise packs, packaged fruit, trail mix, cookies, etc.

OTHER ITEMS
Any and all available communications devices (cell phone, land line phone, text messaging devices, GPS device, wireless laptop, walkie-talkie, signaling devices, weather radio or any radio, portable television, etc.)

Emergency preparedness manual

Help sign

Solar, hand-cranked, or battery-operated radio and extra batteries (try to find those that will also charge your cell phone and other needed devices)

Solar, hand-cranked, or battery-operated light or flashlight and extra batteries

Change of clothes (2–3 days' worth)

Washcloth, soap, towel, toothbrush, toothpaste, comb

Pack of face masks (surgical or N-95)

Feminine supplies

Three-day supply of medications

Pillow, blanket, sleeping bag

Important telephone and contact information

Disposable camera

Map of exit routes for the facility

BASIC CAR KIT

2 roadside flares

12-foot jumper cables

Windshield smasher

Quart of oil

Gallon of antifreeze

Small first aid kit

Extra fuses

Solar, hand-crank, or battery-operated light or flashlight

Multipurpose or separate tools: pliers, wire cutters, knife, saw, bottle
opener, screwdrivers (flat head and Phillips), flies, and an awl

Tire inflator (such as Fix-A-Flat)

Rags

Pocketknife

Small shovel

Disposable or cell phone camera

Permanent marker, pen, and paper

Hat and gloves

Thermal underwear

Sunglasses

Sturdy shoes, work or waterproof boots

Rubber or surgical gloves

Rain gear

Waterproof matches

Roll of paper towels

Roll of duct tape

Spray bottle with washer fluid

Ice scraper

Vacuum-sealed tuna packs, crackers, deli mayonnaise packs

Granola or energy bars

Bottled water

Blanket

Change of Clothes

Help sign

(Make sure your gas tank is at least three-fourths full and your spare
   tire is inflated and in good repair.)

ADVANCED CAR KIT (SAME AS ABOVE PLUS BELOW)
Battery charger

Air compressor

First aid kit (including an assortment of bandages, gauze, adhesive
   tape, antiseptic cream, instant ice and heat compress, scissors, and
   aspirin)

Heavy-duty nylon bag to carry it all in

(Make sure your gas tank it at least three-fourths full and your spare
   tire is inflated and in good repair.)

SCHOOL EMERGENCY KIT

WATER

Place at least one liter bottle in your backpack. Store one gallon of water per person per day in your dorm room. It is recommended that you store a two-to-three-day supply.

FOOD

Place a packet of vacuum-sealed tuna, deli mayonnaise, and crackers or a few granola bars in your backpack.

Keep a three-day supply of non-perishable food in your dorm room—items like vacuum sealed pouches of tuna, crackers, granola bars, deli mayonnaise packs, packaged fruit, trail mix, cookies, etc.

OTHER ITEMS

Any and all available communications devices (cell phone, land line phone, text messaging devices, GPS device, wireless laptop, walkie-talkie, signaling devices, weather radio or any radio, portable television, etc.). Carry at least your cell phone or text messaging device always.

Place at least one solar, hand-cranked, or battery-operated light or flashlight and extra batteries in your backpack. Store at least one in your dorm room.

Emergency preparedness manual

Solar, hand-cranked, or battery-operated radio and extra batteries (try to find those that will also charge your cell phone and other needed devices)

Change of clothes (two-to-three-days' worth)

Washcloth, soap, towel, toothbrush, toothpaste, comb

Pack of face masks (surgical or N-95). Carry at least two masks with you always.

Rubber or surgical gloves

Feminine supplies

Three-day supply of medications

Pillow, blanket, sleeping bag

Important telephone and contact information

Disposable camera or cell phone camera. Carry with you at all times.

Help sign

Map of the campus and or exit routes for the facility.

Sources

BOOKS

Bradford, Zeb B., and Frederic J. Brown. *America's Army: A Model for Interagency Effectiveness*. Westport, Conn.: Praeger Security International, 2008.

Dickson, Paul, and Thomas B. Allen. *The Bonus Army: An American Epic*. New York: Walker & Company, 2004.

Scott, Phil. *Hemingway's Hurricane: The Great Florida Keys Storm of 1935*. Thomaston, Maine: International Marine/Ragged Mountain Press, 2006.

GOVERNMENT DOCUMENTS AND REPORTS

H.R. 5122 [109th]: John Warner National Defense Authorization Act for Fiscal Year 2007.

"Hurricane Katrina Chronology." First Army Command Group, undated.

Jarrell, Jerry D., Max Mayfield, and Edward N. Rappaport. "The Deadliest, Costliest, and Most Intense United States Hurricanes from 1900 to 2000 (and Other Frequently Requested Hurricane Facts)." NOAA Technical Memorandum NWS TPC. Miami: National Hurricane Center, 2001.

"JTF-Katrina Response to Hurricanes Katrina & Rita: Final After-Action Review." Joint Task Force-Katrina, undated.

Knabb, Richard D., Jamie R. Rhome, and Daniel P. Brown. "Tropical Cyclone Report: Hurricane Katrina: 23–30 August 2005." National Hurricane Center, Dec. 20, 2005, updated Aug. 10, 2006.

Knabb, Richard D., Daniel P. Brown, and Jamie R. Rhome. "Tropical Cyclone Report: Hurricane Rita: 18–26 September 2005." National Hurricane Center, March 17, 2006, updated Aug. 14, 2006

Louisiana Department of Health and Hospitals. "Hurricane Katrina: Reports of Missing and Deceased." Aug. 2, 2006.

Louisiana Office of the Governor. "Overview of Governor Kathleen Babineaux Blanco's Actions in Preparation for and Response to Hurricane Katrina." Dec. 2, 2005.

Louisiana Office of Homeland Security & Emergency Preparedness. "Hurricane Pam Exercise Concludes." July 26, 2004.

National Hurricane Center. "Hurricane Katrina," Hurricane Katrina Intermediate Advisory Number 9A, Aug. 25, 2005.

———. "Tropical Depression Twelve." Tropical Depression Twelve Discussion Number 1. Aug. 23, 2005.

———. "Tropical Storm Katrina." Tropical Storm Katrina Advisory Number 4. Aug. 24, 2005.

U.S. Army Corps of Engineers. "The Mississippi River and Tributaries Project." New Orleans, 2004.

U.S. Coast Guard. "Coast Guard Recapitalization Fact Sheet." U.S. Coast Guard Acquisition Directorate, February 2008.

U.S. Congress. A Failure of Initiative: Final Report of the Select Bipartisan Committee to Investigate the Preparation for and Response to Hurricane Katrina. Washington, D.C: U.S. Government Printing Office, February 19, 2006.

U.S. Department of Commerce. "Hurricane Katrina Service Assessment Report." June 2006.

———. "NOAA Issues 2005 Atlantic Hurricane Season Outlook: Another Above Normal Season Expected." NOAA News Online (Story 2438). May 16, 2005.

U.S. Department of Homeland Security. "National Response Plan." December 2004.

U.S. First Army. "Hurricane Katrina Chronology." U.S. First Army Command Group, Jan. 9, 2006.

"U.S. military bars journalists from body-filled areas of New Orleans." Agence France-Presse, Sept. 9, 2005.

U.S. Senate. *Hurricane Katrina: A Nation Still Unprepared. Report of the Committee on Homeland Security and Governmental Affairs.* Washington, D.C.: U.S. Government Printing Office, May 2006.

Weston, Lieutenant Col. Mark C. "Review of the Posse Comitatus Act After Hurricane Katrina." U.S. Army War College Strategy Research Project, March 15, 2006.

White House. "President Addresses Nation, Discusses Hurricane Relief Efforts." Sept. 3, 2005.

———. "President Arrives in Alabama, Briefed on Hurricane Katrina." Sept. 2, 2005.

———. "Statement on Federal Emergency Assistance for Louisiana." Office of the Press Secretary, Aug. 27, 2005.

NEWSPAPER, MAGAZINE, AND ONLINE ARTICLES

Alpert, Bruce. "Bush photo after Katrina big mistake, ex-aide says: Flyover image became symbol of detached response, book says." *Times-Picayune,* May 29, 2008.

Baker, David R. "Hard times in Big Easy: Efforts intensify to evacuate living, recover dead: Thousands dead, 1 million evacuated. Katrina? No, a simulation run last year." *San Francisco Chronicle,* Sept. 9, 2005.

Beriwal, Madhu. "Hurricane Pam and Hurricane Katrina: Pre-event 'Lessons Learned.'" EIIP Virtual Forum Presentation, Dec. 14, 2005.

Blow, Charles M. "Farewell Fair Weather." *New York Times,* May 31, 2008.

Dewan, Sahila. "Holdouts at FEMA Trailer Park Test Aid's Limits." *New York Times,* June 7, 2008.

Dwyer, Jim, and Christopher Drew. "Fear Exceeded Crime's Reality in New Orleans." *New York Times,* Sept. 29, 2005.

"Former FEMA Director Testifies Before Congress." Transcript of House hearings on federal, state, and local response to Hurricane Katrina. *New York Times,* Sept. 27, 2005.

Heightman, A. J. "When the Rules Change." *Journal of Emergency Medical Services* 30, no. 11 (Nov. 2005).

Hillen, Michelle. "Former Louisiana Governor Slams Federal Katrina Response." *Arkansas Democrat-Gazette,* Feb. 21, 2008.

Hsu, Spencer S., Joby Warrick, and Rob Stein. "Documents Highlight Bush-Blanco Standoff." *Washington Post,* Dec. 5, 2005.

"In Case of Emergency: Officials hope eight days of intense training for a catastrophic hurricane will aid recovery efforts if the real thing ever hits." *Times-Picayune,* July 20, 2004; posted on Louisiana Office of Homeland Security & Emergency Preparedness website.

Leinwand, Donna. "Honoré in charge, refusing excuses that slow cleanup." *USA Today,* Sept. 12, 2005.

Lemann, Nicholas. "Insurrection." *New Yorker,* Sept. 26, 2005.

Livingston, Tami. "Apathy on storms baffles officials: As Hurricane Preparedness Week kicks off, 'There's a culture of complacency.' " *Florida Times-Union,* May 24, 2008.

"Louisiana's Blanco vows to rebuild: Governor accepts responsibility for disaster response 'failures.' " CNN, Sept. 14, 2005.

"LSU Researchers Assist State Agencies with Hurricane Response Plans." *LSU Highlights,* Summer 2005.

McCulley, Russell. "The Unlikely Comeback of William Jefferson." *Time,* Dec. 11, 2006.

"Michael Chertoff's Announcement." Text of a press conference by Michael Chertoff, secretary of homeland security. *New York Times,* Sept. 9, 2005.

Murray, Shailagh, and Allan Lengel. "The Legal Woes of Rep. Jefferson: Probe of La. Democrat Provides Fodder for GOP." *Washington Post,* Feb. 16, 2006.

"'One John Wayne dude' tackles relief efforts: Former 2nd ID commander coordinates military hurricane response." *Stars and Stripes,* Sept. 4, 2005.

Povich, Elaine S. "Louisiana governor defends decision not to federalize Guard units." *CongressDaily,* Feb. 2, 2006.

Rosenblatt, Susannah, and Rainey, James. "Katrina Takes a Toll on Truth, News Accuracy: Rumors supplanted accurate information and media magnified the problem. Rapes, violence and estimates of the dead were wrong." *Los Angeles Times,* Sept. 27, 2005.

Sanger, David. "FEMA Chief Was Recalled After High-Level Meeting." *New York Times,* Sept. 11, 2005.

Thevenot, Brian, and Gordon Russell. "Reports of anarchy at Superdome overstated." *Seattle Times,* Sept. 26, 2005.

Thomas, Evan. "Katrina: How Bush Blew It." *Newsweek,* Sept. 19, 2005.

Varney, James. "They came seeking refuge, then suffered days in anguish." *Times-Picayune,* Aug. 29, 2006.

OTHER SOURCES

1A JOC Watch Battle Captain e-mail to multiple recipients, "RE: High Priority—VCJCS mission for LA ARNG—Secure building at 333 Canal St.," Sept. 3, 2005.

American Morning. CNN transcript of Sept. 26, 2005, show.

Cable News Network LP, LLP, and Michael Cary v. Michael D. Brown . . . Director of the Federal Emergency Management Agency. "Plaintiff's Complaint, Application for Temporary Restraining Order and Application for Injunctive Relief." C.A. No. H-05—3170, S.D. Texas, Sept. 9, 2005.

Cable News Network LP, LLP, and Michael Cary v. Michael D. Brown . . . Director of the Federal Emergency Management Agency. "Agreed Order and Final Judgment." C.A. No. H-05—3170, S.D. Texas, Sept. 11, 2005.

"CNN Security Watch: Lessons of Hurricane Katrina." *CNN Presents.* Transcript of Sept. 10, 2005, show.

"Congressman Jefferson commends Lt. Gen. Russel Honoré." News release from the office of Congressman William J. Jefferson, Feb. 25, 2008.

"Congressman William Jefferson's Corruption Charges Lead to Political Uproar on Capital Hill." FoxNews.com, June 6, 2007.

Gibson, Sergeant Joel. F. "Citizen answers call of hunger." 13th COSCOM Public Affairs Office online newsletter, September 2005.

Honoré, Lieutenant General Russel L. E-mail correspondence with Major General Rich Rowe, Sept. 1, 2005.

Honoré, Lieutenant General Russel L. E-mail correspondence with Lieutenant Colonel Ronald J. Rose, Sept. 6, 2005.

King, Rita J. "Big, Easy Money: Disaster Profiteering on the American Gulf Coast." CorpWatch Report, August 2006.

Mandia, Scott A. "The Long Island Express: The Great Hurricane of 1938. What's In Store for New York's Future." Retrieved June 16, 2008, from http://www2.sunysuffolk.edu/mandias/38hurricane.

Martz, Ron. E-mail correspondence with Terri Troncale, *Times-Picayune,* March 24, 2008.

Martz, Ron. Telephone interview with Edward Woerner, June 24, 2008.

"Mayor to feds: 'Get off your asses.' " Transcript of WWL radio interview with New Orleans mayor Ray Nagin, Sept. 1, 2005.

Paula Zahn Now. CNN transcript of Sept. 1, 2005, show.

——. CNN transcript of Sept. 20, 2005, show.

Rodriguez Henry "Junior." Letter to President George W. Bush, Sept. 29, 2005.

Tapper, Jake. "Amid Katrina Chaos, Congressman Used National Guard to Visit Home: Two Heavy Trucks, Helicopter Were Involved in Lawmaker's Trip at Height of Crisis." ABC News, Sept. 13, 2005.

"Transcript of court proceedings for CNN v. Michael Brown." CNN, Sept. 11, 2005.

"U.S. won't ban media from New Orleans: CNN filed suit for right to cover search for bodies of Katrina victims." CNN, Sept. 11, 2005.

Acknowledgments

Hardly a week has gone by since my retirement in early 2008 that my BlackBerry does not buzz with an e-mail message wishing me well from a soldier who served with me during the thirty-seven years I spent in the uniform of the United States Army. Over the course of my career I have commanded and worked with tens of thousands of soldiers who are the heart, soul, and backbone of the Army and to whom I owe a great debt of gratitude for their service and loyalty. It obviously is impossible to name all of them here, but it is necessary for me to give special thanks to a number of people who were instrumental over the course of my career, including during JTF-Katrina, and while researching and writing this book. Although some of the military personnel I will name have retired or been promoted since the Katrina operations, here and in the book I use the ranks they held at the time I worked with them.

I am especially grateful to the people of consequence who did the dirty work in the aftermath of Hurricane Katrina: the police and fire officials, the National Guard soldiers, and the citizens of New Orleans who responded quickly and professionally to the disaster and worked tenaciously to get the city back on its feet. The active forces—Army, Air Force, Marines, Navy, and Coast Guard—that came to Louisiana and Mississippi after Katrina, saved thousands of lives, and eased the suffering of an untold number of other victims of the storm.

President George W. Bush and his staff at the White House, deputy chief of staff Joe Hagin in particular, were extremely supportive of me and Joint Task Force–Katrina, and allowed us to do the jobs we were sent to Louisiana and Mississippi to do. President and Mrs. Bush were also wonderfully gracious hosts during my occasional visits to the White House.

The White House advance team of Scott Levy, a native of Louisiana, Jason Recher, and Scooter Slade was of vital importance to the task force in helping keep our protocol straight during visits from high-priority guests, especially President Bush and Vice President Dick Cheney.

Secretary Michael Chertoff of the Department of Homeland Security, Vice Admiral Thad Allen, his deputy Captain Tom Aykin, their staff at the Federal Emergency Management Agency, and Deputy Secretary of Defense for Homeland Security Paul McHale gave JTF-Katrina the cooperation and coordination needed to work through a number of contentious issues. I would also like to thank Senator Mary Landrieu of Louisiana, Governor Haley Barbour of Mississippi, Governor Kathleen Blanco of Louisiana, Mayor Ray Nagin of New Orleans, and their respective staffs for their assistance and openness during our operations.

I am especially appreciative of the unwavering support of the Army staff, led by Chief of Staff General Peter Schoomaker and Vice Chief of Staff General Dick Cody. Admiral Tim Keating and his staff at Northern Command, particularly Lieutenant General Joe Inge, my predecessor at First Army, and Major General Rich Rowe, the operations officer, helped keep JTF-Katrina on course and provided vital assets when needed.

My friend and former boss, General Dan McNeill, commander of Forces Command, was someone I turned to when in need of wise counsel and assistance in breaking down bureaucratic roadblocks in a hurry. He and the FORSCOM staff worked tirelessly to assist my staff at First Army in finding solutions to difficult problems.

I cannot say enough about the tremendous job done by the First Army staff during JTF-Katrina, which was led at Fort Gillem by Major General Jay Yingling, my deputy, and Colonel Jim Hickey, my chief of staff. It was their professionalism and devotion to duty in running the staff that allowed me to go forward and work the problems we were facing in Louisiana and Mississippi. But special mention also goes to my G-1, Doctor Vicky Dunn; my comptroller, Deborah Murphy; Colonel Bill Mason, the best logistician in the Army; and Gloria Starr, my secretary, who kept me supplied with my favorite cigars during those six weeks away from the office.

JTF-Katrina could not have accomplished half of what it did in the time it did without the marvelous work of the task force command group. Its members included Air Force Major Generals Henry Morrow and Scott Mays, commanders of the Joint Force Air Component; Major General Douglas V. O'Dell, Jr., commander of Marine Forces JTF-Katrina; Army Major General William Caldwell, commander of Task Force All-American; Army Brigadier General Mark Graham, deputy commanding general, JTF-Katrina (Forward); Army Brigadier General Michael Terry, commander of Joint Logistics Command; and Rear Admirals Joseph

Kilkenny, Stephen Turcotte, and Ronald Bayless, commanders of Joint Force Maritime Component.

The Defense Coordinating Officers sent to the hurricane-threatened states were our early warning system that enabled us to react more quickly and decisively than if we had waited until after the storm to move them into place. They included Colonel Tony Daskevich in Louisiana, Colonel Damon C. Penn in Mississippi, Colonel Mark Fields in Florida, and Colonel L. "Bullett" Young in Alabama.

U.S. Coast Guard Admiral Robert Duncan and his Guardsmen were responsible for saving numerous lives in New Orleans by working continuously with helicopters and small boats to find and rescue people trapped in their homes or in the rising floodwaters. Captain Nora Tyson, commander of the USS *Bataan,* and Captain Richard Callas, commander of the USS *Iwo Jima,* and their crews assisted with search and rescue and provided vital medical services and numerous other assets to our overall effort.

The Adjutants General of Louisiana and Mississippi, Major General Bennie Landreneau and Major General Harold A. "Hac" Cross, provided the soldiers, cooperation, counsel, and friendship needed to make the active/Guard relationship work exceptionally well after the storm. Brigadier General Robert Creer and Brigadier General Bruce Berwick and all the personnel from U.S. Army Corps of Engineers were extremely supportive of our efforts, and their speedy work in getting the levees plugged and the city dewatered helped the task force do its job quicker.

My senior mentors during JTF-Katrina, retired Marine General Charles Wilhem and retired Coast Guard Vice Admiral Jim Hull, followed me closely in the first two weeks and gave valuable insights into such complex issues as command and control and Navy–Coast Guard interaction. A special thank-you also goes to Brigadier General Tony Cuculo III and his lessons-learned team, who watched what we were doing and found ways to improve on how it is done the next time.

Colonel Ernie Shows, the garrison commander at Camp Shelby in Mississippi, and Colonel John Hadjis, the commander of the 177th Armored Brigade at Shelby, were wonderful hosts for JTF-Katrina headquarters and provided everything we could have wanted to make things run smoothly. Colonel Chris DeGraff of my staff, who was responsible for the JTF-Katrina headquarters at Camp Shelby, was incredibly efficient and was always in the right place at the right time making the right decisions.

ACKNOWLEDGMENTS

First Army Command Sergeant Major Marvin Hill and 82nd Airborne Division Command Sergeant Major Wolf Amacker executed every order with speed, precision, and a professionalism that was truly awe-inspiring. They are the very model of senior noncommissioned officer leadership that makes the Army what it is today. My driver in New Orleans, Sergeant First Class Richard Linton, and my enlisted aide, Sergeant First Class Craig Cox, were of vital importance to me. Litton was ready to go anywhere at any time and Cox was on hand to make sure I took time to eat during those twenty-plus-hour days we worked.

My public affairs staff, Lieutenant Colonel Rich Steele, and Commander Dora Lockwood, kept me apprised of news developments almost as soon as they occurred and proved invaluable in providing background information on issues that needed to be addressed or alerting me to problems that had already been resolved.

The American Red Cross and its great group of volunteer workers who came from all over the country, along with countless nongovernmental organizations that gave of their time and money, are among the heroes who were instrumental in helping New Orleans get back on its feet again after Katrina. Special thanks also to the media, particularly CNN and the Fox Network, for their around-the-clock coverage of the storm and its victims and for helping us see ourselves. Among those deserving special mention are Barbara Starr and Kyra Phillips of CNN, Rick Leventhal of Fox, and Scott Pelley of *60 Minutes* for their preparation, astute questions, and commitment to balanced reporting. Thanks also to Terri Troncale, editorial page editor of the *New Orleans Times-Picayune,* who provided valuable information about the newspaper's coverage of the storm and my September 2005 meeting with the editorial board.

I am especially grateful to four other members of my staff, two of whom were with me almost continuously from the time we left First Army in Atlanta on August 31, 2005, until we returned six weeks later.

Lieutenant Colonel Ron Rose, my operations officer, and Lieutenant Colonel Lee Gutierrez, my executive officer, went everywhere I went and saw everything I saw and are two of the most outstanding, hardworking, and loyal soldiers I have had the privilege to work with.

Major Jeff Parks, the secretary of the general staff at First Army at the time of Katrina, knows more about who did what and when they did it than any other person alive. If Jeff does not know something, or does not know where to get it, it can't be found. In addition to being the repository for an incredible amount of knowledge about our operations,

Jeff was our point of contact between the White House and my staff and coordinated the visits of all the dignitaries to New Orleans, including the president, vice president, cabinet members, and congressional delegations, to ensure that everything went smoothly and according to protocol.

My aide, Captain Scott "Tiger" Trahan, was a real workhorse during the JTF-Katrina operations and without him the rest of my staff and I would have been lost. No one else could have done what Tiger did when it came to coordinating aircraft, security, ground transportation, food, water, and communications on short notice virtually every day we were in Louisiana and Mississippi. It did not matter where we were going or how short the notice, Tiger always had transportation and support ready when we got to our destination. He was a true "combat multiplier" and a magnificent asset to the task force.

Two other great soldiers and their families deserve special mention here. Major Justin Reese (Tiger II) was a tremendous help during the transformation of First Army. He and his family are very special to me and my family. And Major Joseph Albrecht (Tiger III) is one of the most selfless, devoted, and loyal individuals I have ever met. There are no words adequate to express the gratitude my wife and I have for Joe and his wife, Megan, and their beautiful twin daughters, Paige and Samantha. They were invaluable to us during our transition from the Army to the civilian world. The Albrechts will always hold a special place in our hearts and have been a true blessing to us.

Several people read portions of the manuscript and offered valuable suggestions and insights, particularly Jim Clifton, Doctor Shelia Kearney, and Geoff Brewer of the Gallup organization. My sister, Mary Honoré McAtee, was especially helpful on our family history. If there are errors in this work, they are unintentional and of my own making.

To my children I express my sincere and humble thanks for their love and support during my career and for their encouragement in writing this book. Daughters Stefanie and Kimberly and sons Michael and Steven have made me a better father and a better man.

Index

Abu Ghraib, 68–69
Acadians (Cajuns), 26
Acosta, James Russel, 81
Afghanistan, U.S. Army in, 48, 69–70
Agriculture Dept., U.S., 25, 36
AIDS, 223
Air Force, U.S.:
  and digital mapping system, 166
  resources supplied by, 106, 127, 183
Alabama:
  exodus from, 85
  hurricanes in, 73, 157
  and Katrina, 83, 84, 90, 91
  state of emergency declared in, 88
Allen, Thad, 178, 203
  and FEMA, 145, 158, 170, 176, 186, 187
  handling rumors and reports, 170, 187
Amacker, Wolf, 144–45
animal lovers, 172–74
Army, U.S.:
  Acquisition Corps, 55–56
  in Afghanistan, 48, 69–70
  author's career in, 4, 38, 40–44, 48–50, 51, 53–54, 57–58, 65, 68–69, 205
  budget cuts in, 222
  culture of preparedness in, 6, 45–48, 51, 55, 62, 70, 72, 114
  humanitarian missions of, 140
  and IED/EFPs, 204–5
  initiative taken in, 93
  integration of, 57
  in Iraq, 46, 48, 69–70, 71
  and joint-service environments, 59–60, 65

"leaning forward," 74–75, 197
"lifers" in, 43
logistics vs. tactics in, 114
marijuana use in, 43–44
Materiel Command, 55, 57
National Training Center (NTC), 46–47, 57
Organization Effectiveness in, 48–49
in permissive environment, 93, 140, 165, 211, 213
post-Vietnam, 41, 43–44
protocols in, 72–73, 75, 89
Public Affairs Officers (PAOs), 63–64
Rapid Deployment Force, 51
resources supplied by, 106, 127, 183, 206
restrictions on use in U.S. of, 15–17, 89, 122
tactics examination in, 49–50
Theater Immersion Training, 70–71
training in, 3, 46–48, 69–71, 200, 220
and West Point, 54, 57
See also specific branches
Army Corps of Engineers:
  command of, 137
  dewatering New Orleans, 148
  and FEMA, 74
  and flood control system, 28, 105
  and JTF-Katrina, 137
Army Reserve:
  in Iraq, 71
  ROTC, 36–38, 41, 54
  training of, 3, 69–71, 200